On the Heels of Freedom

*The American Missionary Association's
Bold Campaign to Educate Minds, Open Hearts,
and Heal the Soul of a Divided Nation*

Joyce Hollyday

A Crossroad Book
The Crossroad Publishing Company
New York

Dedication

For those whom history would designate "unsung heroes"—
the students, teachers, advocates, and activists who lived this story.
May the simple serenade of praise on these pages swell
to a resounding chorus of acclamation in the hearts of those
who are moved by your sacrifice and courage.

The Crossroad Publishing Company
481 Eighth Avenue, New York, NY 10001
Copyright ©2005 by Joyce Hollyday

Typographic specifications: Body text set in Benguiat 9/11
and display type is Caxton Book

Printed in the United States of America

Proceeds from the sale of this book will benefit congregations
from the American Missionary Association tradition whose stories
appear on its pages.

Library of Congress Cataloging-in-Publication Data

Hollyday, Joyce.
On the heels of freedom : the American Missionary Association's
bold campaign to educate minds, open hearts, and heal the soul
of a divided nation / Joyce Hollyday.
p. cm.
Includes bibliographical references (p. 216).
ISBN 0-8245-2348-2 (alk. paper)
1. American Missionary Association--History.
2. African Americans--Missions. I. Title.
BV2360.A8.H65 2005
266'.022'08996073--dc22
2005014737

1 2 3 4 5 6 7 8 9 10   10 09 08 07 06 05

Contents

Foreword

The best way to capture the importance of the book Joyce Hollyday has written is to ask this question: What if none of this had ever happened? What if no God-fearing, pietistic Christians had ever joined the *Amistad* Africans in their fight for freedom? What if no New England missionaries had gone south to ensure that emancipated blacks were prepared for citizenship? What if their worship practice invoking the God of goodness in creation had not informed their public practice of "goodness" toward unknown neighbors?

The answer to all these questions is the same: our world would look nothing like it does today. What is more, little of what has offered hope for the future from generation to generation is not somehow linked to the efforts of those whose stories are so carefully told here and others like them. This is a big statement to make, and I make it without exception. If we remove the efforts of the American Missionary Association and their ilk from the history of this nation, the present is incomprehensible.

This story is certainly my story, and the story of my family. As my late wife, Jean, once reminded me, our parents would not have had an education if it had not been for the United Church of Christ and its foreparents in the Congregational and Christian churches. Neither would either of us have had such an opportunity. Jean was born and raised in the one Alabama county that has produced more black PhDs than any other in the United States of America. This astounding fact is due to a single American Missionary Association school—Lincoln Academy in Marion, Alabama—and the extraordinary community that gave life to it and to which it gave life abundant.

Our family story is not unique. We can add to the list of people touched by this tradition every black leader of any import in this country, from the best known—Martin Luther King and Barak Obama—to the unknown legions of teachers, preachers, and community sustainers in every city and town in America. If we lift our questions up to the world stage, the answer is no different. Had there been no Glasgow Missionary Society in South Africa, there would be no Fort Hare University, the first university in southern Africa to accept non-whites, and therefore no Nelson Mandela, no Thabo Mbeki, and no Albert Luthuli. If the Christian missionaries in that same region in 1893 had not offered hospitality and refining political debate to Mohandas Gandhi, there would have been no nonviolent movement for social change in India. In other regions of the world, the same is true.

The power of this story does not lie solely in the events of the glorious past it recalls, however. Its power lies in the creative tension in which faith calls us to live, and the power of persons of faith to create the future by choosing to live in that tension. There is no privatized dream of a better world in these stories, but a vision of a public good in which every living soul is cherished and every opportunity is made for thriving, where neighborhoods everywhere are strengthened by leadership developed in schools, churches, and intentional, nurturing communities *somewhere*.

This is the creative tension to which the great truths of all religious faiths inevitably lead. It is the clash of the forces of the world for good and those at work against it. That same struggle exists in our present world. The power of the history told here is its reminder to us that the choice is still ours to make.

ANDREW YOUNG
ATLANTA, GEORGIA
HOLY WEEK 2005

Prologue

The sun beat fiercely on the car as we emerged from under a canopy of live oaks draped with Spanish moss on the campus of Tougaloo College. Passing back through the ironwork arch at the entrance, we turned toward the highway for the long journey home. Heat rose in waves from the black soil of Mississippi's cotton fields and a landscape dotted with makeshift stands peddling bags of boiled peanuts and plates of pit-smoked barbecue.

As the miles fell away behind us, Milton Hurst began to talk about sharing hot, summer nights with his maternal grandparents as a child in Alabama's Black Belt. Each evening, as a red sun sank low toward the horizon, rags were set on fire in a pot, the smoke intended to keep away mosquitoes. "My grandmother said nothing about slavery," Milton remembered. "She sat on those evenings around the smudge pot on the front porch, with a pipe lit, as my grandfather told stories. And he would say, 'Is that right?' and she would say, 'Yes, that's right.' But she did not share her story." He paused. "Sometimes we don't tell the story because it's so painful."

Milton's grandfather had witnessed the murder of his sister when she was a young woman. When she saw some white men beating another slave, she "went into hysterics and started screaming," recounted Milton. She would not stop. "And so they took her out, put a millstone around her neck, and threw her in the Alabama River." His grandfather raged about slavery.

But like his mother's mother, Milton's paternal grandfather found slavery and its aftermath too agonizing to talk about. When he confronted the white owners of the land he sharecropped about cheating him, he was ordered immediately off the land. "According to my father's information, he could not move," said Milton. "He just sat there on the porch, leaning against the wall, looking out across the fields." Milton's grandmother had to walk to a neighboring landowner to ask if they could work his fields.

Milton Hurst, who serves as pastor of First Congregational United Church of Christ in Talladega, Alabama, believes that one of our difficulties today is that we do not tell the stories of courage and faithfulness to younger generations: "To relive history, and to realize that your people have been through adversity, means that you're informed about survival—about coming through, getting over, getting by. It also gives more than a hint of those specific places where God has deliberately touched down and moved a church or a people. You can see it in the retelling of the story. You can feel in your bones the fact that this was an act of God, because there is no other explanation for it. The stories inform us, give us direction about what we ought to be doing, and give us the opportunity to rededicate ourselves to a mission. They remind us that we're all part of the same fabric."

Susan Mitchell, co-pastor of Sankofa United Church of Christ in Atlanta, Georgia, chimed in from the driver's seat, "When you actually hear the stories from people who had the experience themselves, it increases your faith and your understanding of how things came to be the way they are. And it gives you the courage to want to move forward, to press through the things that we face today, just as they pressed through in the past."

The day was Sunday, July 11, 2004. We had just completed a five-year project that had involved conducting interviews in churches across the Southeast, logging close to fifteen thousand miles in the process. Moments before, in Tougaloo's renowned Woodworth Chapel, Susan had preached for the last time her sermon based on 2 Timothy 1:6-7: "I remind you to rekindle the gift of God that is within you . . . for God did not give us a spirit of fear, but rather a spirit of power and of love."

Borrowing from this scripture, we had named our oral history project "Rekindle the Gift." From the outset, we were intent on documenting a stunning, but little known and rapidly fading, legacy. The story has roots in the 1839 mutiny by captured Africans on the ship *Amistad*. The Congregationalists who raised money for their legal defense and return trip to Africa formed the American Missionary Association (AMA), which grew to be the largest abolitionist organization in the nation. At the close of the Civil War, AMA missionaries from the North went south. In partnership with newly emancipated citizens, suffering ostracism, mob violence, and in some cases death, they established more than five hundred schools and aided the planting of two hundred Congregational churches that grew up in their shadows.

These American Missionary Association churches and schools have produced many of our nation's most outstanding activists, artists, and political leaders, from Booker T. Washington, W .E. B. DuBois, and James Weldon Johnson to Andrew Young, Septima Clark, and Coretta Scott King. Fisk University gave us the Jubilee Singers, who popularized the spirituals. Dorchester Academy in Georgia hosted citizenship schools during the civil rights era. For more than a century and a half, the impact of these institutions on local communities and the nation has far exceeded their size.

The AMA story resides in the archives of a few research institutions, but perhaps most poignantly and powerfully in the hearts of the oldest members of the Congregational churches—now part of the United Church of Christ—who were among the last generation to attend the AMA elementary and secondary schools. Milton Hurst, Susan Mitchell, and I crisscrossed the South to capture their testimonies—from lessons about equality learned as schoolchildren to leadership in local civil rights struggles—before they were lost to us all forever. We knew before we began that in our churches all across the Southeast Conference of the United Church of Christ—in Alabama, Georgia, Mississippi, South Carolina, and eastern Tennessee—we would find living witnesses to the power of faith and courage to transform the nation. Our hope, as our project motto described it, was "to remind the church of the power of the past, to make it come alive in the present, in order to serve God's future."

At the outset, we wondered whether our prepared questions were adequate to draw out people's stories. We soon learned that our questions were virtually extraneous. On our first visit, to Rush Memorial United Church of Christ in Atlanta, after sharing Sunday morning church service, we simply explained why we were there and turned on the tape recorder. The stories poured out, like water rushing through an opened floodgate. When I commented to an older gentleman that I was amazed at how easily the stories flowed, he paused a moment, and then said softly, "Nobody ever asked before." We were touched that young members of the congregation lingered after the service to listen, hanging on every word as their elders told courageous tales from the civil rights era and the years leading up to it.

The stories were not the only gifts that were bestowed upon us as we made our visits. Hospitality was generous and gracious at every stop. We were treated to an extravagant feast of chicken and greens in Midway, Georgia; local catfish in Marion, Alabama; shrimp in Charleston, South Carolina; and the world's best barbecued ribs at First Congregational United Church of Christ in Atlanta. We shared a huge birthday cake with members of First Congregational in Savannah in a fellowship hall decorated with a spring profusion of dazzling azaleas and wisteria blossoms, and we were treated to a lavish seafood buffet near the Gulf in celebration of the pastor's birthday in Thomasville, Georgia. In nearby Beachton, members of Evergreen Congregational United Church of Christ sat us in front of the church at the end of Sunday service and showered us with beautiful homemade quilts, toiletries, and eight pounds of local sausage, while the choir surrounded us and sang a hymn to send us on our journey home.

Upon our arrival in Montgomery, Alabama, we were greeted with a huge fruit basket and given special copies of the fortieth anniversary edition of *To Kill a Mockingbird*. Our stay in Nashville, Tennessee, included a three-hour tour of the "Music City," which began with a family-style meal in an old mansion. In Alpine, Alabama, we shared prayers and hymns with members of King's Chapel before conducting interviews, and in Athens, the children of Trinity Congregational United Church of Christ danced and sang a tribute.

We included stops at poignant and inspiring civil rights sites: Kelley Ingram Park, Sixteenth Street Baptist Church, and the Civil Rights Institute in Birmingham; Ebenezer Baptist Church and the memorial fountain in Montgomery; the Martin Luther King Jr. Center for Nonviolence in Atlanta. We stopped by to see the renowned Amistad murals at Talladega College and toured Connecticut sites related to the *Amistad* story: monuments and museums in New Haven, the captives' home in Farmington, and the Hartford courtroom where they were granted their freedom. During a December blizzard, we visited the museum in Mystic Seaport where a full-size replica of the ship was built. In late January 2002, while the exaggerated glitz and hoopla of the Super Bowl, Mardi Gras, and city elections collided outside, I spent a week in quiet isolation at the Amistad Research Center in New Orleans, drawing inspiration from hundreds of original letters penned by late-nineteenth-century AMA missionaries.

As Susan, Milton, and I passed by Meridian, Mississippi, headed toward the Alabama border, we acknowledged the bittersweet tenor of the day. We expressed deep thanks for having been part of so rich a ride through history together, and at the same time a touch of sadness that the journey was coming to an end. As we passed into Alabama, I was powerfully aware that the "race mixing" in our car would have been dangerous a generation ago and paid silent tribute to the many brave souls who had risked—and sometimes lost—their lives on these very roads to change laws and hearts. Through our travels, I had come to embrace a renewed appreciation for the apostle Paul, who began his epistles to the churches he had visited on his missionary journeys by thanking God for their courage, their faith, and the power of their witness. I now had personal experience of such gratitude.

Milton Hurst, grandson of slaves, attended Talladega College, one of the American Missionary Association's early schools. He spent thirteen years serving as a professor, dean of students, and assistant to the president of the college. His granddaughter is a student there now, as his daughter was before her. "The AMA," he said, "provided an experience that could only be dreamed of, wished for, longed for. It was an experience of hope in the midst of despair, of trust for a future beyond the present history, of daring to dream that you are not held by your circumstances." The AMA was not without its flaws and blind spots, which are documented in the pages that follow; but Milton's words rang true wherever we visited.

Today, the United Church of Christ continues to uphold a vision of God's "extravagant welcome." Just as the church's forebears were in the forefront of the struggle for racial equality and inclusion, more recent history has found the denomination at the center of controversies because of our churches' acceptance of all who come, without regard for gender, ability, economic status, or sexual orientation. "Then as now," said Milton Hurst, "these churches represent hope. Even now in this present, in these circumstances, we represent openness, inclusion, tolerance, a spirit of mercy and grace. One phrase that I like to use when I think of the United Church of Christ and the American Missionary Association is, we dare to struggle. We will not give up. We will not say it cannot be done. We still dare to struggle."

Susan Mitchell wondered aloud about how her life might be different, and how she might have dealt with trials and difficulties, if she had heard the stories when she was growing up. "As I listen to the stories of faith and freedom, and see how they unfold in a variety of contexts that are wonderfully unique," she said, "I grapple with a longtime question of mine: How did we ever make it through? How did we as a people ever make it through the Maafa—what is commonly known as the Middle Passage—enslavement,

Jim Crow laws, segregation, and physical, spiritual, and mental oppression? Part of the answer is revealed when we acknowledge that each of us has the gift of God within us."

Toward the end of her "Rekindle the Gift" sermon, which she tailored for each congregation we visited, Susan always talked to the elder members about "Big Mama, PaPa, Ma Dear, Grandad, Auntie, Junior, Pops, teachers, preachers, and community leaders" who instilled the idea that "no matter what society said, you knew on the inside you were just as good as anyone else in the world." She exhorted them to "remember that you caught the faith from an older generation and then expressed it in new ways. Pass on the faith to our youth, and trust that God will guide them to continue on the mission to which we were called."

Susan concluded with words that hold wisdom for us all in these fearful and troubled times: "Faith was, and is, the best weapon for the conquest of fear. Demonstrate your faith by adding fuel to your fire, and don't let fear prevent you from rekindling the gift of God within you. Just proclaim the word of God and press on. Add some fuel to your fire, so that your flickering flame becomes a bellowing blaze." For, as the apostle reminds us, "God did not give us a spirit of fear, but rather a spirit of power and of love."

JOYCE HOLLYDAY
LENT 2005

From Mystery to Mission

A School for "Contraband of War"

Hot, heavy mist clung like a shroud to the coast of what is known today as the state of Virginia. The year was 1619. The August day was blistering, and the times were beyond hard for the land's recent settlers. When a ship wrapped in mystery slowly emerged from the fog, it looked to them like salvation. Cannons yawned on its deck under furled sails. The drooping flag on its stern was Dutch. Its cargo was twenty Africans, robbed from a Spanish vessel during one of many raids intended to break up the maritime monopoly enjoyed by Spain and Portugal.

The inhabitants that the ship's crew encountered at Jamestown, the first permanent English settlement in North America, were a rough lot. All male at its founding, many had come to this shore as indentured servants; some were criminals escaping the gallows back in England. The settlement's mission, outlined in a charter granted by England's King James, was to preach, baptize, and "recover out of the arms of the Devil a number of poor and miserable souls."[1]

The dream of a "promised land" in the New World had turned quickly into a nightmare. Two years after the settlers' arrival came the brutal winter of 1609-1610—"the starving time." Propelled by gnawing hunger, they scoured the forests for nuts and berries to eat, finally becoming so desperate that some dug up graves and ate corpses. Of the nine hundred settlers who arrived in the first three years, only sixty were still alive by the spring of 1610.[2]

Determined to carry on, they discovered that their survival was wrapped in leaves of tobacco. Cultivating the crop that would shift their status from tenuous to tenacious was extremely labor intensive, and only endless, arduous work made it possible for them to hang on through another decade. From their perspective, the Dutch ship that penetrated the fog in 1619 arrived just in time. The vessel's crew exchanged their captives for food. Thus began the slave trade that would eventually entangle the lives of millions of human beings in bondage and cruelty in America.

Two and a half centuries later, in the spring of 1861, on the same spot of coast, three weary fugitives from slavery emerged from the smoky haze of cannon fire and made their way to Fortress Monroe, seeking protection. The war that would ultimately determine their fate raged around them. The fort stood near

Hampton Roads, a patch of southeast Virginia named for the network of coastal paths that had carried several generations of Africans from the horrific holds of newly arrived ships into the shackles of slavery.

On May 27, 1861, when a Confederate officer arrived at the fort under a flag of truce to claim the three men who had fled from work on a Confederate battery, General Benjamin Butler, in charge of Union forces at the fort, faced a dilemma. Citing international law, he declared the vulnerable trio "contraband of war"—confiscated enemy property—thus circumventing the Fugitive Slave Act that required the return of escapees to their owners. Word spread among slave communities, and the next day eight more "contrabands" appeared at the fort. Forty-seven runaways, including several babies and frail, elderly women, arrived the day after.

By fall a seemingly endless parade of destitute fugitives, clothed in rags and wrapped in tattered blankets, overwhelmed the fort. They came at night, drawn by the flickering light of Union campfires on the dark horizon as others had been guided by stars in the heavens pointing north. They were stooped old men, gaunt young women, and parents clinging tightly to frightened and hungry children, their flesh shivering from the cold and their souls trembling with the hope of freedom.

Renowned New York abolitionist Lewis Tappan contacted General Butler, offering assistance. A minister with ties to the American Missionary Association (AMA) was sent, Rev. L. C. Lockwood, who reported being moved by the singing of the fugitives, who hailed him as an answer to their prayers. Lockwood, who unnerved his sponsors during his tenure with the occasional use of tobacco for his asthma, immediately made a requisition to the AMA for "1,500 Sunday-school primers with pictures attached."[3] The fugitives wanted a school.

On September 17, 1861, in a small brown cottage not far from where the first Africans were forced onto this shore, Mary S. Peake opened a classroom to twenty students. The daughter of a free African American mother and an Englishman, Ms. Peake had for years secretly welcomed scores of enslaved persons who snuck at night to the cabin she shared with her husband, teaching them to read when it was considered a crime to do so. White masters were known to administer brutal whippings, apply iron muzzles, or cut off thumbs or parts of fingers of slaves caught in the act of reading or writing. Yet all across the South—from Nashville to New Orleans; in Alexandria, Virginia, and Talladega, Alabama; in Savannah, Georgia, and Wilmington, North Carolina, and corners unknown—African Americans were pioneers in their own education, taking great risks to form clandestine schools. Ms. Peake's was the first to benefit from Northern benevolence and the protection of federal guns.

In waning health, for the sum of a dollar and a half a week, Mary Peake taught children in the mornings at Fortress Monroe, and adults every afternoon. She established a school that rose from its humble inception to become known the world over as the Hampton Normal and Agricultural Institute. Her physician advised her to abandon the work, fearing she would be "lost to earth," but she persisted.[4] Just five months after she had begun her school, in her final days, Ms. Peake gathered her students around her bed and taught until she succumbed to tuberculosis. An observer wrote: "From the room above the school, on Saturday, February 22, 1862, as the 'All's well' of the midnight watch sounded through the window of the cottage from the war-ships in the Roads, her brave soul crossed the bar."[5]

By early 1862 almost two thousand fugitives had taken refuge at Fortress Monroe, one-third of them children. The educational effort near the fort and in the surrounding areas of Virginia expanded rapidly. Schools were started in the former home of ex-U.S. President John Tyler and in an unoccupied portion of the Hampton courthouse, its roof rebuilt after a fire. "There in sight of the whipping tree," wrote Rev. Lockwood, "with its bark lacerated with the same strokes that fell on quivering flesh, we are teaching a free education and a free religion."[6] African American teachers launched schools in Norfolk and Newport News; other schools followed when missionary teachers were sent to Suffolk, Portsmouth, and Yorktown.

When she first learned that she was dying, Mary Peake had penned to the officers of the American Missionary Association that she was "assured that their cause would triumph; that the Association was sowing seed which would spring up and become a great tree for the shelter of a down-trodden people."[7] Little did she know how massive that sheltering tree would grow to be from so small a seed. The AMA's educational and evangelistic crusade eventually involved hundreds of teachers and tens of thousands of students, setting the stage for the birth of scores of Congregational churches that came to life in the shadows of the schools. Years later, African American intellectual and activist W. E. B. DuBois would dub this massive missionary effort, which touched virtually every corner of the South with its transforming power, "that finest thing in American history."[8]

This unprecedented campaign was launched with a simple inquiry from Lewis Tappan to General Benjamin Butler in 1861.

But the groundwork for the endeavor had been laid two decades earlier when Mr. Tappan responded to an equally pressing and challenging need. Like the first slave ship shrouded in mist and mystery that altered the life of the Jamestown settlement in 1619, the *Amistad* would change the course of history in 1839—altering first its own course, as its determined captives took control of the vessel, and ultimately their own destiny.

1

A Detour in Destiny

The Journey of the Amistad

The timbers of the low, black schooner creaked as it listed in the waters off Long Island, its hull weighed down with barnacles, its sails tattered. On board were thirty-nine Africans, fatigued and hungry, some naked, others dressed in the garish silk shirts and satin pantaloons of Spanish aristocrats. For days after the eerie vessel was first sighted less than a mile from shore, it was an object of curiosity and controversy. Some observers claimed it was a ghost ship, others that it was full of pirates.

Sweat beading on his forehead, Lieutenant Thomas R. Gedney of the *U.S.S. Washington* put down his spyglass on this sweltering August afternoon in 1839 and sent a small boat with six armed men to investigate. Their leader, Lieutenant Richard W. Meade, immediately recognized the ship as a slaver, built low for speed, with wide hatchways. Beneath the large, gilt eagle head on its bow, he spied the word *Amistad*—"Friendship" in Spanish.

When the military men boarded the schooner, two frightened Spaniards burst from its hold, one exclaiming loudly, "Bless the Holy Virgin, you are our preservers," as both men fell to their knees. Overcome with emotion, the older of the two, Pedro Montes, rose and lunged forward, throwing his arms around Meade. The startled lieutenant reacted by drawing his pistol, thrusting it into the old man's face and threatening to shoot if he didn't let go.[1]

Soon an astounding story unfolded of this ship that had sailed off its course, now winding its way toward the pages of history. Two months earlier, the *Amistad* had departed from Havana for a three hundred-mile voyage to the Cuban port of Puerto Principe, where its human cargo of forty-nine men and four children was to be delivered into slavery. Most of the captives were from the Mendi region of Africa. They had been rice farmers, leopard hunters, blacksmiths. Gbatu was the son of a nobleman; Fang, of a king. Pugnwawni, who had filed teeth and a much-tattooed body, had been sold by his uncle to pay for a coat, and Moru was enslaved as an orphan. Of the children, Kali and Teme had been kidnapped, and Kagne and Margru had been sold by their fathers to men to whom they owed debts.[2]

All had survived the brutal Middle Passage across the Atlantic Ocean, most on the *Tecora*, which the captive Bahoo described later in a legal deposition: "(We) were two moons coming from Africa to Havana, where (there were a) . . . good many in the vessel, and many died; were tight together; two and two chained together by hand and foot night and day."[3] More than a third of the captives on board the *Tecora* died en route. Those who refused to eat their provision of rice were whipped and had vinegar rubbed into their wounds.[4]

In Havana, they were driven into the large barracoons erected to hold enslaved persons before auction. After examining their bodies and teeth, Jose Ruiz bought the men for $450 apiece. Pedro Montes purchased the boy and three girls. The buyers secured passports that classified their captives as *ladinos*—slaves who had been imported from Africa before the 1820 ban in the Spanish territories—rather than as what they were: *bozales*, illegally imported slaves.

Under cover of darkness, with only the dim glow of harbor lamps around them, Ruiz and Montes forced their captives onto the *Amistad*, which had been built and fitted in Baltimore for the coastal slave trade, on the evening of June 28, 1839. Loaded with weapons, provisions, medicine, and the false passports listing Spanish names for each of the Africans, the chartered vessel set sail at midnight.

The journey to Puerto Principe was expected to take only two days. But a day out, the winds shifted, and Captain Ramon Ferrer realized it might take as long as two weeks. He ordered that food for the Africans be cut to one banana, two potatoes, and a small cup of water per day. Sengbe Pieh (sometimes known as Joseph Cinque, the Spanish name assigned to him), a rice planter from a Mendi village who had been stolen from his wife and three children on an African road, gave part of his meager ration to the children.

Heavy neck irons were used on the Africans at night, wrist and ankle chains during the day when they were allowed up from the hold onto the deck in groups of ten to eat and exercise. Suffering from severe thirst, one captive, Burnah, took some water from a cask on deck. He was caught and whipped by the crew throughout the night. Four other Africans were beaten the next day, their wounds rubbed with salt, gunpowder, and rum.

The cruelty raised the captives' anger and frustration. Sengbe used sign language to ask what was to be their fate. In cruel jest, Celestino, the cook, grinned and signaled that the Spaniards planned to slit their throats, chop up their bodies, salt them, and eat them as dried meat. Enraged, Sengbe searched for a key to freedom, finding a loose nail, which he hid under his arm until an opportunity presented itself.

On the third night of the voyage, when a fierce thunderstorm covered the noise and distracted the crew, Sengbe used the nail to pick the locks on the neck irons. Wielding large cane knives they found in boxes on board, a group of captives attacked the crew. Celestino was the first to be killed. As the Africans surrounded Captain Ferrer, he yelled to his crew, "Throw some bread at them!" Montes, seriously wounded, saved himself by crawling behind a barrel and hiding under an old sail. Ruiz surrendered, and Antonio, the cabin boy, who begged for mercy, was spared and tied to the anchor.[5]

Sengbe and his companions seized control of the *Amistad*. They broke open the cargo in the cabin and hold, finding glass doorknobs and gingham parasols, exotic jewelry and fancy dishes, perfume, two hundred boxes of macaroni, a few saddles, and an entire trunk filled with gold doubloons. They rifled through trunks of colorful Spanish silks, satins, and shawls, festooning themselves in outlandish costumes.

Montes was discovered the next day, barely conscious. He was dragged onto the deck and ordered to sail the ship east, toward the rising sun, to Africa. By day, he heeded the instructions, though he kept the sails loose and flapping in the wind, so the vessel made little headway. At night he steered the ship northwest, hoping that one of the British vessels on anti-slave-trade patrol, so dreaded before, would discover and rescue him and Ruiz. For two months the ship zigzagged its way up the Atlantic coast of the United States. Provisions gave out, and some of the Africans, delirious from thirst, broke open bottles of medicine, consumed the contents, and died. Others succumbed to starvation.

A few merchant ships came close to the *Amistad*, but backed away when they caught sight of the strangely dressed men on board brandishing knives. On August 25, carrying handfuls of Spanish gold doubloons, Sengbe and some others went ashore and managed to buy two dogs, a bottle of gin, and some sweet potatoes. Their purchase was closely watched, and the next day the men of the *Washington* captured the *Amistad* and towed it to New London, Connecticut.

As soon as the tow line had been secured, Sengbe loaded up as much gold as he could into a makeshift money belt and jumped overboard. He sank immediately from the weight of the coins, but managed to struggle back to the surface. He dived and surfaced, keeping a boat in pursuit of him turning in circles for almost forty minutes, until he surrendered. When he was returned to the *Amistad*, his companions wept, laughed, and danced for joy. But he announced to them soberly, "You had better be killed than live many moons in misery."[6]

When the Africans reacted to these words with screams, Lieutenant Gedney ordered that Sengbe be brought to the *Washington* and manacled, to prevent him from jumping overboard again. The next morning, Sengbe convinced the lieutenant that if he would allow him to be reunited with his friends, Sengbe would give him a handkerchief full of gold, which he had hidden away. Upon his return to the *Amistad*, Sengbe gave a speech that began, "My brothers . . . you have only one chance for death and none for liberty."[7] His words created such a riot that Sengbe was removed once more. He spent the following night on the deck of the *Washington*, staring at the *Amistad* until dawn.

On the morning of August 29, a federal district judge conducted an inquiry on board the *Washington*. Sengbe appeared before him, manacled, with a snuffbox hung on a cord around his neck, wearing a red flannel shirt and duck pantaloons. The judge determined that the Africans should appear before the next circuit court, on September 17, in Hartford, Connecticut, where a judgment would be made as to whether they should stand trial for murder, mutiny, and piracy on the high seas. He ordered the U.S. marshal to transport them to the New Haven jail. The marshal noted with curiosity that while he was attempting to direct the captives, none of them responded to the Spanish names on the warrant, though the names had been carefully copied from their passports issued in Havana.

Five days later, on September 3, New York abolitionists appointed Lewis Tappan, Joshua Leavitt, and Simeon Jocelyn as the Amistad Committee, assigning them the task of raising money for the Africans' legal defense. Both Leavitt and Jocelyn were Congregational ministers. Jocelyn was a founder of New Haven's antislavery society and a conductor on the Underground Railroad, aiding escaping slaves to freedom, and Leavitt was the editor of an antislavery newspaper, *The Emancipator*. The three issued a national "Appeal to the Friends of Liberty," describing the state of the captives who "after having been piratically kidnapped from their native land, transported across the seas, and subjected to atrocious cruelties, have been thrown upon our shores..."[8] Donations flooded in from sympathizers around the country.

But the committee faced stiff opposition and an array of challenges, including communicating with the captives. Day after day, persons from near and far who could speak any African language were taken to the jail, with little success. Josiah W. Gibbs, a professor of theology and sacred literature at Yale Divinity School and a renowned linguist, learned to count to ten in the Mendi language by holding up fingers before the captives, whose initial blank stares turned eventually to excited comprehension. Gibbs then walked up and down the wharves of New York harbor, counting loudly over and over, "*eta, fili, kiauwa, naeni, loelu . . .* " until James Covey, a former slave employed on the British warship *Buzzard*, overheard him. Covey agreed to come to New Haven and serve as translator. His appearance and first words at the jail elicited a shout of joy from the captives.

Students at Yale Divinity School, founded by the Congregationalists, began coming every day, instructing the Africans in English, as well as in the Bible and religious studies. They began with simple picture cards of animals and letters. Gradually the lessons evolved into a school inside the jail, with classes being conducted four or five hours a day. One of the captives' teachers wrote, "Those who have been with them have not infrequently seen the tear start at the mention of the aged father, or the defenseless wife and child, and stout men turn aside and weep, and the little children cry as if their hearts would break." Asked if they wanted to return to Africa, one of the children replied in broken English, "Tell the American people, that we very, very much want to go to our home."[9]

Hawkers and gawkers were a constant distraction. Four thousand curiosity seekers paid twelve-and-a-half cents each to file through and stare at the Africans. The captives were becoming folk heroes, with thousands of children carrying in their pockets pictures of Sengbe and tickets to an exhibit of masks molded in black wax from the Africans' faces. Every day families gathered on the New Haven village green to watch the Africans exercise. The men leapt over one another, turned somersaults, flips, and cartwheels, to cheers and fervent applause.

Sengbe left the jail every afternoon with an escort to sit for a portrait at the home of the painter Nathaniel Jocelyn. Jocelyn portrayed Sengbe draped in a white robe and holding a staff, a classical motif that had previously been reserved for heroic white figures. In the antebellum period, Africans were rarely pictured at all, and particularly not as individuals with dignity and strength.

Jocelyn was the first American artist to depict an African as more than a slave. The portrait created a controversy in the art world, and in 1841 the Artist Fund Society of Philadelphia refused to exhibit it, stating that it "might prove injurious both to the proprietors and the institution." Outraged, Jocelyn resigned his membership, while his portrait of Sengbe emerged as a symbol of justice and freedom.[10]

William Cullen Bryant wrote a poem immortalizing the captives' leader:

Chained in a foreign land he stood,
A man of gentle frame,
Amid the gathering multitude
That shrunk to hear his name—
All stern of look and strong of limb,
His dark eye on the ground—
And silently they gazed on him
As on a lion bound.
Vainly, but well, that chief had fought—
He was a captive now;
Yet pride, that fortune humbles not,
   Was written on his brow.
The scars his dark broad bosom wore
   Showed warrior true and brave;
A prince among his tribe before,
   He could not be a slave.[11]

On September 14, a throng of thousands jammed the banks and hung off the bridges of the canal leading to New London harbor. The Africans, wrapped in white woolen blankets and huddled on a canal boat, floated past all the curious gazes. The girls had been given shawls, which they styled into high turbans. While disembarking, one of them stooped down and wiped the dust off her first pair of shoes with her new handkerchief. At New London, they all boarded wagons for the remainder of the journey to Hartford.

As in New Haven, throngs of people came to see the captives in Hartford. Among their visitors was Thomas Gallaudet, founder of the first school for deaf persons in the United States. He worked on developing a sign language with the Africans, hoping to help them communicate with the courts.[12]

The thirty-nine surviving captives landed in the middle of a great controversy. The U.S. antislavery movement was in an uproar over political tactics, the role of churches, and women's rights, while relations were tense between England, Spain, and the United States over slavery. Debate raged over the Africans' fate: Ruiz and Montes claimed that they were Spanish property,

Lieutenant Gedney of the *U.S.S. Washington* also laid claim to the *Amistad* and its cargo, and abolitionists argued that the Africans were innocent of all charges and had acted in self-defense on behalf of freedom.

In the courtroom, the children wept with terror, desperately clutching the marshal's hands as he tried to calm them with pieces of fruit. After hearing all arguments, the judge referred the case to the November 19 district court for a decision to be made as to whether the Africans were legally slaves. Meanwhile, Lewis Tappan arranged for the Africans to bring civil suit against Ruiz and Montes for assault and battery and false imprisonment. Both were arrested on October 17 in a New York hotel.

Jose Ruiz wrote a poem in January 1840, published in *The Colored American*:

The slaves are ours:
The pound of flesh, which I demand,
Is dearly bought, is mine, and I will have it.
If you deny me, fie upon your law!...
I stand for justice: answer; shall I have it?[13]

Tensions escalated between the United States and Spain. Under pressure from the Spanish government, fearing a breach in international relations, U.S. President Martin Van Buren ordered that the schooner *Grampus* be anchored off New Haven during the district court trial, ready to spirit the captives back to Cuba. Abolitionists took turns keeping watch over the jail and the harbor to prevent such an action. The British queen entered the fray, taking the side of the captives.

The second trial, postponed after a day of testimony until January 1840, lasted five days. The odds were not in the Africans' favor. Connecticut was considered the most hostile of the New England states to abolitionism, and Hartford had recently been the site of a race riot. Judge Andrew T. Judson presided at their trial. A few years earlier, he had led the opposition to Prudence Crandall, a young white woman who had opened a school for African American girls. Judson, a lifetime member of the American Colonization Society, which advocated the forced return of blacks to Africa, presided over the town proceedings that led to the closing of Crandall's school. Lewis Tappan and his brother, Arthur Tappan, had financed her defense. Judson claimed during Crandall's trial that the abolitionists' purpose in supporting education for blacks was to prepare them to instigate slave insurrections in the South, and he told the jury that the United States is "a nation of *white men,* and every American should indulge that *pride* and *honor*, which is falsely called prejudice, and teach it to his children . . . Who of you would like to see the glory of this nation stripped away and given to another race of men?"[14]

Roger Sherman Baldwin, a renowned attorney who would later become governor of Connecticut, represented the Africans. Despite the odds, the second trial of the *Amistad* captives went in their favor. At a critical moment, with questions flying fast and furious from the attorneys, Sengbe rose and riveted the court with his passionate plea, "Give us free! Give us free!" The judge granted Sengbe his wish, declaring that the Africans had been illegally enslaved and deserved to be set free and transported back to Africa.

With jubilant hope, they began making plans, urging one of their teachers from the divinity school to return with them to teach their families, promising to "give him a house and abundance of food, take the best care of him and not let him be sick."[15] When he asked what they would do with him if he grew weary traveling in Africa where there were no horses, Sengbe took a blanket, tied the ends together, put a broom handle through it, and rested it on his shoulder and that of a companion, showing the teacher how they would carry him in a sling.

But the wheels of justice—and injustice—ground on, momentarily crushing hopes of Africa. Under the influence of Van Buren, prosecutors appealed the district court decision, deferring the Africans' dreams of reaching home for more than a year. The captives survived a long and bleak winter by beginning each morning with prayers and filling the day with classes. Eleven-year-old Kali wrote a letter saying, "We write every day; we write plenty letters; we read most all time; we read all Matthew and Mark and Luke and John, and plenty of little books. We love books very much."[16]

On February 22, 1841, the case of the Africans landed in the U.S. Supreme Court, with proslavery Chief Justice Roger B. Taney presiding and both the U.S. president and the government of Spain against them. Twenty years later, Taney would be decisive in the infamous Dred Scott case, which declared that blacks had "no rights which the white man was bound to respect." Leading the defense for the Africans was former U.S. President John Quincy Adams, an old man who hadn't argued a case before the Supreme Court in thirty years. He wrote in his diary: "The world, the flesh and all the devils in hell are arrayed against any man who now in this North American Union shall dare to join the standard of Almighty God to put down the African slave trade; and what can I, upon the verge of my seventy-fourth birthday, with a shaking hand, a darkening eye, a drowsy brain, and with my faculties dropping from me one by one, as the teeth are dropping from my head—

what can I do for the cause of God and man, for the progress of human emancipation, for the suppression of the African slave trade? Yet my conscience presses me on; let me but die upon the breach."[17]

"Grand Old Man Eloquent," as Adams was called, gave an eight-and-a-half-hour argument on behalf of the Africans, pointing three times to the Declaration of Independence on the court wall, a document his father had helped to write. A moving letter in broken English from Kali to Adams was published in *The Emancipator*. The boy's poignant plea ended with the words, "All we want is make us free."[18]

On March 9, 1841, as a previous judge had given Sengbe his wish, so Kali got his. The highest court in the nation declared the Africans free, designating them illegally kidnapped persons who were entitled to return to their native land. For the first time since its founding, the U.S. Supreme Court determined that people of color had rights equal to whites. It took two days for the news to reach the Africans. At Sengbe's request, young Kali read the Supreme Court's decision to the others.

The now free Africans presented a Bible to Adams, inscribed with their thanks and their names. Kali included a letter that read: "Dear Friend, . . . We love you very much and we will pray for you when we rise up in the morning and when we lie down at night. We hope the Lord will love you very much and take you up to heaven when you die . . . Wicked people want to make us slaves but the great God who has made all things raise up friends for Mendi people he give us Mr. Adams we write our names for you."[19]

The abolitionists needed time to raise money for the Africans' passage home. They arranged for them to stay in Farmington, Connecticut, a key station on the Underground Railroad. The canal in Farmington was frozen, so the Africans arrived by rail and were met by a dozen sleighs. Temporary quarters were created on the second floor of a store, where the men slept on straw and blankets and were provided flannel shirts and trousers. A barn was eventually transformed into a dormitory, and the Africans raised corn, potatoes, and other vegetables on fifteen acres of land. A school was created over the store, and studies resumed with a Yale Divinity School professor.

Charles Ledyard Norton, who was a child in Farmington at the time, later recalled that "there was consternation among the timid souls in the quiet village. Stories of cannibalism were plentifully circulated, and there were formal protests against forcing such a burden upon the community . . . Anxious mamas at first trembled and kept their children behind bolted doors, but before long it was no uncommon sight to see the big grown-up blacks playing with little white children in village dooryards."[20]

Among the captives' strongest supporters throughout their ordeal was Rev. James W. C. Pennington, the first African American pastor at Dixwell Avenue Congregational Church in New Haven, founded in 1820 when a group of twenty-four former slaves met with Simeon Jocelyn, who served the church for its first fifteen years. On May 10, Rev. Pennington, then pastor at Talcott Street Congregational Church (also known as the First Colored Congregational Church) in Hartford, called together African American colleagues from five states, with Sengbe and four other *Amistad* Africans as their honored guests. That day they founded the Union Missionary Society, which claimed to be the "peculiar property of Anti-Slavery Men."[21] Pennington was elected president, and the society took as its mission raising funds for the *Amistad* Africans and recruiting African American missionaries for Africa.

To help raise money, the Africans made tablecloths and napkins in Mendi fashion, adding fringe to the edges of cotton and linen squares. Through the spring and summer of 1841 they went on tours, organized by the Union Missionary Society and the Amistad Committee, to New England churches, where their handiwork was sold and Sengbe and Kali emerged as stars. Sengbe acted out their story, while Kali spelled any word given to him from the Gospels, without mistake.

Back in Farmington, spirits were sinking as time dragged on. In August, Foone, known as a good swimmer, drowned in a canal, leading some to draw the conclusion that he had committed suicide out of despair and homesickness. The tragedy convinced Lewis Tappan and the other abolitionists that the Africans could not wait much longer to return home. He received notes full of sorrowful pleas. Sengbe wrote, "Now we want to go home, very much, very soon . . . We want to see no more snow . . . Cold catch us all the time."[22]

Finally, almost three years after they had initially been stolen from their homeland, the time had come for the thirty-five still-surviving Africans to go home. On November 17, 1841, their Farmington friends hosted a farewell ceremony. The Africans sang. Kinna, Kali, Foole, and Margru read Bible verses, and hundreds of their friends pressed forward to say farewell. At five o'clock the next morning, they boarded the ship *Gentleman* as a hundred townspeople gathered at the canal basin to see them off. When the captain announced that they were leaving, the Africans seized hold of their friends, and tears flowed profusely.

Ten days later they set sail from New York harbor for the fifty-two-day voyage to Freetown, Sierra Leone. Accompanying them were James Covey, two black teachers from Farmington, and three white missionaries, who established the first mission station in Africa. Kinna wrote to Lewis Tappan that the group had arrived safely in Sierra Leone. "We have been on great water. Not any danger fell upon us. Oh, no . . . Our blessed saviour Christ have done wondrous works . . . Dear Mr. Tappan . . . I pray Jesus will hear you; if I never see you in this world, we will meet in heaven."[23]

A February 1842 report in a publication of the Union Missionary Society described the *Amistad* Africans' fate: "They were seized, manacled, incarcerated, shipped, famished, landed, sold, liberated, re-shipped, re-imprisoned, tried, acquitted, re-liberated—all in the course of two brief years."[24] Their courage galvanized antislavery elements, creating a catalyst for increased activism, moving abolitionism from a nascent movement to a powerful moral force.

The *Amistad* event was a milestone in other respects as well. The partnership between the Africans, and both white and African American Congregationalists, made it a truly interracial endeavor and a model for future efforts for equality. More than a century and a half later, the *Amistad* event is still referred to as "the nation's first Civil Rights case."[25] Judge Constance Baker Motley has called it "the first legal milestone in the long, difficult struggle in the courts by persons of color for equal justice under the law."[26]

The wake of the *Amistad* is wide and sweeping. The event has been commemorated in poetry and novels, a lyric opera and a Hollywood film. A bronze sculpture in front of New Haven's City Hall, in sight of the famous exercise green, depicts Sengbe's capture, trial, and return home. The *Amistad* murals, painted by renowned artist Hale Woodruff, adorn the walls of the library rotunda at Talladega College in Talladega, Alabama, and a depiction of the schooner is embedded in its terrazzo floor.

In 1992, in commemoration of the 152nd anniversary of the mutiny, members of the Sierra Leone National Dance Troupe traveled to Farmington, Connecticut, to thank the town for its kindness and courage a century and a half earlier. In a traditional African ritual of honoring ancestors, they broke cola nuts over the grave of Foone, who was buried in the town's cemetery after he drowned in its canal.

The Amistad Chapel is the centerpiece of the Cleveland, Ohio, denominational headquarters of the United Church of Christ. Congregationalists merged with members of the Christian, and subsequently Evangelical and Reformed, traditions, to form the denomination in 1957. Dedicated in May 2000, the chapel houses a font of perpetually running water—a symbol of the *Amistad*'s sea journey and a reminder of the call of the biblical prophet Amos to "let justice roll down like waters, and righteousness like an ever-flowing stream." (Amos 5:24) The chapel celebrates both the pivotal role that Congregationalists played in the *Amistad* story and the critical place the event holds in the history of this denomination, widely recognized for its commitments to education, equality, and social justice.

On a cool, hazy morning in March 2000, while the sound of traditional African drums reverberated in the air and Ambassador John E. Leigh of Sierra Leone pronounced it "a great day for Africa and the United States," a full-size replica of the original *Amistad* was launched from Mystic Seaport in Connecticut. A parade of dignitaries tolled the ship's bell, once for each of the original fifty-three captives. The prayer of invocation, offered by United Church of Christ President and General Minister John H. Thomas, began, "Remind us, O God, that we are here today because a courageous band threw off their chains to declare that freedom is a cause worth dying for, that home is a place worth struggling for . . . Remind us, O God, that we are here today because determined people of faith and conscience confronted evil and challenged indifference that our land might reach toward its nobler instincts and be led by a purer vision."[27] Made of wood from Connecticut, South Carolina, and Sierra Leone, and blessed at its launching by actress Ruby Dee with water from Connecticut, Sierra Leone, and Cuba, the ship is a floating museum that carries the *Amistad* story and travels to promote freedom and racial justice.

In the forty years after the *Amistad* Africans returned home, the United States experienced a time of unprecedented upheaval and transformation, marked by civil war, the abolition of slavery, Reconstruction, and restoration of a violently divided Union. The *Amistad* legacy was carried on in the American Missionary Association, which flowered into the nation's largest abolitionist organization before the war, and became the leader in educational efforts for emancipated citizens after it, out of the tiny seed of the Amistad Committee of three.

In Africa during those years, the first U.S. mission struggled but survived. Both Kali and Kagne worked there for several years, until Kali became crippled by disease and Kagne succumbed to a fever. Margru returned to the United States as a young woman to study at Oberlin College, then went back to Africa to serve as principal of the mission school.

Sengbe, who, one story reports, returned home to discover that his family and village had been destroyed during a war while he was gone, disappeared for many years. But he returned to the mission as an old man in 1879, announcing that he had come there to die. He was buried in the mission's small cemetery by Reverend Albert P. Miller, a young black missionary from the United States.[28]

A poignant irony lingered in the air as Rev. Miller pronounced funeral prayers over Sengbe. The young minister had, only the year before, graduated from the recently founded Fisk University in Nashville, Tennessee—one of the institutions birthed by the American Missionary Association that had evolved from a rudimentary classroom into a renowned university. That day, he was burying the man who, forty years before, on a stormy night at sea, grasped freedom and set into motion the events that made his education possible.

2

"God with Us!"

The Founding of the American Missionary Association

A rdent supporters called it "Aunt Mary Ann." Others referred to it less affectionately as "After Money Again." The American Missionary Association began with assets totaling $387.22 and grew into the most extensive, most well organized, and most racially integrated abolitionist organization in the country.[1] To those who questioned the association's fervent fund-raising practices, AMA officials proclaimed, "We are not beggars, but the 'Lord's collectors.'"[2]

The mid-1800s had brought a burst of missionary activity to the United States, with dramatic growth in Bible societies and benevolence organizations. Distressed by the number of missionary societies that refused to condemn slavery in the United States, James W. C. Pennington, Lewis Tappan, and Arthur Tappan determined to create a union among those that did. All three were men of rare conviction and courage.

Born enslaved in Maryland, Pennington had escaped north on the Underground Railroad, became a proficient linguist in Greek, Hebrew, and German, and was acknowledged among many Congregationalists as "the most eloquent pulpit orator" of his era.[3] He officiated at the wedding of fiery abolitionist Frederick Douglass and publicly banned slaveholders from his communion table and his pulpit. Rev. Pennington wrote a book on the biblical and historical origins of Africans, which was published while he was awaiting word of the Amistad captives' fate. His autobiography, *The Fugitive Blacksmith*, considered by historians to be one of the most important slave narratives, appeared just as the Fugitive Slave Act was passed. Pennington had kept his status as an escaped slave secret for many years, and he was eventually released from the threat of re-enslavement when a friend bought his freedom for $150.

The Tappan brothers, descendants of Benjamin Franklin, had grown up in a family of pious evangelical Congregationalists in quiet, conservative Northampton, Connecticut. Their ancestors in the faith, the Pilgrims, had risked everything to come to this country in pursuit of religious liberty and intellectual freedom. At the age of fifteen, Lewis, the youngest son in the family, left home with eight dollars in his pocket and a Bible from his father, boarding a sleigh headed for Boston.

In time, the Tappans became highly successful merchants and renowned philanthropists in New York City. Lewis maintained his evangelical sentiments, roaming the city's wharves and taverns and counting houses to pass out religious tracts. He and his colleagues claimed to have dispensed six million pages. A fellow merchant said of Arthur, "I would give Arthur Tappan $10,000 a year if he would only sit in a chair in the front window of my store—his character is enough."[4]

The Tappan brothers were opposed to slavery on religious grounds, believing that God had created humanity for equality and freedom. They became notorious crusaders for the abolitionist cause. For years they received death threats, were attacked in the press, and were burned in effigy. Their business was a target of arson and an economic boycott. One opponent sent Lewis a slave's ear, and rumors circulated that proslavery merchants had ordered that he be kidnapped, tarred and feathered. On a hot summer night in 1834, a mob, led by a man on a white charger, broke into his home, threw furniture, bedding, and pictures out of windows into the street, and burned the pile. The following year a detractor offered $100,000 for the bodies of Lewis and Arthur, payable upon delivery to any slave state. In response to the perpetual threats, Lewis Tappan steadfastly carried only one "weapon"—his New Testament, kept in his breast pocket.

The Amistad Committee and Pennington's Union Missionary Society took the lead in calling for a meeting of antislavery organizations. They became the core of the American Missionary Association, formed in Albany, New York, on September 3, 1846—seven years to the day after the formation of the Amistad Committee. Rev. J. H. Payne, who had been elected president of the meeting, addressed the gathering: "There are in the slave states of this country nearly three millions of our colored brethren in slavery the most malignant and cruel in existence. The personality of its victims is annihilated by laws: the image of God is effaced; the man is regarded as chattel. He is denied the Bible, and made the sport of the wanton, the avaricious, the intemperate, and the merciless, while the religion of a portion of the country defends the atrocity, and a large portion shelters and fellowships the transgressor . . . To bear such crimes in silence . . . is enough to paralyze the faith and hope of the Church . . . "[5]

The AMA's constitution was unanimously adopted following Rev. Payne's address. It declared that the organization was open to "any person of evangelical sentiments, who professes faith in the Lord Jesus Christ, who is not a slave-holder, or in the practice of other immoralities, and who contributes to the funds."[6] The first issue of its publication, *The American Missionary*, laid out its mission: "to preach the gospel to the poor, assist feeble churches, sustain missionary operations amongst the freed colored population, and preach deliverance to the crushed and stricken slave." [7]

The AMA sustained the work of the Mendi mission in Sierra Leone for twenty-seven years, though its challenges were severe. Over time, forty-nine missionaries were sent from the United States. Sixteen died from disease, and thirteen returned because of illness. But one missionary remained for twenty-four years, two for seventeen, and another for thirteen.[8]

The mission work expanded to Siam (now Thailand), Jamaica and Puerto Rico, the Sandwich Islands (now Hawaii), and the territory of Alaska. The AMA opened missions among Native Americans in the Southwest and Midwest and Chinese immigrants in California, as well as among the thousands of former slaves who had made their way on the Underground Railroad to freedom in Canada. It later served "highlanders," mountain families in rural Appalachia, opening Pleasant Hill Academy in the Cumberland Plateau wilderness in Tennessee. But from its founding, the American Missionary Association was most preoccupied with the sin of slavery and its victims.

Though the AMA considered itself nonsectarian, its officers and the majority of its members were Congregationalists. Lewis Tappan was elected treasurer, and George Whipple, an abolitionist and ordained minister who was greatly esteemed by his colleagues, served as the first corresponding secretary. Rev. Whipple had to sell his home to continue in the low-paying job. He wrote thousands of letters of encouragement, and occasionally gentle rebuke, to missionaries in the field, often working in his New York office well past midnight, then wrapping himself in a blanket and curling up on his desk to sleep a few hours before picking up his pen again before daybreak. Upon his death, George Whipple was hailed as "a discreet and sleepless friend" of the nation's African Americans.[9]

Many of the Congregationalists' Pilgrim forebears had been legislators and merchants who were beneficiaries of slavery's profits. In its 1872 Annual Report, the AMA spoke of northern complicity with, and responsibility for, slavery: "The Pilgrim and the Slave came to America in 1620. How different their character, yet how blended their history! The one was the bearer of a civilization founded on liberty and intelligence; the other a victim of barbarism based on bondage and ignorance; and yet the Pilgrim as the representative of the North, became, in a measure, responsible for the guilt of slavery, and the sweat of the Slave and the blood of the Pilgrim alike have moistened the soil of the South. The Pilgrim's guilt was that of consent . . . and fearfully did he atone for his complicity for slavery, for he gave as many sons to destroy it as the old masters to save it."[10]

Among the first ministers to receive a commission from the AMA for its antislavery work was John G. Fee, whose unflinching courage inspired many to join the crusade. Fee was raised on a Kentucky farm with slaves. In 1840, six years before the founding of the AMA, as a student at progressive Lane Seminary in Cincinnati, Ohio, Fee knelt at a natural altar in a grove of trees and cried out to God, "Lord, if needs be, make me an Abolitionist."[11] When God answered his prayer, he wrote to his father about his conversion and received an immediate reply: "Bundle up your books and come home; I have spent the last dollar I mean to spend on you in a free State."[12]

The father loaded up on proslavery literature for Fee and offered to pay the bills if he would attend Princeton Theological Seminary. Fee refused. After finishing at Lane, he returned to Kentucky, believing his family and neighbors could be converted. Instead, he entered into a struggle with his father that lasted more than a decade.

His father was on the verge of selling Julett Miles, a mother of nine children and grandmother of several more, who had been enslaved on the Fee farm for years. John Fee agreed to buy her, and then he immediately set her free. His father banned Ms. Miles from the farm, and when she returned to see her children, he threatened to sell her back into slavery before sundown. She fled to Ohio, but returned for her five younger children and three grandchildren when she got word that John's brother planned to take all the Fee slaves to New Orleans. She was apprehended at the Ohio

River and thrown in jail. Fee's father then sold all of his slaves, including her children and their families.

John Fee was attending an annual meeting of the American Missionary Association in New York at the time. He went directly to his father and confronted him, then tried to get Julett Miles released from jail. But she was tried and convicted of having stolen slaves and died a few years later in prison. Of this tragedy, Fee reflected: "The torture of the body is terribly cruel, and yet it is the smallest part of the crime of human slavery. I have seen women tied to a tree or a timber and whipped with cow-hides on their bare bodies until their shrieks would seem to rend the very heavens . . . Yet this torture of the body was the least part of the agony of slavery. The acme of the crime was on the soul. The crushing of human hearts, sundering the ties of husband and wife, parent and child, shrouded all of mankind in the long night of despair."[13]

Declaring "Enter not my door again," Fee's father dismissed him from his home. Fee, whose only convert after ten months of preaching in his hometown was a young woman who later became his wife, was happy to receive a commission from the American Missionary Association.

Cassius M. Clay, who owned six hundred acres of land encompassing present-day Berea, Kentucky, admired Fee and offered him a small farm if he would move there and establish a church. From his ridge above a lush valley, Fee wrote, "I am engaged in the effort to build up a church having no fellowship with slaveholding, caste, secret societies, dram-drinking, and other known sins . . . We distribute Bibles to such slaves as can read, and anti-slavery documents to slaveholders and non-slaveholders."[14]

Mr. Clay often joined Fee on speaking tours, which stirred controversy and opposition around the state. Speaking in the courthouse in Mount Vernon, Clay placed the Constitution of the State of Kentucky on one side and a Bible on the other. Between them he placed a revolver, announcing, "And here, gentlemen, flanked on either side by the charters of civil and religious liberty, I propose, if it shall be challenged, to vindicate my right to say today whatever I shall deem best."[15]

In 1855, on his way, he believed, to a discussion about slavery, Fee was met instead by a mob. He described finding "the accustomed good and attentive audience absent . . . and a lawless band of wicked, profane men (about forty) in their stead." The group demanded that Fee promise not to preach anymore in the area. He refused, explaining later that it would be "treacherous to God, to my own soul, and to their highest interest if I should do so." Fee described what happened next: "They . . . took me by force, put me on my horse, then with boards and sticks forced my horse along, pouring upon me vile abuse and constant threats of violence. Then it was that I felt the force of the words uttered against Christ, my Saviour: 'Away with him! away with him!' In many respects this was to me a trying occasion . . . Yet to me it has been a blessing. It has driven me nearer to God my strength. It has given me such sympathy with Christ as I had not before, and could not have otherwise."[16]

In February 1858, Fee was preaching at Big Bend when a mob of thirty or forty armed men appeared and demanded that he desist. Fee again refused. One man pulled out a rope, threatening to hang him. Another vowed to "duck him in the river till there was no breath left in him." They marched Fee and his companion, a Mr. Jones, to the Kentucky River, where they "descended into a dark, lonely ravine upon the bank." The angry crowd again tried to get Fee to promise to keep silent, and once more he refused, saying, "It is not impossible that some of you may yet want me to come and pray with you, and I should hate to be under a pledge not to do it."[17]

The leader stripped Jones and beat him severely with three heavy sycamore whips. Turning to Fee, he warned, "I will give you five hundred times as much, if you do not promise to leave the country and never return." Fee knelt down and said, "I will take my suffering first." A voice in the crowd shouted, "Don't strike him." The man hesitated, then dropped his whips.[18]

Soon Fee wrote to the American Missionary Association in New York, "We need a college here—an anti-slavery, anti-caste, anti-rum, anti-tobacco, anti-sectarian, pious school under Christian influence, one that will furnish the best facilities for those with small means who have energy and character that will lead them to work their way through this world."[19] On those principles, Fee founded Berea College, a "co-racial" institution for young people in the mountains that became world famous. The college was revolutionary in its commitment not only to equality between black and white, but also between women and men.

In 1859 Fee went to the AMA's annual meeting in New York and then on a fundraising tour, preaching at abolitionist Henry Ward Beecher's church in Brooklyn under arrangements made by Lewis Tappan. Anti-slavery insurrectionist John Brown had just been thrown into prison for his raid at Harper's Ferry, West Virginia. Fee's call for more people with such spirit was misquoted, and rumors circulated that he was shipping arms into Kentucky.

Seven hundred and fifty men pledged to remove Fee and his cohorts from Berea "peaceably if they could, forcibly if they must."[20] A mob mounted on horses charged onto the Berea campus and ordered the teachers to leave the county within ten days. Fee was prevented from returning by the outbreak of the Civil War, but Berea College remains a vital institution to this day, and Fee set a standard for courage and vision that many who followed him in the AMA carried on.

The American Missionary Association struggled for funds and friends in its early years, its members walking by faith, trusting that the resources would appear to sustain the work. At its fourth annual meeting in 1850, the AMA had responded unequivocally to the Fugitive Slave Act's demand that fugitives from slavery be returned to their masters: "Resolved, that we believe the Christianity of the nation is about to be tested, in view of the late act of Congress for recovery of fugitive slaves, which appears equally at variance with the principles of the Association, the Constitution of the country, and the law of God, and that as Christians we do solemnly covenant with each other and our colored brethren that we cannot obey it, nor any law that contravenes the higher law of our Maker, whatever persecution or penalty we may be called to suffer."[21]

That year a group of Boston whites surrendered fugitive Thomas Sims back into slavery. An anonymous eyewitness told of the sad day, when Sims was marched to the end of a wharf and fastened into the foul-smelling hold of the ship *Acorn*. "A tug hauled the *Acorn* out into the harbor; her sails were raised, and like a guilty specter she stole away in the gray of the morning, leaving humiliated and disgraced the city of John Hancock, Samuel Adams, and Paul Revere."[22]

The angry and despairing crowd that had watched the tragedy reassembled in a packed Tremont Temple that night. The eyewitness continued: "I cannot remember which of the speakers first struck the note to which so many hearts responded: 'When God is with us, why do we forget him in this war with slavery?' and from that moment the war-cry was that of old crusaders, 'God with us! God with us!' The name of the American Missionary Association ever since that evening has been in my memory inseparably connected with that meeting. Whether I then first heard its name, or whether it was commended as a model for uniting men in opposition to slavery upon Christian as well as moral grounds, I cannot now recall, but from that night opposition to slavery in the free states took on a new form."[23]

Five days later, a convention was called, which some historians consider one of the most important ever held in New England.

According to the anonymous eyewitness, the American Missionary Association was again "highly commended" by the speakers as "the best agency for the protection of the colored race" and "a model for effective opposition to the increasing aggression of the slave power." He asserted that "it will ever remain a truth of history that opposition to slavery made no substantial progress until it came upon the ground of the Association, to enlist the powerful agencies of the pulpit and the church, and that the first attempt to raise this opposition to that high level was the organization and work of The American Missionary Association."[24]

Another boost to the AMA's work came when Rev. Charles Avery of Pittsburgh, Pennsylvania, donated $100,000. "Walking by faith was well," wrote a historian of the AMA, "but the sight of a hundred thousand dollars in its treasury strengthened faith immensely."[25] In its first eighteen years, the American Missionary Association founded and/or supported 285 antislavery churches and commissioned forty-five abolitionists as itinerant ministers in the United States.[26]

Intensifying salvos from the North against the slave economy of the South launched rumors below the Mason-Dixon Line about dissolving the Union. In December 1860, reacting to the election of Abraham Lincoln, South Carolina became the first state to secede. By February 1, 1861, all the states of the Deep South had followed. Two months later, the Confederate cannon that lit up the night sky as it rained the first blasts against Fort Sumter in Charleston harbor became the starting gun of the Civil War. The Union flag over the fort came down, as bells pealed throughout Charleston and its joyful inhabitants left their slumber to rush into the streets to celebrate.

Almost immediately after President Lincoln called for a response to the bombardment of Fort Sumter, the American Missionary Association understood that history was calling it to grander service: "The whole country is in great excitement. War has begun. The President of the United States has issued his proclamation calling for troops, and multitudinous hosts are responding to the call. When the war ceases the slave states will, we believe, present one of the grandest fields for missionary labor the world ever furnished. Should the prayers of the friends of freedom be speedily answered in the emancipation of the slaves, a field of usefulness may be opened before us that will call for renewed exertion on a greatly increased scale compared with which our past efforts have been preparatory work."[27]

A month after the start of the war, the first band of fugitives appeared at Fortress Monroe in Virginia, seeking protection and requesting a school. Two months after their school opened, in November 1861, Union forces captured the Port Royal Islands off the coast of South Carolina, opening another "field of usefulness" that would prepare the way for a full-scale educational effort after the war.

3

Harbinger of Hope
The Port Royal Experiment

In the golden glow of twilight that wraps the sea islands off the coasts of Georgia and South Carolina, darkening expanses of marsh disappear as stark silhouettes of ancient oaks emerge, eerily draped with beards of Spanish moss, some so massive their branches rest on the sandy ground. In the quiet just after nightfall, echoes older than the trees whisper in the gathering breezes. They reverberate from the crumbling, lichen-covered walls of former slave quarters, formed from tabby, a mixture of oyster shells, lime, and sand.

Still in the air is the lilting cadence known as Gullah, the creolized language that melded the richness of African dialects and the tongue of the master. Still echoing are the "trickster tales" that were told around fires to wide-eyed children—the stories of small and seemingly powerless Bruh Rabbit who always outwitted big Bruh Bear. Just audible are the hushed tones of new parents giving their children "basket names" in the African tradition—names such as Rain or Hardtimes, Boney or Handful—that reflected a trait of the child or conditions at the time of the birth.

Still hanging in the ocean air are the lullabies of resistance, sung to sleeping infants while maternal hands crafted baskets for rice from bulrushes and pine needles, laced with strips of palmetto in the African way. Still lingering are the "shouts"—the rhythmic clapping and movement that accompanied the singing of spirituals and the soaring of ecstatic prayers—that went on, sometimes all night long, in the "praise houses."

The echoes remain, but only as vestiges of a once-flourishing culture of African folklore and tradition on the sea islands. Once-abundant, artfully sewn cast nets are rarely flung in tidal creeks after shrimp and crabs, roots seldom cure, and graves that were once lavished with mirrors, cups, and utensils for those who would need them in the next life now lay largely unadorned. Almost gone are the intricate dance steps known as the Buzzard Lope and the Kneebone Bend. Silent are the goatskin drums that once accentuated the dancers' rhythms, summoned the ancestors, and transmitted messages to the community. Almost lost are the terrible tales of the plat-eye—a one-eyed, web-footed ghost—and the hag, who could slip through keyholes, remove her skin, and hang it up while she rode a victim at night—prevented, according to myth, only by sprinkling pepper and salt, or by placing a broom across a door.

Some of the lingering whispers hover on special spots of coast, the particular haunts of ghosts and legends, filtering through curtains of night air as dark and soft and thick as black velvet. On St. Simons Island, at Georgia's edge, mythic voices rise out of the misty marshes, chanting in chorus, "The sea brought us, and the sea will bring us home." Here, a group of men and women from the Ibo tribe of southern Nigeria walked off the ship *Monrovia*. They turned their backs on slavery and walked toward the water, following the ship captain's slave and their chief into the sea, chained to one another, grasping hands as they went, chanting as the roiling water overtook them and carried them down to their deaths—or, some say, back to Africa.

During the eighteenth century, almost half of the enslaved persons imported from Africa first touched American soil at Sullivan's Island, just off the coast from Charleston, South Carolina. After a time of quarantine in the island's "pest houses" to ensure that they were free of disease, they were put to work all over the sea islands, clearing forests and draining swamps, enduring blazing sun and lurking alligators and snakes. Rice, indigo, and unique long-fiber cotton flourished here. An intricate system of sluice gates and canals capitalized on the force of ocean tides to flood and drain fields, and West African rice growers were particularly treasured on the islands' plantations. By the outbreak of the Civil War, ten thousand enslaved persons, comprising 80 percent of the local population, labored on the islands.[1]

White plantation owners left the sea islands for almost half the year, fleeing from malaria and the fevers that raged during the hot months. Their absence, the area's geographical isolation, and the smuggling of slaves directly from West Africa that went on here long after importation was declared illegal made the islands a haven for fugitives and a center for a thriving Africa-based culture. When plantation families were present, this culture of resistance lived alongside the burgeoning white resistance to participation in the federal Union.

One observer remarked that the Episcopal Chapel of Ease on St. Helena, the largest of the sea islands, held "as high a concentration of aristocracy per pew as gathered anywhere along the South Atlantic."[2] Frogmore, the village at the center of the island, was named after the traditional honeymoon castle of English kings. Entertainment on St. Helena included horse races and dog fights, and special occasions were often marked with the presentation of a cowhide plantation whip to island gentlemen. When members of the elite Agricultural Society gathered to hunt, they rotated providing dinner afterward; the fare became so lavish that the Society began imposing a fifty-cent fine on members who provided more than six courses of meat at the Club House, to "prevent competition." One observer noted that at these meetings "no man was permitted to go home sober."[3]

A visitor to Beaufort, the region's largest town, wrote, "For a quiet and rather dull place, it has become another name for sedition."[4] The sea islands were considered the seedbed of secessionism in South Carolina, which initiated the Southern exodus by leaving the Union five days before Christmas in 1860. White inhabitants on the islands immediately destroyed lighthouses that the federal government had built the previous year, unwilling to let them guide Union forces. They constructed forts of palmetto logs and sandbags. The women of the islands made the sandbags, rolled bandages, and sewed uniforms for Confederate troops, resorting to making pants out of bed ticking when they ran out of other cloth. Most of the pants were blue, but striped cloth that resembled peppermint candy was reserved for the pants of commissioned officers.[5]

On a bright, cloudless November afternoon in 1861, a Union flagship approached St. Helena's Port Royal Sound, a strategic entry point for supplies to Charleston and Savannah, Georgia. At the first sound of cannons, some of the white inhabitants ran to their upper windows to watch the battle. A cluster of Confederate wives and daughters gathered on the veranda of the Tom B. Chaplin Plantation, while several others slipped away to the Chapel of Ease to pray. Fear overtook the group on the veranda when they saw flags on two forts in the bay being lowered in defeat. The families in the chapel heard the rumble of gunfire give way to the thunder of hoofbeats, followed by the clatter of spurs up the church's aisle by a messenger, sent by the women on the veranda with the dreaded news.[6]

As soon as the Union bombardment of Port Royal ceased and the occupying forces appeared on the horizon, white landowners and their families set fire to piles of cotton bales, loaded a few select possessions on flatboats, and fled from their mansions, some leaving dinner on tables or cooking on stoves. Union troops discovered only one white person remaining in the area, "Old

Pritchard" in Beaufort, who had been left behind because he was too drunk to climb into a boat. He had a reputation as a cruel and hated master, and local lore has it that he spent his last days fishing, sitting under shade trees, and begging favors from the people he once owned.[7]

Slave communities on the islands long remembered November 7, 1861, as "the day of the big gun-shoot."[8] A young boy hearing the heavy gunfire reported to his mother that he heard thunder. She replied that it wasn't thunder at all, but "the Yankee come to (give) you Freedom."[9] Masters tried to force their human property to escape with them, threatening that the Yankees would round them up and send them to Cuba to worse slavery. But most ignored the threats. Some hid in the marshes and fields. A few were burned to death in cotton warehouses by their owners. One story reported that thirty slaves were shot for their resistance.[10] Those who survived stayed to offer tentative welcome to the Northern occupiers and to confront the precarious future that awaited them.

Word of the Union seizure of Port Royal spread throughout the South, and African Americans, facing starvation or capture where they were, streamed toward the sea, hiding during the day and traveling quietly at night. One enterprising basket maker made a waterproof, coiled grass boat that carried him safely to Port Royal.[11] Many people, especially children, died of exposure or starvation on the long journey.

The thousands of island residents and hordes of incoming refugees faced desperate circumstances. White plantation families had either taken or destroyed whatever food and supplies they could. Union soldiers plundered most of what was left, stealing crops, boats, and livestock. Enslaved persons had typically received cloth for making clothing twice a year, and the Union victory at Port Royal came just before the winter issue, leaving them to face cold weather in worn, thin clothing.

Soon after the Union declared victory on the islands, the strongly antislavery secretary of the treasury department, Salmon P. Chase, arrived to determine the fate of "abandoned" lands. Commodore Samuel F. DuPont, who had led the Union naval attack, shared Chase's humanitarian concern for the destitute African Americans, as well as his embarrassment about the pillaging by Union troops. DuPont reported that most of the people on the islands were "almost starving and some naked or nearly so."[12] The men decided that a different future was possible only if a new cotton crop could be planted by mid February. Mr. Chase wired a young Boston attorney named Edward Pierce, who had been at

Fortress Monroe when the first "contrabands" appeared there and had supervised their work and education.

But before Mr. Pierce could arrive to offer assistance, another Northerner with an interest in cotton appeared on the islands. In early December, Lieutenant Colonel William H. Reynolds, an officer from Rhode Island, presented a letter to Secretary Chase from his state's young governor, recommending Reynolds to oversee the collection of contraband cotton. Since Governor William Sprague was about to become Chase's son-in-law, and Chase had every reason to trust him, the secretary agreed to the recommendation and sent Reynolds to Beaufort.

When Mr. Pierce did appear on the scene, he discovered that Mr. Reynolds had made himself quite at home. Reynolds had begun his reign on the islands by confiscating all the volumes in the Beaufort Library, including several rare biographies, shipping them north atop bales of cotton. He had instituted an exploitive arrangement with the African Americans who were picking cotton, paying them a dollar for every four hundred pounds of unginned cotton delivered at the steamboat landing, deducting the value of any salt, molasses, or other staples they used from plantation stores. And he had arranged to have all the cotton ginned in New York instead of on the islands.

Lieutenant Colonel Reynolds was among the first wave of a myriad of Northern speculators and carpetbaggers who flooded the desperate South, seizing an opportunity for personal economic gain. One observer wrote that the federal government had "sent out a cotton agent for every bale of cotton, with the rank of Captain."[13] Commodore DuPont wrote to a Northern friend, "We have had all kinds of agents out here(:) cotton collectors, statistic collectors, humanitarians, philanthropists, etc., the best among them the people of God, starting schools."[14]

Edward Pierce, a man of God, was about starting schools—and about aiding African Americans on a path to self-determination. So was Rev. Mansfield French, who arrived on the islands about a week behind Pierce, at the request of Lewis Tappan and George Whipple of the American Missionary Association. These joined forces with a local army officer, Chief Quartermaster Rufus Saxton, who shared their concern about the desperate plight of the African Americans.

Mr. Pierce also enlisted the aid of a Boston friend, Rev. Jacob Manning, assistant pastor at Old South Church. Rev. Manning, known as a radical spirit, had pronounced John Brown's raid on Harper's Ferry "an unlawful, a foolhardy, a suicidal act," which, he said, he stood by "wondering and admiring."[15] Rev. Manning agreed to recruit missionaries and teachers in Boston, while Rev. French agreed to do the same in New York.

Mr. Pierce traveled throughout the North, raising funds for the Port Royal Experiment, which involved planting schools as well as sustaining cotton production on approximately two hundred former plantations with fairly paid labor. At stake, in Pierce's mind, was an answer to the loud and prevalent voices around the nation shouting that African Americans were unable to handle freedom responsibly and would never be "productive citizens." His plan was derided by some as a "very mad scheme," but many others were compelled by his vision. One observer commented that abolitionists would do well to concentrate their energies on the Port Royal project because "the success of a productive colony there would serve as a womb for the emancipation at large."[16]

Secretary Chase paved the way for Mr. Pierce to meet with President Lincoln about the experiment. Feeling pressured by those who wanted to push him ahead of public opinion on slavery and grieving the critical illness of his young son, the president showed Pierce little patience, stating his disinterest in the details and wondering aloud why there was such an "itching" to get African Americans inside Union lines. When Pierce explained that the sea islanders had lived there for some time and that it was their masters who had fled, Lincoln wrote a brief note to Chase authorizing him to give Pierce whatever seemed "judicious."[17]

Back in Boston, Mr. Pierce organized a committee dedicated to "the industrial, social, intellectual, moral and religious elevation of persons released from Slavery in the course of the War for the Union."[18] In New York, the American Missionary Association led the organization effort. The two groups collaborated with great speed, and within two weeks of Pierce's return to Boston, forty-one men and twelve women were in New York, waiting to catch a boat to South Carolina. The night before they left, they gathered in the home of the Collector of the Port of New York, placed their hands on a Bible in groups of six, and took the wartime oath of allegiance. In return, they received passports to Port Royal.

March 3, 1862, dawned with a cold drizzle. Large trunks and barrels of clothing, medicine, tools, and seeds were dragged into the hold of the paddleboat *Atlantic*, which headed out in a curtain of fog. On its deck were doctors, teachers, seminary students, and engineers. The expectant group offered prayers and sang hymns as the boat churned its way south.

John Murray Forbes, a prominent businessman on board, referred to the missionaries as a "villainthropic society," adapting a phrase from author Charles Dickens.[19] Boston engineer Edward

Philbrick reflected, "A good many look like broken-down school-masters or ministers who have excellent dispositions but not much talent."[20] Some soldiers on board derisively called them Gideonites, referring to followers of the great biblical deliverer whose vastly outnumbered Israelite army used trumpets and torch-es to send its enemies fleeing. The proud missionaries adopted the term, from then on referring to themselves as Gideon's Band.

A few days of turbulent travel later, the *Atlantic* came to the entrance of Port Royal Sound. Too late in the day for high tide, the boat had to spend the night drifting about, waiting for the sea to rise in the morning and carry her into the harbor at Hilton Head. Edward Pierce told the missionaries that night that "not even the Mayflower" had carried "a nobler mission" than theirs, and that by their efforts would be settled, "one way or the other, the social question of the age."[21]

At Hilton Head, the whole company and their cargo were trans-ferred to a small river steamer, the *Cosmopolitan*, for the trip to Beaufort. About halfway into the fifteen-mile trip, the boat ran aground on an oyster bed. After a long delay, the group finally reached their goal, being ushered to Beaufort on a moonlit path, singing hymns and a rendition of "John Brown's Body" that gar-nered baleful looks from the boat's captain.

They arrived around midnight on what turned into the coldest night of the winter. They decided to sleep on board the boat, and discovered the deck to be covered with hoarfrost in the morning. But the day turned warm and gave them their first glimpse of their new home. A grove of magnificent live oaks was about all that seemed intact in their view. The streets were covered with sand, and formerly lovely homes showed evidence of the massive loot-ing and destruction that had taken place. Soldiers had converted one plantation mansion into a slaughterhouse for livestock. The missionaries picked their way through broken furniture and smashed pianos. Lieutenant Colonel Reynolds and his agents had made a point of confiscating the usable furniture from any home the newcomers decided to use.

Most Union soldiers considered the missionaries meddlesome interlopers. One army official stated that Gideon's Band had descended "like the locusts on Egypt."[22] Drunken parties among the soldiers were not uncommon; nor were their abuses of African Americans, including beating the men, raping the women, and exploiting the labor of all. The self-righteous missionaries were far from a welcome presence. Edward Pierce's confrontation of one particularly brutal colonel led to the officer assaulting and badly beating him.

Mr. Pierce quickly established a headquarters and several supply depots, and he delivered teachers and superintendents in an army wagon to their far-flung posts. The task facing the island residents and the missionaries seemed overwhelming. Planting season for cotton was slipping away, the plantations were widely scattered and isolated from one another, and white owners, soldiers, and cotton agents had all taken a turn doing damage.

Only one missionary in the group had listed "farmer" as his occupation, and inexperience was a serious problem. The primary image of missionary labor on the islands was of a divinity school student overseeing several former plantations, with an even younger companion teacher whose primary contribution was enthusiasm. One superintendent had allowed cotton seed to be used for fertilizer and cattle feed, leaving too small an amount for planting. Pierce drastically miscalculated the quantity of replacement seed needed, and he had to return most of an order to New York. An observer of the missionary operation lamented, "I don't believe in putting Reverends in places where prompt business men are required. Some of them don't get through morning prayers and get about their business till nearly noon."[23]

The missionaries also had not counted on African American resistance to planting cotton. Understandably, people who had been forced to labor for long hours, under threat of the whip or worse, were not anxious to put their energies back into the backbreaking cotton crop. Because of its long growing season, cotton was greatly subject to the arbitrariness of nature; too little or too much rain, blight, or worms could all devastate a crop, and harvest time came at the height of hurricane season. Enslaved persons sometimes worked all night by the light of the moon to get in a crop before it was blown down. Once freed, most of the African Americans on the islands preferred to grow corn, potatoes, and other staples to feed their families, supplementing these with fish and oysters that were readily available. The missionaries' insistence on putting cotton above all else agriculturally was a devastating blind spot. At its worst, this preoccupation extended plantation-era master-slave dynamics and patterns of white control over black labor.

Internal tensions among Gideon's Band were also an issue, with personalities clashing and a rift developing between the more "intellectual" Bostonians, most of whom were Unitarians, and the more pious, "evangelical" New Yorkers, who were mostly Congregationalists. Their perspectives differed widely on education, the role of labor, and their relationship to African American religious practices. The complications intensified when a group of new recruits arrived from Philadelphia, bringing their own opinions.

Among the best of the new arrivals was Laura M. Towne, who had listed her vocation as "abolitionist," and who was a practitioner of homeopathic medicine as well. She had brought with her a large quantity of new and used clothing for distribution. As a prank, the soldiers handling the freight on the arriving boat drew sketches of their imagined view of Ms. Towne on each of the boxes of clothing, all of which bore her name. Their images of a gaunt, bony female bearing a frightful expression and straddling a keg of molasses were far from an accurate picture of this strong, quiet, compassionate woman, who in her early twenties was superintendent of two former plantations, who valiantly battled the islands' smallpox and yellow fever epidemics, and who remained on St. Helena Island for forty years.

Ms. Towne was particularly concerned with the health of the islands' female inhabitants, who had suffered from frequent pregnancies under the burden of producing more slaves for their masters. One woman had been buried up to her neck in earth as punishment a few days after giving birth to a stillborn child. Another, unable to keep up her tasks as a field hand late in a pregnancy, was whipped so brutally that she miscarried.[24]

Ms. Towne and her companion teacher, Ellen Murray, started Penn School, which stayed in operation for almost a hundred years. They began with nine pupils in the living room of a former plantation mansion. Soon they had eighty scholars and moved their classes into the old Brick Church on St. Helena. Ms. Towne wrote in her diary that her earliest students, who were unfamiliar with a classroom, talked loudly, fell asleep frequently, and walked off in the middle of lessons: "They got up by the dozen and made their curtsies, and walked off to the neighboring fields for blackberries, coming back to their seats with a curtsy when they were ready. They evidently did not understand me, and I could not understand them, and after two hours and a half I was thoroughly exhausted."[25] Despite many challenges, Ms. Towne stayed with the school until her death, relying in lean times on her own and her family's money to keep it going.

The arrival of a large barge in 1863 created quite a stir. On board was a prefabricated, two-room, frame school building sent by the Pennsylvania Freedmen's Association. Ms. Towne adorned its tower with a brass bell patterned after the Liberty Bell and inscribed with "Proclaim Liberty," which was rung every morning to summon the island's children to their classes. Every teacher, wrote Ms. Towne, was obliged "to make herself heard over three other classes reciting in concert, and to discover talkers and idlers among fifty scholars while one hundred and fifty more are shouting lessons and three other teachers bawling admonitions, instructions, and reproofs."[26]

The new school was a clear improvement, though it was not waterproof, as Ms. Murray recorded after a particularly hard rainstorm: "The recitation rooms, flooded, are abandoned, and books are hurried into desks. The oldest pupils slide into the driest seats, and the girls exclaim as the water drips on some cherished finery. One teacher, subject to rheumatic attacks, holds her umbrella over her as she teaches. In another class the giggling pupils are all perched, like chickens on a roost, on top of the desks, the floor below them being a pool."[27]

The pupils came to school at great sacrifice, working in their lessons between chores and field work. The school was filled with young students caring for babies, who often cried "from a disinclination to remain five hours foodless" in the arms of their siblings, who were "rather careless of infant comfort in their zeal for knowledge," according to Ms. Towne.[28] One Edisto Island teacher described a young student, Hector, who had to bring his younger brother, his baby sister, and a bucket of rice with him every day. He spent his day reading his lessons while rocking the baby and putting rice into her mouth at regular intervals to keep her from crying.[29]

Superintendents on the farms continued to meet some resistance from local island residents, but teachers were universally and joyfully accepted. Class attendance by both children and adults was regular, even though some pupils had to walk several miles every day to school. In Beaufort, the school grew too large for Rev. Solomon Peck and his daughter to handle, so they hired four African Americans as teachers.

Relationships of respect and affection developed, particularly between island women and their female teachers, who frequently returned from their visits to local homes with their pockets full of fresh eggs, the traditional gift of friendship on the islands. Other gifts appeared from time to time on the porches of missionary houses—articles that the local residents had appropriated one step ahead of the soldiers and cotton agents. These were seen as signs of gratitude and acceptance.

Generally a positive lot, a few among the missionaries were dishonest or interested in personal gain. One unfortunate soul, James A. McCrae, was sentenced to walk up and down Beaufort's Main Street for a week bearing a placard around his neck that read "I sold whiskey to a private soldier." In addition, he was ordered to pay a fine of five hundred dollars or be imprisoned at hard labor for six months, and he was eventually sent home.[30]

For many, the high point of every week on the islands was Sunday services, when local inhabitants, teachers, and superintendents came in a parade of carriages and carts down sandy streets and converged on the Brick Church to pray, sing, and exchange news. People crammed into the pews and aisles, and sat on every available window ledge. Those who couldn't fit inside sat out under the oaks in the churchyard, leaning against the marble gravestones of permanently departed masters.

About a month after Ms. Towne arrived, one of the worst episodes in sea island history occurred. In May 1862, Major General David Hunter was named commander of Union forces in the South. Determined to recruit African American troops, Hunter ordered fifty thousand stands of arms and an equal number of red breeches be sent to Port Royal. African Americans experiencing newfound freedom generally did not want to leave their homes, nor did they desire to fight their former masters. Some feared that the recruitment strategy was a trap to lure them back into slavery.

On May 9, Hunter issued a proclamation declaring all slaves in South Carolina and Georgia free, on the grounds that these states were under martial law. Jubilation evaporated quickly when another order immediately followed. All able-bodied African American males between the ages of eighteen and forty-five were to report to Hilton Head at once. Early on the morning of May 12, several companies of soldiers fanned out over the islands, rounding up men, spreading consternation and panic as they went. Women sobbed as they clung to husbands and sons being dragged away and drafted for fifty cents and a plug of tobacco. Five hundred men were forced into the army that day.

Laura Towne and Edward Pierce were livid. Mr. Pierce protested to Major General Hunter and Secretary Chase that the men were needed for the fields, and that the damage done by Hunter's actions to black trust for Northerners might be irreparable. Hunter's only concession was to return plowmen and foremen. Three days later, President Lincoln rescinded Hunter's order.

Slowly, circumstances began to improve on the islands. A few of the more sensitive missionaries made changes to accommodate prevailing realities. At one of the most successful former plantations, the superintendent gave each African American family a piece of land and complete freedom to plant whatever they wanted. Laborers were assigned only as much cotton land as they wanted to work and were compensated fairly for their hours of planting, tending, and picking.

Money arrived from the sale of the first contraband cotton, providing enough to compensate the missionaries and increase the number of teachers. As word of the venture spread in the North, contributions grew. The arrival of a large shipment of mules bought by the Treasury Department greatly helped the agricultural effort. Though the venture was still tenuous, by June 1862 the worst of the poverty, exploitation, and abuses had been eradicated on the islands.

But just as circumstances began to stabilize, a new threat visited the missionary effort. By the end of July, the thermometer was creeping toward one hundred degrees, and the mosquitoes were almost intolerable. Several superintendents became sick with fevers by fall, and a few went north to recover. Francis Barnard became the first martyr among the missionaries. As he lay dying, hundreds of African Americans surrounded his home, praying through the night. Three other missionaries died that season, including a nephew of renowned abolitionist Wendell Phillips.

Good news came when Rufus Saxton was promoted to general and put in charge of military operations on the islands. But many of his troops ridiculed him for supporting the missionary endeavor and regularly undermined his efforts. The general found himself unable to stop Union soldiers from stealing and killing the African Americans' livestock. The practice was so widespread on Ladies Island that people took their chickens into their cabins at night. The soldiers routinely stripped corn stalks of their ears and tore up miles' worth of fences, burning the rails for firewood.

Word came to the islands that the Union army was in trouble in Virginia, and Hunter was ordered to send reinforcements from among his men. Troops abandoned some of the most productive land and concentrated on the most defensible parts of the islands. Despite protests by the locals and the missionaries, sixteen hundred African Americans, along with their pigs, chickens, and personal possessions, were carried for safety from more isolated areas to St. Helena Island on large flatboats that were camouflaged with tree branches to protect them from Confederate sharpshooters.

On September 22, 1862, President Lincoln announced the promise of emancipation in a Preliminary Proclamation, which would take effect on January 1, 1863. Saxton decided to recruit African American troops and succeeded where Hunter had failed. Officers visited island farms, and black soldiers were promised pay equal to whites. With the war being seen as a battle for freedom, many African American men enlisted—despite the Confederate threat that any captured black soldiers would be immediately shot. Suspicions slowly gave way to trust, and by early November the first full company of black soldiers was formed.

Saxton chose Thomas Wentworth Higginson, a well-known Massachusetts abolitionist and prominent backer of John Brown, to command the black regiment. The regiment had many successes on the islands, driving off Confederate forces, demolishing salt works, and freeing slaves in isolated corners. Teachers followed the companies with their primers, instructing soldiers and those they freed along the way.

Charlotte Forten, a young African American woman, arrived on St. Helena in October 1862. Ms. Forten had begun her teaching career at the age of sixteen, after repeatedly witnessing with terror—from behind drawn curtains in her grandfather's home—the pursuit of runaway slaves by mobs on Philadelphia streets. Bearing a letter of recommendation from poet John Greenleaf Whittier, Ms. Forten had asked the Philadelphia Port Royal Relief Association to enlist her as a teacher. When association officials contacted her, they asked her to be ready to set sail the next day with the party of a Quaker gentleman, Mr. Hunn, who was on his way to open a store at Port Royal.

Ms. Forten's journal is a treasure trove of information about the Port Royal Experiment, beginning with her voyage by sea to South Carolina. "Of all the doleful, dismal, desperate experiences," she wrote, "sea-sickness is certainly the dolefulest, dismalest, and desperate-est!"[31] She spent much of the trip wrapped in a shawl, sitting on a coil of rope on deck, barely surviving a dreadful storm that nearly swallowed the ship one night. Ms. Forten provided rich and poetic details about the people of the islands, the schools, the dangers, and the rare beauty of the environment she called home for almost two years. Just before arriving, she wrote: "Early this morn Mr. H(unn) came to our door to tell us that we were in sight of the blockading fleet in Charleston harbor. Of course we sprang to the window eagerly, and saw the masts of the ships looking like a grove of trees in the distance . . . T'was a strange sight as our boat approached the landing at Hilton Head. On the wharf was a motley assemblage,—soldiers, officers, and "contrabands" of every hue and size . . . (A)fter an hour's delay, during which we signed a paper, which was virtually taking the oath of allegiance, we left the 'United States' . . . and took a steamboat for Beaufort."[32]

A crew of African American boatmen rowed the group to St. Helena. "The row was delightful," wrote Ms. Forten. "It was just at sunset—a grand Southern sunset; and the gorgeous clouds of crimson and gold were reflected in the waters below, which were smooth and calm as a mirror. Then, as we glided along, the rich sonorous tones of the boatmen broke the evening stillness. Their singing impressed me much. It was so sweet and strange and solemn, 'Roll, Jordan, Roll.'"[33]

Laura Towne's carriage carried them through pines and palmettos to the superintendent's house, where a cheerful fire glowed in the grate, and Ms. Forten declared that she "soon began to feel quite at home in the very heart of Rebeldom." But, she added, "It is all a strange and wild dream, from which I am constantly expecting to wake."[34] She faced the austere conditions awaiting her with graciousness, though she wrote of getting little sleep, "what with the headache, the fleas, and Miss H(unn)'s *tremendous* snoring."[35]

She described her first day on St. Helena: "We went into the school, and heard the children read and spell. The teachers tell us that they have made great improvement in a very short time, and I noticed with pleasure how bright, how eager to learn many of them seem. The singing delighted me most. They sang beautifully in their rich, sweet clear tones, and with that peculiar swaying motion which I had noticed before in the older people, and which seems to make their singing all the more effective . . . Dear children! Born in slavery, but free at last! May God preserve to you all the blessings of freedom, and may you be in every possible way fitted to enjoy them. My heart goes out to you. I shall be glad to do all that I can to help you."[36]

On warm days, school was convened outside. "Imagine our school room," wrote Ms. Forten, "the soft brown earth for a carpet; blue sky for a ceiling, and for walls, the grand old oaks with their exquisite moss drapery."[37] She petitioned friends in the North to send picture cards and alphabet blocks for the school. Her writings reflected the shared resolve of those who labored at Port Royal: "(L)et us labor earnestly and faithfully to acquire knowledge, to break down barriers of prejudice and oppression. Let us take courage; never ceasing to work,—hoping and believing that if not for us, for another generation there is a brighter day in store,— when slavery and prejudice shall vanish before the glorious light of Liberty and Truth."[38]

One Sunday she witnessed the baptism of 150 people, many attired in colorful dresses and white aprons, in a creek near the church. Enslaved persons had been prohibited from marrying, so weddings became a common occurrence after Sunday services, attended often by Ms. Forten, who wrote delightful commentary on the grooms, dressed in the best attire they could muster, and the brides, adorned in homemade headdresses crafted from ribbons and bright island flowers. When whooping cough struck many of the children and adults, rendering them unable to get to church, she gathered them on Sunday mornings in her room to read the Bible's Sermon on the Mount and teach them the Twenty-third Psalm.

Ms. Forten was a frequent observer of the African Americans' practice of "shouts," a custom that the McIntosh County Shouters of Georgia have kept alive into the twenty-first century and that is considered "the oldest African American performance tradition surviving on the North American continent."[39] The ritual of the ring shout that Ms. Forten observed was a fusion of lively percussion, call-and-response singing, and expressive movement, with roots in Africa. "Shout," often traced to the Afro-Arabic word *saut*, which was a fervent dance around the Kabaa in Mecca, refers primarily to movement rather than to sound. A "sticker," or "stick man," beat out the rhythm with a broomstick on the wooden floor while vocalists sang a spiritual that accelerated in tempo. The "shouters" moved in a counterclockwise circle, taking small steps, often with arm movements, and never crossing their feet. As one nonagenarian participant explained, "(I)f you cross your feet you were dancing . . . (and) you were turned out of the church because you were doing something for the devil . . . (S)houting is . . . praising God with an order of thanksgiving."[40]

The shouts often happened late at night, after a prayer service in the island praise house, when wooden benches were pushed aside and the shouters took the floor, moving with increasing fervency, sometimes all night long. The shout was particularly common on New Year's Eve, at Watch Night services. Plantation owners usually balanced their books at the end of the year, and frequently they announced on New Year's Day which of their slaves would be sold. Enslaved families spent the long night praying and shouting and hoping against hope to stay together another year.

There were those among the missionaries, particularly the rather staid Boston Unitarians, who considered the African Americans' practice of shouts to be primitive, even barbaric. The American Missionary Association New Yorkers were generally more open to such emotional expressions of faith. And Charlotte Forten found them absolutely inspiring. She wrote about her first shout in her diary, detailing the circle of eager faces and the whirling movement, the excited gestures of an elderly blind man, the red glow and dancing shadows cast on the praise house walls by a burning pine knot: "There is something in it that goes to the depths of one's soul."[41]

The missionaries' lack of respect for the rich African American culture of the islands, and their systematic attempt to eliminate those elements that they found incompatible with their brand of Christianity and "civilization," is perhaps the greatest travesty of the Port Royal endeavor. Their hubris and racism were nowhere more evident than in their insistence on white, Northern ways of worship. Charlotte Forten, with prophetic foresight, recorded in her diary that she passed by a funeral one day and heard local African Americans singing hymns—"not their own beautiful hymns, I am sorry to say. I do so fear these will be superseded by ours, which are poor in comparison."[42] The culture that the missionaries began to undermine in the nineteenth century was virtually obliterated by the land speculators and luxury-resort developers who invaded the islands in the twentieth.

Ms. Forten invited John Greenleaf Whittier to write a Christmas hymn for her students to sing, which they did with great pride under a spray of Spanish moss, holly, and casino berries that she had crafted for the church. On Christmas Day she distributed a home-made apron and an orange to each of the children and an apple pie for every family. She sewed a flannel jacket for elderly, grieving Harriet, three of whose children had been sold away from her to pay bail for her master's son, who had killed another man in a duel.

Ms. Forten was particularly eloquent in her descriptions of the island's natural beauty, and the joy it brought her, in the midst of the dangers and hard work she endured. She reflected on the exquisite majesty of magnolias and the vivid hue of ferns, and she wrote of daffodils in bloom in February: "What sunbeams they are to warm and cheer my heart."[43] She commented on a dazzling display of lightning, trees "aflame with sunlight," and the serene splendor of the beaches and their shells. A cypress swamp filled with tall, gnarled roots reminded her of an "old cathedral, with monks cloaked and hooded, kneeling around it."[44] At times the unique beauty of the islands seemed surreal to her: "The young moon—just a silver bow—had a singular, almost violet tinge, and all around it in the heavens was a rosy glow, deepening every moment, which was wonderfully beautiful. I shall never forget how that rosy light, and the moon and stars looked to us as we caught them in glimpses, riding through the dark pines. How wild and unreal it all seemed and what happiness it was."[45]

When she received reports that Confederate gunboats were on their way to the area, Ms. Forten calmly darned a pair of stockings and waited. "Though not particularly brave at home," she wrote, "it seems as if I *cannot* know fear *here*."[46] She reported hearing shells exploding regularly. When startled by an unfamiliar noise one night, she woke a colleague and recorded their response: "She lit the candle and we took our revolvers,—all ready for rebels. Waited awhile. Then as all continued quiet, put our pistols under our heads and composed ourselves to sleep."[47]

Rumors of Confederate raids were frequent. Of the rebel cavalry, she wrote, "It is said they can blow brandy into their horses' noses and that will enable them to swim a long distance. And so it is tho't they may have been able to cross from Edisto over some of the little creeks . . . Reports are most numerous here, always. So it is better not to believe them at all."[48]

On a journey to Edisto Island, Ms. Forten and her colleagues followed winding creeks through dense thickets in a parade of small boats. On this trip, she discovered that the best antidote for seasickness was pound cake and lemonade. The party spent a night in a deserted plantation mansion, using overturned bureau drawers for chairs and boat cushions as beds. There they discovered a bathtub—"quite a treasure in these regions," she reflected, delighted to get to make use of it. In the morning they had to traverse a large marsh at low tide to get back to the boats: "Mr. T rolled his pantaloons up, took off boots and stockings, and waded across. Lieut. R and Mr. F were each carried across on the back of a sailor. But what were we ladies to do? Suddenly the bathing tub suggested itself to somebody. A brilliant idea, and one eagerly acted upon. Mrs. F and I, successively, seated ourselves in the tub which was raised to the shoulders of four stout sailors, and so, triumphantly, we were borne across. But through a mistake the tub was not sent back for Misses T(owne) and Murray and they had to be brought over on the crossed hands of some of the sailors, in the 'carry a lady to London' style, where at we were all greatly amused."[49]

The challenging sea islands beckoned to many more missionaries in the years that followed, the Gideonites who arrived in March 1862 being only the first wave of Northerners to these exotic shores. Their Port Royal Experiment, the first large-scale, comprehensive program of education and relief for freed slaves, was a harbinger of a more massive effort that would eventually spread throughout the South after the Civil War.

Their agricultural endeavor fell short of success. The cotton yield was low, and the best seed had been lost as a result of ginning the 1861 crop in New York. But the educational effort reached some 2,500 children, and many more adults acquired basic literacy skills. Despite their often condescending paternalism, the missionaries offered island inhabitants critical protection from the abuses and exploitation of the Union soldiers and cotton agents. Through a systematic relief and empowerment effort, they staved off the poverty and starvation that had seemed the inevitable fate of those who had been newly freed, staking a claim on the future.

Like the constancy of waves on sea island shores, currents of resistance and hope have simmered just beneath the surface through time, erupting in torrents of nation-changing force when beckoned by history. The *Amistad* captives and those who came to their aid, along with the newly freed citizens behind Union lines and their teachers, were part of a long stream of courage and faithfulness, flowing with passion and power, eroding, reshaping, transforming the social landscape. Pushed by the principles of liberty, equality, and education, this stream would flow on, over miles and years, joining that mighty river of hope that became the civil rights movement. This long reach toward freedom, which still goes on, made a significant advance with a president's proclamation in 1863.

Charlotte Forten called New Year's Day 1863 "(t)he most glorious day this nation has yet seen."[50] The white tents of the African American regiment spread out over the grounds of the former Smith Plantation on a picturesque point of Ladies Island south of Beaufort, billowing in the wind and offering a backdrop to the soldiers' dark blue coats and bright red breeches. Five thousand people from around the sea islands were expected to gather. Large stores of molasses, bread, and tobacco had been prepared, and a dozen oxen were roasting on spits over pits filled with burning coal. Long before daylight, throngs of people riding in carts or on oxen, coming by foot or by boat, headed toward the platform that had been erected in a grove of massive live oaks. Anticipation and excitement wafted on the ocean breezes.

Prince Polite, who became a renowned island basket maker, was a young boy in 1863. He recounted the details of that marvelous day.[51] Prince's grandfather, Big Pa, who had been a chieftain in Africa before he was sold into slavery, was a hundred years old, with hair white like cotton. Prince thought his grandfather was too frail to walk to the celebration, so he decided to stay home with him. But Big Pa had another idea, telling him, "Son, I was borned free and I's goin' to die free! Bring me my stick, 'cause we're going to get our freedom!"

Many of the formerly enslaved inhabitants believed that they had to be present for the reading of the Emancipation Proclamation in order to be free. The youngest of babies were carried in arms so as not to be left out. "So we started out to get our freedom," recounted Prince Polite. He and his grandfather walked six miles to the ferry, and on the way Big Pa's eyes "burned like fire." He clutched his walking stick in one hand and his grandson's hand in the other. "It seem like Big Pa grow stronger and stronger as he walked. I ain't never going to forget that walk so long as breath is spared in my body. There been aplenty of people on the road, all hastening to get their freedom too!"

Except for a small scandal involving the superintendent in charge of refreshments being accused of watering down the government-supplied molasses for the feast, the day went off in grand style. Dr. William H. Brisbane, a sea island planter turned abolitionist, who had carried his slaves to freedom in the North, read the Emancipation Proclamation to the crowd. "I couldn't get the understanding of it," said Prince, "but Big Pa, he look like he could go on listening until Judgment Day!" Hymns were sung, and prayers and poems offered. An American flag was handed to Colonel Higginson, who began to wave it exuberantly.

Then, said Prince, his grandfather gripped him hard on the shoulder and began to sing. "My country 'tis of thee, sweet land of liberty, of thee I sing!" Before he finished the first line, another voice in the crowd joined in, and then another. And then, said Prince, "It seemed like all the colored people of a sudden know that that flag belonged to we people and that for the first time we had a country of our own—and nothing could keep them from singing it out."

Colonel Higginson later wrote in his journal of that poignant moment: "I never saw anything so electric. It made all other words cheap, it seemed like the choked voice of a race at last unloosed . . . Art could not have dreamed of a tribute to the Day of Jubilee that should be so affecting, history will not believe it, and when I came to speak of it after it was ended, tears were everywhere."[52]

After the singing, Big Pa "lost all his strength and fell where he stood." Prince laid him under a giant oak tree, thinking his grandfather was dead. Big Pa lay quiet for a long time, then suddenly he opened his eyes and said, "Go tell the colonel please I must see him before I die."

Colonel Higginson came to his side. "Colonel, is you plum sure I is a free man?" asked Big Pa. The colonel said Big Pa was as free as he was. "And does the flag belong to colored people same as you?" Big Pa wanted to know. Higginson answered affirmatively. And then he asked, "If I had been a soldier, could that flag cover my coffin at my funeral?" Big Pa's voice trembled as he pleaded, "Please, Colonel, you couldn't let me enlist today, could you? I know I'se an old man but I'se got some strength in my arms still, and I could serve my country and my flag for one day. I could die proud and happy! I ain't got but one wish in all the world now, and that is to have that flag cover me when I die!"

Colonel Higginson bent over, took the old man's hand, and promised him the flag on his coffin. "My country's flag, my country's flag," exclaimed Big Pa. "Thank the Lord, I born free and I die free!" Then, said Prince, "He just smiled and shut his eyes. He never opened them no more on earth."

Charlotte Forten wrote in her diary that evening: "Ah, what a grand, glorious day this has been. The dawn of freedom which it heralds may not break upon us at once; but it will surely come, and sooner, I believe, than we have ever dared hope before. My soul is glad with exceeding great gladness."[53]

4
"Go Up and Possess the Land"
The Post-Emancipation Struggle

The shrill whistles of three Union gunboats pierced the quiet night along South Carolina's Combahee River on June 3, 1863. A short woman in a turban—whom John Brown had called "General" and the hundreds of African Americans she had guided along the Underground Railroad to freedom in Canada had named "Moses"—shepherded a group of startled slaves toward the waiting boats. Some carried steaming pots of hominy, others had children in tow, and many were herding squealing pigs and squawking chickens toward the river, the oaths and threats of their overseers ringing in the air behind them as the whistles summoned them forward.

Harriet Tubman had been at work as a spy for the Union, passing on the information about Confederate movements and supply lines she gleaned from local people. Her raid on the plantations along the Combahee, in league with Union Colonel James Montgomery, was a stunning success. The boats slipped up to the Beaufort pier early the next morning, their decks crowded with 727 African Americans, who had been escorted by 250 black soldiers from the newly formed 2nd South Carolina Volunteers.

The "contrabands" were housed temporarily in a church, where Colonel Montgomery proudly proclaimed victory and the rescued serenaded him with the spiritual "There Is a White Robe for Thee." Harriet Tubman, it was reported, "created a great sensation" with a speech of "sound sense and real native eloquence." When she finished, all the able-bodied men were promptly inducted into Montgomery's regiment.[1]

Emancipation was six months old by that time. But many enslaved people in isolated corners had not received the word, and many plantation owners made a point of keeping the news from them. In the months that followed the official proclamation, the future of four million former slaves was anything but clear. Much of the controversy regarding their status swirled around the issue of land ownership.

Most of the Gideonite missionaries felt that the newly emancipated citizens were entitled to gain possession of the land on which they had labored, with the New Yorkers of the American Missionary Association advocating land ownership most strongly, sometimes in confrontation with the more business-minded Boston superintendents. As early as February 1862, General Rufus Saxton had suggested that land be parceled out in equal measure to African American families. But a year later, soon after emancipation was proclaimed, the U.S. Congress was at work trying to pass legislation to put confiscated Confederate lands up for open sale, a move that would have destroyed the social experiment at Port Royal. Laura Towne convinced General Hunter to intervene, and, citing military necessity, he issued a General Order to stop the sales as arranged.

President Abraham Lincoln supported the effort to reserve large tracts of land for people formerly enslaved, and the terms of the land sales were changed to enable that possibility. On March 9, 1863, exactly one year after the arrival of the Gideonites on the sea islands, the first land sales took place. A substantial portion of the islands went to the federal government. Local African Americans, who pooled their meager resources, cooperatively bought several former plantations, comprising about two thousand acres.

About a third of St. Helena Island went to Edward Philbrick, the Boston engineer who on the journey to Port Royal had assessed the missionaries as "broken-down schoolmasters and ministers" lacking talent. Philbrick planned to conduct a massive free-enterprise agricultural effort based on cotton production. He had the support of most of the Boston missionaries but the strong disapproval of the New York American Missionary Association contingent, which accused him of instituting a system of wage slavery motivated by profit and self-interest.

The AMA missionaries strongly and persistently advocated that the nation owed a debt to its former slaves and that a stable economic future could be secured only through land ownership, while those in Philbrick's camp felt that any assistance to newly emancipated citizens was not only unnecessary but harmful. William Gannett, a Boston Unitarian in Port Royal, wrote of the formerly enslaved, "Very little, very little, should be given them; now in their first moment of freedom is the time to influence their notion of it." Gannett felt that it would be "most unwise and injurious" to give African Americans plots of free land, because to do so would encourage idleness and "remove the benefits accruing to the people from the struggle to obtain them."[2]

The debate was momentarily sidelined by developments in the war. On the same day as the Combahee River raid, the first Northern regiment of free African American soldiers arrived in South Carolina. Sent off in grand style a few days before from Boston, the famed 54th Regiment of Massachusetts arrived on June 3, 1863, to an equally spectacular welcome in Beaufort. Bands played and the crowds sang in this Southern town—reported to contain at that time more abolitionists per capita than Boston—whose streets its Northern occupiers had renamed with letters and numbers in the manner of Washington, D.C.

Boston abolitionists had pushed for the creation of the 54th Regiment, with the strong advocacy of Massachusetts Governor John Andrew. He felt that it was critical that African Americans have a hand in defeating the Confederacy; otherwise, he said, they would be in the situation of having "lost their masters, but not found a country."[3] The young Robert Gould Shaw was named colonel of the regiment.

Union attention became riveted on an assault on Charleston, the symbolic heart of the Confederate rebellion. Battery Wagner, a fort near Charleston harbor, was the chosen first target. The black troops of the Massachusetts 54th slogged through marshy terrain for two days without sleep or food, and with little water except for what fell on them from the sky. They arrived at the fort at sunset on July 18, fatigued, wet, and cold, but determined to be the lead regiment in the attack. Their dedication was all the more compelling given that they were serving without compensation, refusing to take an insulting cut in pay after the army withdrew its pre-enlistment promise of regular soldiers' wages.

Walking in sand and water up to their knees, buffeted by unrelenting waves, the black troops marched forward in the gathering darkness and were greeted with a blistering hail of gunfire. Of the six hundred men who launched the attack, 270 were killed, wounded, or missing when it was over. Colonel Shaw stood for a brief moment on the fort's parapet, holding high his sword and shouting, "Forward, Fifty-fourth!" before being shot through the heart.

After the failed assault, Confederates stripped Colonel Shaw's corpse of his uniform and gold watch. The fort's commander ordered that he be buried in the common trench with his black soldiers as a sign of shame. Later, when Union forces regained the fort and decided to recover the body, Shaw's father refused to allow it. He wrote to the AMA's Edward Pierce, "We can imagine no holier place than that in which he is, among his brave and devoted followers, nor wish for him better company—what a bodyguard he has!"[4]

Charlotte Forten had been inspired by both Harriet Tubman and Robert Gould Shaw. On a visit to see Ms. Tubman in Beaufort, Ms. Forten listened raptly as the heroic old woman told her story and was moved to tears when she sang choruses of jubilant songs. Ms. Forten had taken Colonel Shaw to a shout in an island praise house, which he much appreciated, asking for copies of the hymns to send home. Ms. Forten said of him, "The bravest are the tenderest."[5] On July 20 she wrote in her diary: "For nearly two weeks we have waited, oh how anxiously for news of our reg(iment) which went . . . to take part in the attack on Charleston. To-night comes news, oh so sad, so heart sickening. It is too terrible, too terrible to write . . . That our noble, beautiful young Colonel is killed, and the reg(iment) cut to pieces! . . . I am stunned, sick at heart. I can scarcely write . . . It seems very, very hard that the best and the noblest must be the earliest called away. Especially has it been so throughout this dreadful war."[6]

Edward Pierce informed Ms. Forten that Colonel Shaw had left instructions before the attack that, if he should fall, one of his horses should be given to her. Shaw had three very fine, spirited ones that he had brought from the North, according to Ms. Forten. She was greatly surprised and moved by the gesture, writing that she would "treasure this gift most sacredly, all my life long."[7]

In the wake of the fighting, many of the missionaries, including Charlotte Forten, went to Beaufort to help tend the injured and write letters home for them. Island residents sent fresh melons and vegetables by the cartload to the soldiers, with expressions of gratitude for their sacrifice. Among Ms. Forten's tasks was mending the patients' pants and jackets: "It was with a full heart that I sewed up bullet holes and bayonet cuts. Sometimes I found a jacket that told a sad tale—so torn to pieces that it was far past mending."[8]

The courage of the black soldiers at Battery Wagner riveted the nation, and the assault was seen as a turning point—the moment, according to one historian, when the African American soldier changed "from a chattel to a person."[9] Public opinion in the Union turned in favor of enlisting black troops, and by the end of 1863, sixty African American regiments were being organized.

In the sea islands, this meant a return to tactics of terror. Over General Saxton's protests, Major General Hunter sent squads of soldiers to seize African American men at night and herd them forcibly into army camps during the day. When a group of local women attacked soldiers with their hoes, the troops fired on them.

A Treasury official wrote that the men were being "hunted like wild beasts" and that the islands were in "a perfect panic." A few men had been killed for their resistance, and many others had taken to hiding in the swamps. The official said that he could "conceive of no greater terror and distress on the coast of Africa after a slave hunt" than he had witnessed on the islands. The conscription by terror required 1,045 Union troops to raise 2,831 African American soldiers.[10]

By the fall of 1863, General Ulysses S. Grant's Union troops had defeated General Robert E. Lee's Confederates at Gettysburg; the cities of Vicksburg, Mississippi, and Chattanooga, Tennessee, had fallen into Union hands; and Union forces controlled the length of the Mississippi River. As the fighting shifted, attention in the sea islands returned to the issue of land ownership. On September 16, 1863, President Lincoln outlined plans for the disposition of the sixty thousand acres the federal government had acquired in the land sales the previous March. Included in his plan was the sale of twenty-acre lots to "heads of families of the African race" at the rate of $1.25 per acre.

A few weeks later, on a clear October day, Reverend Mansfield French of the American Missionary Association stood outside a small church on Port Royal Island and pulled out his Bible. He preached to a crowd of island residents, black soldiers, and fellow missionaries that they were facing a historic moment like that of the biblical Israelites and the prophet Moses when they stood at the edge of the Promised Land. Rev. French exhorted them, as according to scripture God had instructed the Israelites, to set aside their fears and "go up and possess the land." Local residents sang the spiritual "Children of a Heavenly King, as we journey, let us sing . . . " General Rufus Saxton explained the president's instructions and invited island residents to inspect a sixteen-by-twenty-foot cabin, constructed of poles and planks without nails, a prototype of one that each family was entitled to buy at a cost of twenty-five dollars.

On November 3, Saxton formally invited African American families to come to his headquarters with a deposit of money and a clear description of the land they wanted to buy. What he did not realize—or chose to ignore—was that only sixteen thousand of the federal government's sixty thousand acres were for sale—an amount woefully inadequate for the needs of the islands' African Americans. Government officials accused Saxton of trying to establish "squatter sovereignty" in the region. They ordered a survey and, ignoring winding creeks and marshy inlets, former plantation boundaries, and the lay of cotton fields, created small, square tracts and many odd, unusable triangles of land.

On New Year's Day 1864, island residents huddled in a bitter east wind under an overcast sky to hear General Saxton proclaim a bold hope for their future on the anniversary of emancipation. Saxton outlined his idyllic vision of the islands as he imagined them in two years: "(W)e may see these islands covered with neat cottages, each the centre of a happy home, little farms well tilled, school houses built and teachers hired to instruct your children..."[11]

Missing from the crowd that day was Rev. French, who had gone to Washington to persuade Secretary of the Treasury Salmon Chase to grant formerly enslaved persons preemption rights to sea island land. French was successful in his mission, and island officials accused him upon his return of having tricked Mr. Chase. All federal lands not reserved for military or educational purposes were made available to African American families at the $1.25-per-acre rate in twenty- or forty-acre tracts—forming the genesis of the famous postwar expectation of freed slaves that the federal government would provide each of them with forty acres of land.

On January 17, St. Helena's Brick Church was overflowing with island residents and missionaries who came to hear Saxton and French describe, as one observer put it, how they were going to "reorganize the whole system of Southern Society."[12] Speakers droned on through the day, and weary listeners finally lost patience when Judge Abram D. Smith of the federal land commissioners explained at length the Latin roots of the word "preemption," then spit out a large plug of tobacco. In the days following, the commissioners were flooded with preemption claims, many marked with the petitioner's *X*, a few signed with names in the shaky penmanship of new literacy.

Pride and hope soon turned to bitter disappointment, as the commissioners refused even to acknowledge the petitions. A weekly sea island paper accused them of being "cruel and contumacious," their response marked by "shuffling insincerity."[13] Secretary Chase removed Judge Smith, perhaps the most sympathetic commissioner, from his post for drunkenness. It was said of the judge, "If you catch him before ten, you will find him sober and clear; but then he doesn't get up till quarter of ten."[14] Smith's fall from official favor coincided with Chase's retraction of preemption rights for former slaves.

Within days, one of the commissioners was assuring a prospective land speculator in Massachusetts that it was safe and profitable to buy land in the sea islands and that African Americans would gladly work for him. When the sales went forward, land sold for an average of more than eleven dollars per acre. In its report, the land commission stated smugly, "You will readily see therefore what an imposition upon the government it would have been to have had these lands pre-empted at $1.25 an acre."[15]

Rev. French, referring to the biblical Israelites who grieved in exile by hanging up their musical instruments on the branches of trees, wrote to Chase: "The willows bend again under the weight of broken harps. The voice of joy and thanksgiving has given place to mourning."[16] In all his church services, including funerals, French exhorted the former slaves to move onto the land they needed, plant crops, give prospective buyers as much trouble as possible, and defend their right to stay with their hoe handles, if necessary. Critics accused him of treason.

Some of French's hearers paid heed to his fiery sermons. A group of former slaves planted corn in Edward Philbrick's Coffin Point cotton fields and refused to pull it out. Those who had bought land cooperatively were seeing success in their efforts. But most African Americans were left with few options, and many felt forced to work for Northern businessmen such as Philbrick, who was in his second successful season of cotton production, turning a large profit by underpaying his black labor force. Philbrick eventually sold his land in the fall of 1865, for five times the price he had paid for it.

Thwarted at home, sea island residents, in a bold and audacious move, decided to send a full South Carolina contingent from among them to the Republican National Convention in Baltimore in May 1864. Sixteen delegates, four of them African American, were elected at a rally in Beaufort. One observer disparaged them as "three or four army sutlers (provision peddlers) sandwiched between contrabands." William Gannett, though harboring hopes that the delegates would be officially recognized, declared the effort "premature and foolish."[17]

The South Carolina flag flying from Guy's Hotel in Baltimore during the convention created a sensation, and many delegates pursued the Port Royalists staying there and took an interest in the reorganization going on in South Carolina. Members of the Port Royal delegation received seats on the floor of the convention but were denied official recognition. Their efforts to bring the question of black suffrage to the floor—the first organized public attempt to raise the issue—were skillfully circumvented. One observer commented, "All were ready to have the negroes fight for the Union, die for it, but were hardly ready to let (them) vote for it."[18]

The war that tore the nation in half was coming to a close. By mid-November 1864, the city of Atlanta lay smoldering under a pall of smoke and Union General William Tecumseh Sherman was ready to launch his infamous March to the Sea. As he and his sixty thousand troops marched in four columns toward the coast, sowing destruction as they went, a throng of freed people followed them, seeking protection.

Seven hundred of them arrived in Beaufort on Christmas night, shivering and starving, "in a state of misery which would have moved . . . a heart of stone," according to one observer.[19] One woman whom soldiers had found foraging for food, her legs still in shackles put on by her master to prevent her from running away, was alternately carried and dragged for miles before the men found the means to cut her chains. A mother managed to get her eleven children safely to the city by tying them together along the length of a rope. Stories were told of other mothers who felt driven to kill their youngest children, when they could walk no farther, in order to save their oldest.

The sea island residents responded generously to the newcomers, sharing their meager resources, but there simply was not enough to go around. Laura Towne, who was inundated with sick patients, wrote to AMA officials in New York, "The poor Negroes die as fast as ever. The children are all emaciated to the last degree and have such violent coughs and dysenteries that few survive."[20] January 1865 was icy and wet, and victims of malnutrition and pulmonary diseases died at the rate of three or four each day. Refugees continued to arrive at the rate of a hundred a day.

General Sherman had been quoted as saying that he believed that "Massachusetts and South Carolina had brought on the war, and that he should like to see them cut off from the rest of the continent, and hauled out to sea together."[21] His rough troops, heady in victory, were notorious for abusing island inhabitants and destroying property. But Sherman emerged as an advocate for those formerly enslaved at the most important point of their future security and survival. On January 16, 1865, he issued his Special Field Order Number 15, which declared that the sea islands from Charleston south to St. John's River, and the corresponding coastal land thirty miles into the mainland, were reserved exclusively for settlement by African Americans on tracts of land not to exceed forty acres.

On Skidaway Island, African Americans laid out a village plan, numbered their lots, put the numbers in a hat, and drew them. A reporter from the *National Freedman* wrote of the venture, "It was Plymouth Colony repeating itself. They agreed if any others came to join them, they should have equal privileges. So blooms the Mayflower on the South Atlantic coast."[22] By the summer of 1865, General Rufus Saxton had overseen the settlement of forty thousand freed people on the land.

Wherever the former slaves established farms, the Northern missionaries set up schools. They redoubled their efforts in the North for acquiring medicine and clothing to meet the growing crisis. And they pressured the federal government to establish a national bureau to aid the African Americans, declaring that at Port Royal they had demonstrated that the typical emancipated citizen was "willing and able to fight as a soldier; willing and able to work as a laborer; willing and able to learn as a pupil."[23] Taking the Port Royal experience into its consideration, on March 3, 1865, the U.S. Congress passed the Freedmen's Bureau Act. It included the provision that "every male citizen, whether refugee or freedman," be granted forty acres of land for rental for three years, after which time he could purchase it.

General Oliver Otis Howard, who had led a column of troops in Sherman's March to the Sea, was named head of the Bureau of Refugees, Freedmen, and Abandoned Lands, popularly known as the Freedmen's Bureau. Secretary of War Edwin Stanton summoned General Howard to his office and handed him a large bushel basket loaded with papers, saying, "Here, General, *here's your Bureau!*" The stunned general was unable to receive the gift, having lost his right arm in battle. Recommended by General Saxton and abolitionist preacher Henry Ward Beecher, Howard had visited Laura Towne's school on St. Helena (where his empty sleeve made quite an impression on her young scholars) and was sympathetic to the plight of the freed people and well liked by the missionaries.[24]

On April 9, 1865, General Robert E. Lee surrendered his army at Appomattox. Five days later—exactly four years and one day after the Union surrender of Fort Sumter—a throng of freed people, abolitionists, teachers, missionaries, and politicians converged on Charleston to witness the raising of the old flag over the battered fortress in the city's harbor. Abolitionist William Lloyd Garrison burst into tears when a regimental band played "John Brown's Body," exclaiming, "Only listen to that in Charleston's streets!"

Rev. Beecher, his long gray locks whipped by the ocean wind, had to clap his hat firmly upon his head and hold his speech with both hands, causing some of his listeners to register their disappointment that the famous orator read, rather than preached, his text. Far from offering reconciliation and hope to the defeated Southerners in his audience, Beecher berated them and held forth an image of secessionist aristocrats—"these guiltiest and most remorseless traitors"—on Judgment Day being "caught up in black clouds, full of voices of vengeance and lurid with punishment

. . . whirled aloft and plunged downward forever and forever in end-less retribution."[25]

Wildly misjudging what lay ahead, Beecher continued, *"One nation, under one government, without slavery,* has been ordained, and shall stand. There can be peace on no other basis. On this base reconstruction is easy, and needs neither architect nor engineer." The Port Royal missionaries likely wondered where Beecher got such a notion, or the idea that Southern whites would simply acquiesce to Reconstruction efforts. Laura Towne over-heard a Charleston woman at the gathering say, "See those nasty Yankees," and her friend respond, "I wish I had their winding sheets to make when the yellow fever comes."[26] Another Southern woman declared that she avoided the Yankees "as studiously as if they were as many rattlesnakes."[27] These comments were a more accurate reflection of what lay ahead.

The task of Reconstruction was complicated considerably by the fact that on the same night as the Charleston celebration, President Abraham Lincoln was killed in Ford's Theater in Washington, D.C. The assassination spread confusion and uncer-tainty among residents across the sea islands. One former slave was heard to say, "Uncle Sam is dead, isn't he?"[28] Fear was strong that, with the man they acknowledged as their liberator gone, they would have to return to slavery.

Within a month, the first of the dispossessed plantation own-ers drifted back to the islands, and by summer the return was a flood. Laura Towne wrote, "Secesh are coming back thick."[29] They were shocked by what they encountered. Planter Thomas Elliott, who returned without his family, said of Beaufort, "The town is not fit for a white Lady to stay in, Yankees and negroes are all the rage."[30] His kinsman William Elliott returned to find that two black-ened chimneys rising out of a pile of ashes and rubble were all that remained of his family's mansion. He took up residence in an outhouse with a few of his father's former slaves and put in a cot-ton crop.

Many stories were told of formerly enslaved persons who took pity on their indigent former masters, advancing them small loans and performing kindnesses. But fear and hostility greeted other former plantation owners. Stephen Elliott reported of his former slaves, "(T)hey firmly and respectfully informed me: We own this land now. Put it out of your head that it will ever be yours again."[31]

But the white planters seemed assured that they would get their land back, a confidence that was not without foundation. President Andrew Johnson's view of Reconstruction was that returning

Confederates had only to acknowledge the end of slavery and submit to federal authority. On May 29 he granted general amnesty to all participants in the rebellion, with the assurance of restitution of all property except slaves. General Howard worked quickly to distribute as much land as possible to African Americans before Johnson's policy went into effect.

On September 23, former planters from Edisto Island, futile in their pleas to the Freedmen's Bureau, successfully petitioned President Johnson for the return of their land. Johnson ordered General Howard to go to the island to inform the residents. They were in a state of panic by the time he arrived and refused to come to order until a woman began singing the spiritual, "Nobody knows the trouble I've seen; nobody knows but Jesus." Trouble indeed. General Howard reluctantly broke the already suspected news that the planters still held legal title to their land.

Laura Towne went to Washington to plead with President Johnson and Secretary Stanton on behalf of the freed people on the islands. Her pleas were fruitless, and she returned with the further bad news that General Saxton was to be removed from his position and the Freedmen's Bureau was to be subordinate in its affairs to the military occupation forces, which were accused of having more interest in maintaining order and forcing African Americans to work than in treating them fairly. By March 1866, all formerly enslaved persons not in possession of land who refused to make contracts to work for restored planters were forced to leave the islands.

The cessation of the war, and the painful settlement of the land issue, signaled the end of the radical experiment at Port Royal. Before arriving to participate in the endeavor, James Thompson, a young member of Gideon's Band, had said, "To make another Massachusetts of South Carolina it is only necessary to give her freedom and education. To these ends we devote our best efforts."[32] The radical idealists who converged on Columbia, South Carolina, in 1868—among them many AMA missionaries—did their best to institutionalize this hope. They created a new state constitution based on democratic principles that eliminated race inequality and laid the legal foundation for a universal, free, public education system. "The skeleton of an educational system will be already there," the missionaries claimed of their contribution, "waiting only to be filled up."[33]

In a letter to Edward Pierce, Laura Towne credited the presence of the Northern missionaries and teachers with molding South Carolina toward loyalty after the war, which she claimed was absent in the states without their influence. Mr. Pierce claimed that no moment since Christian martyrdom or the Reformation called for such devotion and "exhilaration of moral sentiments" as was found in the South at the close of the war.[34]

To the missionaries' great dismay, the settlement of land disputes had slammed one door of hope for those who had been enslaved. But the shared commitment between pupil and teacher to education lived on and spread with vigor throughout the South after the war. Port Royal came to be viewed as a "dress rehearsal" for experiments in equality and education that sprang up in virtually every corner, largely through the stepped-up efforts of the American Missionary Association. The city of Savannah, Georgia, emerged as a focal point of both the best and the worst of the ongoing educational missionary endeavor. As the effort marched on into this new territory and beyond, remnants of the missionaries' influence among the freed population lingered on the sea islands—in cooperative agricultural efforts and schools, in empowered African American communities, and in a small throng of schoolboys bearing the first and middle names Rufus Saxton and Edward Pierce.[35]

5

An "Invasion of Light and Love"

Flooding the South with Teachers

Children clung desperately to their mothers, and husbands encircled wives with protective arms, their warm tears mingling with the cold, driving rain. Huddled together in the horse stalls of the Ten Broek racetrack near Savannah, Georgia, 429 men, women, and children owned by Pierce Butler were known that bitter day in March 1859 simply as "Allotment A." Husbands and wives, sisters and brothers, elders and infants, some only days old—all had been loaded onto railroad cars and carried to the racetrack to be auctioned off by the infamous peddler of human property, Joseph Bryan.

Bryan's Slave Mart was a dreaded symbol among Savannah's black population. A somber brick building with grated windows, it was the usual auction site for enslaved persons arriving in the city. But this sale—the largest ever in coastal Georgia—was too massive to fit within its walls. Slave speculators came to the racetrack from all across the South, inspecting the human merchandise for days before the selling began.

Pierce Butler had inherited both a fortune built on the backs of enslaved Africans on the Georgia sea islands and a familial predisposition for privilege. Butler's grandfather, Major Pierce Butler of Ireland, had arrived on American soil in 1767 as part of the 29th Regiment of Foot to King George III. Major Butler, who viewed slaves as "plantation equipment," was responsible for drafting the fugitive slave article to the U.S. Constitution and the infamous "three-fifths rule," which deemed every slave equivalent to three-fifths of a person.[1] His grandson came into possession of the family's holdings on Butler and St. Simons Islands, one of the largest plantation complexes in the country, encompassing 1,500 acres planted in rice, cotton, and sugar, and exploiting the labor of some eight hundred slaves. [2]

In 1836 Mr. Butler married Fanny Kemble, a popular English actress who was appalled at the miserable condition of Butler's human property, and at her husband's pronouncements that blacks were "incapable of mental, cultural or moral improvement" and that teaching them to read "impairs their value as slaves, for it destroys their contentedness."[3] Ms. Kemble observed no contentedness among those who were enslaved on the Butler plantation—only wretched hovels, ragged clothing, and sick slaves lying on the ground unattended and groaning in pain. She flooded her husband with petitions on their behalf for more food, clothing, and rest after childbirth.

Ms. Kemble's persistent concern for the slaves, and Mr. Butler's considerable propensity for sexual infidelity, eventually led to a very public divorce in 1848. Within a decade, Mr. Butler, once one of the wealthiest men in the nation, had squandered most of his fortune through mismanagement and dissolute living. His mansion was sold to pacify creditors and meet gambling debts. All that was left to sell in 1859 were his slaves. Half of them were carried to the racetrack auction.

Mortimer Neal Thomson, a writer for the *New York Tribune* who pretended to be a speculator at the sale, wrote: "The buyers were generally of a rough breed, slangy, profane and bearish, being for the most part from the back river and swamp plantations, where the elegancies of polite life are not, perhaps, developed to their fullest extent." He overheard one particularly brutish man say, "You can manage ordinary niggers by lickin' 'em, and givin' 'em a taste of the hot iron once in a while when they're extra ugly; but if a nigger really sets himself up against me, I . . . just get my pistol and shoot him right down; and that's the best way."[4]

On the first morning of the auction, Pierce Butler walked among his slaves and spoke affectionately to each one. Then he commenced selling them, wrenching them from home, family, and community, subjecting them to whatever brutalities their new owners would force upon them. They stood for two days in a drenching rain, wind howling around them, clutching bits of baggage and one another as they were paraded into the racecourse's grandstand—an event that came to be known throughout generations as "the weeping time."

Though Mr. Butler stated his desire that families not be separated, few remained intact. The reporter Thomson wrote: "(T)he man and wife might be sold to the pine woods of North Carolina, their brothers and sisters be scattered through the cotton fields of Alabama and the rice swamps of Louisiana, while the parents might be left on the old plantation to wear out their lives in heavy grief, and lay their heads in far-off graves, over which their children might never weep."[5]

The fate of Jeffrey and Dorcas—"chattel No. 319" and "chattel No. 278"—was typical. Mr. Thomson recorded his observations about an hour after they were sold apart: "I see Dorcas in the long room, sitting motionless as a statue . . . and I see Jeffrey, who goes to his new master, pulls off his hat and says, 'I'se very much obliged, mas'r, to you for trying to help me (by buying my wife) . . . thank you—but—it's—berry—hard'—and here the poor fellow breaks down entirely and walks away covering his face with his battered hat, and sobbing like a child."[6]

When the sale was over, Mr. Bryan feted the buyers with champagne and cigars. Pierce Butler had $303,850 in his pocket. Before leaving the racetrack, he walked among his former slaves once again, carrying two canvas bags filled with twenty-five-cent pieces. He doled out a dollar to each as salve for their burning grief.

The Emancipation Proclamation brought an end to such cruel, public spectacles and wrenching, private sorrows. But it did not end the loss of home and community. For most African Americans, emancipation meant being uprooted, leaving behind plantation life and seeking a new start. For those in Georgia, Union General William Tecumseh Sherman led the way to freedom—or to death.

In November 1864, the general had turned his eyes from the scorched ruins of Atlanta toward the Georgia coast and vowed to make Savannah his Christmas gift to President Lincoln, a goal he achieved. All along his path, destitute and desperate African Americans fell in behind his troops, swelling to twenty-five thousand by the time Savannah came into view. A few fortunate ones owned mules or wagons, which were loaded up with kitchen goods, bundles of clothing, and children. But most of the refugees walked two hundred miles or more, carrying infants and the elderly, staving off starvation by foraging and winter's chill with thin blankets, hoping for safe haven on the coast.

General Sherman had rallied his rough, hardy, ragtag troops for their grueling and unprecedented assignment with the declaration, "I propose to demonstrate the vulnerability of the South, and make its inhabitants feel that war and individual ruin are synonymous terms."[7] As they moved toward Savannah, Sherman's men burned towns, and destroyed bridges and railroads. They wrestled through deep mud for most of their journey and tried to dodge Confederate land mines planted around the city. Like the refugees, they foraged for survival, tackling turkeys and pigs, rounding up thousands of cattle and horses, raiding storehouses for sugar, molasses, and coffee. The troops were often hungry, and as they closed in on Savannah, many were barefoot as well. One soldier, in a letter to his family, speculated that "by the time we reach home our legs would be worn clear up to the knees."[8]

In addition to the troops' ransacking the homes and stealing the food of vulnerable southerners, reports circulated of abuse of civilians, including rapes against women and a few hangings of homeowners who refused to reveal the hiding places of their valuables. One woman who tried to drive away some foragers by throwing scalding water in their faces was dunked in a barrel of molasses. But kindnesses were extended as well. Most celebrated was a Christmas Day gesture, in which a captain and ninety troops tied tree branches to the heads of mules to make "reindeer," hitched them to wagons, and distributed food to families in a particularly impoverished area outside Savannah.[9]

To many troops, the refugees who shadowed them were a drain on precious resources and food. In the most notorious incident of cruelty, at Ebenezer Creek near Savannah, one army corps ordered the African Americans following them to stay behind on the bank of the large stream, then pulled up their pontoon bridge once the last wagons and troops had crossed. The abandoned refugees stampeded into the frigid water, determined not to be cut off from their only protection. Several women carrying babies, it was reported, were swept downstream and drowned. A few contrite soldiers threw logs across the stream, which were fashioned into a raft that carried across as many refugees as could get on board before Confederate forces began firing. Many of the African Americans lost their lives, and several were captured.

Temporary camps, crowded and unsanitary, were established on Savannah's docks. William Gannett, who came from Port Royal to assist with resettlement, described an arrival scene he witnessed: "One half of the number had to be helped up the plank;

they would drop half away from weakness. Four men only were strong enough to carry up those who could not lift a limb. Long, bony, and still, they lay along the decks, the flies swarming around them, as if they lit upon the dead. The silence of four was that of death; and before I had them all landed, the four were six. And yet their case has been that of thousands."[10]

That winter Savannah's population almost tripled with the influx of impoverished African Americans. Finding food, clothing, and shelter was seen as critical to survival. So was getting an education. In December, only days after Union troops occupied the city, a committee of African American church leaders met with General Sherman and Secretary of War Stanton, requesting support for the education of Savannah's freed blacks. From this meeting the Savannah Education Association (SEA) was formed, and a plan for an organized system of free schools was designed.

The SEA's constitution called for funding elementary schools through voluntary subscriptions. Though most parents were handed utter destitution along with emancipation, they made overwhelming sacrifices to enable their children to attend school. In a January 1865 letter to American Missionary Association officials, Rev. William T. Richardson recorded the scene at a meeting when parents were invited to bring forth their subscriptions: "Men and women came to the table with a grand rush—much like the charge of Union soldiers on a rebel battery. Fast as their names could be written by a draft penman, the Greenbacks were laid upon the table in sums from one to ten dollars, until the pile footed up the round sum of seven hundred and thirty dollars as the cash receipt of the meeting."[11]

The money raised was enough to support five hundred children in school for a year. An executive board of nine men examined teaching candidates, and within a week they had hired fifteen instructors and acquired several buildings for use as schools. Louis B. Toomer, who had taught a clandestine school before the war, served as the principal teacher.

Rev. Richardson's letter continued, reflecting great pride about a procession, the "Grand Rally of the Children," that took place on the first day of school: "Tuesday morning we met some five hundred of them in the lecture room of the church. After the proper arrangements were made they were marched forth through the streets of the city, to the buildings assigned for schools. This army of colored children moving through the streets seemed to excite feeling and interest second only to that of Gen. Sherman's army. Such a gathering of Freedmen's sons, and daughters, that proud city had never seen before! Many of the people rushed to the doors and windows of their houses, wondering what these things could mean! This, they were told, is the onward march of Freedom . . . "

But enthusiasm on the part of Northern officials soon faded when they realized that Savannah's African Americans desired to maintain control of the educational effort. Rev. S. W. Magill wrote to AMA headquarters that those in charge of the local effort were good men, but inexperienced. He was angry at their lack of responsiveness to Northern interference, charging that the nine men on the executive board were barely literate, calling their organization "radically defective," and accusing them of "exclusiveness" because they did not want white teachers in their schools. The board expressed openness to receiving financial assistance from the American Missionary Association, but it suggested that, if white teachers came to Savannah, they should serve as assistants to the local black teachers. "(T)he whole thing," wrote Magill, "is preposterous."[12]

In the spring, Rev. E. A. Cooley arrived from Massachusetts to take over AMA operations in Savannah. He immediately began installing white instructors and demoting black teachers to the status of assistants. Rev. Magill petitioned the military to create a new position and appoint him Director of Education among the Colored People for the District of Savannah.

Using its financial aid as leverage, the AMA succeeded in subverting the Savannah Education Association, which could not carry its schools into 1866 without resources from outside. Faced with closing down the educational effort or accepting Northern financing and control, the SEA gave in to the American Missionary Association. In April of that year, Rev. Cooley triumphantly proclaimed, "The field is now virtually our own and another year we can enter it with a great vantage ground in having a house, school buildings, and no opposition."[13]

The Savannah chapter in the AMA's history could have portrayed a stellar model of empowerment and mutual respect. Instead, this early venture showcased Northern white arrogance, racism, and control. The Savannah Education Association, which was the most impressive of Georgia's local black education organizations, was ideally situated for a cooperative venture with the AMA. It met the AMA's stated desire to support strong, local, collective efforts with a high degree of commitment exhibited through generous contributions of time and money. But it apparently violated a largely unspoken assumption: that African American groups desiring Northern aid were required to relinquish all control of school operations. That paternalism on the part of some AMA officials and superintendents, representing the worst of the American

Missionary Association, would plague the organization for the duration of its nineteenth-century education crusade.

Representing its best were the teachers, who walked into unknown territory armed with courage, creativity, and commitment, determined to bring hope to despairing, desperate corners. During the Civil War, they had followed closely on the heels of Union soldiers as the troops penetrated the South and liberated the enslaved. One of them, Mrs. S.F. Venatta, became the AMA's first martyr when a six-pound Confederate cannon ball struck her between the shoulder blades near Helena, Arkansas. One teacher wrote, "History never recorded, and prophecy has scarcely foretold, scenes of greater joy than were witnessed in many cities of the South as our teachers, following closely upon the steps of victorious armies, gave to the freedmen additional assurances, promising them education and the open Word of God."[14]

When General Ulysses S. Grant and his Union troops were victorious over the Confederate rebellion, and the last of the cannons finally were stilled, the American Missionary Association, along with several other benevolence groups, put out a call for teachers to flood the South. Their goal was to reach as many of the nation's four million emancipated citizens as possible. Wrote one historian, "Abraham Lincoln's pen and Grant's sword created the greatest internal problem which the Christian philanthropy of any nation was ever called to face."[15] The May 1869 issue of the AMA's official publication, *The American Missionary*, summed up in one sentence the association's view of its bold response to the crisis: "The war with bullet and bayonet is over at the South; the invasion of light and love is not."[16]

Over the next several years, hundreds of teachers answered the call, the vast majority of them young women, their median age twenty-eight. The youngest teacher was fifteen, the oldest eighty. These women comprised 83 percent of the American Missionary Association's Southern personnel during the first year after the war.[17] According to one observer, they "taught and wrought with a heroism rarely equaled, never surpassed, by women of America or of the world—enduring privations and persecutions which made glory of their shame."[18]

The missionary teachers were generally intensely idealistic, anxious to risk as much as their brothers and fathers had during the war. Precursors of the modern feminist movement, they were committed to breaking free of the genteel spheres of domesticity and dependence to which women of their station and time were relegated. Desiring more meaning and adventure than the confines of New England parlors and submissive marriages, or prospective marriages, would allow them, in their crusade against the ravages of slavery they also battled the stereotypes and conventional notions of what women should be and do.

Jennie Stowell's three brothers had all fought in the war, and only one returned home to Massachusetts alive. Her parents discouraged her from enlisting in the education campaign, accusing her of being headstrong. Over their protestations, at the age of twenty-seven she received a commission from the AMA to teach for one year in Macon, Georgia.[19]

Sarah Jane Foster of Maine, who had her commission to teach with the Freewill Baptists in West Virginia revoked because she socialized freely with her students and their families, applied for a position with the AMA. She wrote in her application, "I am not subject to any physical derangements that I know of," and said of the educational effort, "I never was in a work that so thoroughly aroused my whole being, and gave life such a zest."[20] Ms. Foster served for a year in the low country of South Carolina outside Charleston before yellow fever killed her at the age of twenty-eight.

By contrast, the AMA had great difficulty attracting male teachers. The war had taken a serious toll on available males, and men generally had more opportunities open to them and were less willing to work so hard for so little pay—or, as writer Ednah Cheney put it, "to devote two or three of the best years of life to hard duty for a despised people, in a dangerous climate, and for a small remuneration." But the women, wrote Cheney, were "strong and brave enough for any work, and we have not feared to send them even where men were asked for; and they (have) neither flinched from danger, nor been discouraged by toil."[21]

The teachers were filled with evangelistic zeal, generally viewing themselves as part of a great moral crusade to uplift degraded former slaves and impose New England-style civilization on the South. Most of these self-described "Christian soldiers waging a battle against illiteracy, ignorance, and sin"[22] had never been in the South and had little idea what would confront them in this alien land devastated by war, ravaged by poverty, and plagued by disease.

Their travails frequently began on the journey to their often isolated outposts, requiring overland travel to New York City, a four-day ocean voyage by steamship to a Southern port, and transport by train or wagon the remainder of the way. Missionary letters from the period reflect the challenges: "I arrived at Savannah on the 13th—the voyage occupying four days. We came near perishing during the first part of the trip. The steam in the pipes that heat the cabins froze in New York, through the carelessness of the Engineer who made no effort to have it melted, and so we had a cold cabin, and cold berths all the way. Add to this seasickness, and you can imagine our misery.[23]

"We arrived safely after a terrible lashing at sea, in a wonderful damp condition. Mrs. Warner's trunk got soaked and nearly all her clothes spoiled. It was our vote unanimous that heaven could not be perfect without being the land promised 'where there shall be no more sea.' The owners of the (steamship) line got the full benefit of our board, we certainly got none of it. [24]

"You are aware that we were some 10 days on the old Saragassa—got a thorough 'pickling' in salt water which has improved my health by the addition of a cold and troublesome cough. I spent a part of the time in great danger of turning into "fish bait"—have not yet decided how far 142 lbs. of 'missionary' would go when used for that purpose.[25]

"I had a hard, and expensive, journey from Beaufort to Macon (Georgia). There were heavy rains the whole week. I was out in several, and spoiled a dress which cost nine dollars, a hat worth $2.50. An umbrella is but little protection in the rains we have here. With a salary of fifteen dollars this comes rather hard. Owing to these heavy rains it was found when we were within twenty five miles of Macon that the track was washed away . . . so we could (not) reach Macon for four days."[26]

While the AMA established "mission homes" with a superintendent and several teachers in larger cities, teachers in more isolated areas frequently arrived at their assigned posts only to discover that they had no place to stay and no building for a school. Fannie Campbell lived and cooked in a tent in Vicksburg, Mississippi. Minnie Owen slept in a pantry. One teacher on a Georgia plantation found lodging in former slave quarters, and another retired to her small room one winter night to discover her bed covered with snow. Facing unbearably cold floors in Talladega, Alabama, Josephine Pierce tied a string to a square of carpet and dragged it with her from bed to washstand to writing table.

Schools were begun in cotton warehouses and churches, in abandoned barracks and barns, in open fields and under magnolia trees. One South Carolina school was started in a former billiard room, and another in Alabama found a permanent home in a former headquarters of the local Ku Klux Klan. A school in Atlanta was begun in an abandoned railroad boxcar. Some pupils studied in sheds where slaves had been whipped not long before.

"I am teaching in what was, till the fall, the *poultry-house*," wrote a Georgia teacher. "Had the comfort of the feathered tribe been more thought of in its erection, mine would have been better secured at present. The crevices are numerous, and the keen winds easily find them. On the most exposed side, I have nailed up an army blanket, and if I could only get more to tapestry the rest of the building, it might make the hens sigh for their old quarters."[27]

Sophia E. Russell wrote from Brunswick, Georgia: "Our school house is an old church, about a mile from our 'home'—not very good looking but very comfortable—right in the midst of the 'pine barrens' & completely isolated from all the rest of the world, except fleas and mosquitoes, plenty of those."[28] Helen M. Dodd's Virginia school was convened in a loft over a stable. Although it was cold and smelled unpleasantly pungent, she concluded that it was "no less suitable for a dispensary of knowledge and righteousness than for the birthplace of our blessed Saviour."[29]

Most teachers tackled the challenges presented by their circumstances with ingenuity and a sense of humor. One young woman, lacking sheets, made her own by splitting open her petticoats. Another made a pillow from the sawdust in which her jars of fruit had been packed. Still another used an army ammunition crate for a table, a tin plate for a mirror, and a potato for a candlestick.[30] A teacher in Midway, Georgia, wrote in 1868: "We were here three days without even a bed; at last, by our united efforts, we succeeded in obtaining that. We are still minus chairs and dishes and about every other article of furniture. Add to this the fact that our stove smokes most outrageously, causing us to shed a great many tears, and you have some idea of our internal arrangements.

"(We have) unceiled and unplastered walls, whose rough, barnlike boards are well adorned with wasps' nests; these, however, have nearly disappeared since our arrival, owing to a vast amount of poking and pounding. We wash our own windows, do our own cooking, kill our own lizards, cut our own fingers, burn our own faces, and hold no one responsible. Our house at night is made luminous by the light of one tallow candle set in a tin pepperbox . . . Add to our other blessings a contented mind, and you will see we have very much for which to be grateful."[31]

Georgia teacher Julia Shearman was considerably less grateful and amused by her circumstances. She was so angry when her complaints about her hard husk mattress went unheeded by AMA officials that she ripped it up, removed some hard objects she found inside, and sent them to New York with the suggestion that the AMA secretaries try sleeping on them.[32] Virginia teacher John Taylor left his post soon after he arrived, saying that he "could not live anyplace where the land was so level."[33] But fortunately, as one superintendent noted, "the fainthearted and peculiar were few in number."[34]

Winter brought dangerous drafts to the schoolrooms, and summer wafted in with unrelenting fevers. Sooner or later, most teachers were struck with influenza, malaria, or dysentery. Three teachers died of typhoid fever at the mission home in Hampton, Virginia. All six teachers at LeMoyne School in Memphis contracted yellow fever during the epidemic of 1876, and three died. Scores of others succumbed to varieties of illnesses resulting from overwork, lack of rest, and limited diets.

Teachers were expected to teach day, night, and Sabbath schools, often with as many as a hundred pupils spanning several generations, from young children to grandparents. "Here is seated a middle-aged man, intently studying the first principles of arithmetic," wrote one teacher. "Yonder is his wife, as diligently poring over her primer. Here, a mother just commencing to read; there, her son of sixteen, trying to conquer the multiplication table. In this class is a man just learning his letters; by his side are children five years old at the same lesson."[35] The missionary teachers also tutored, visited the sick, gave out food and clothing to the destitute, read and wrote letters for the freed citizens, and usually did their own cooking and cleaning, as well as splitting and hauling wood. In addition, many planted gardens, picked blackberries, preserved fruits, and canned vegetables to supplement their meager diets.

"I have Abraham Lincoln as a visitor in my school almost every day & evening," wrote Ellen E. Adlington from Berne, Georgia, "so you see I keep good company. This is a little . . . baby, whose sister says that 'every where she go she have to tote dis big boy' & whose mother brings him to nightschool. He has got so that he puts out his little black fists to be taken & laughs & crows at sight of me. I think he will learn to read spontaneously, he is so constantly breathing in the atmosphere of learning."[36] Many formerly enslaved people changed their names after emancipation, and it was not unusual for them to name their children after popular heroes, often Lincoln, but occasionally Confederate president Jefferson Davis. One teacher observed in her classroom: "Washington, Bunyan, Jeff Davis and Abraham Lincoln played and studied together most amicably. I confess it was not without a tinge of regret that I let big Jeff take his place above little Abe, once in the spelling class, albeit he had earned the same."[37]

Given the hardships they faced—the "tax of brain and nerve," as the AMA put it—it is no surprise that among its *Six Qualifications for Missionaries among the Freedmen*, issued in July 1866, the AMA required of its teachers "Health" and "Energy": "This is not a hygenic (sic) association, to help invalids try a change of air, or travel at others' expense." The *Six Qualifications* also included

ON THE HEELS OF FREEDOM

"Culture and Common Sense" and "Experience," as well as "Missionary Spirit": "As our work is to be carried on in a country devastated, and in a society demoralized, and generally made hostile by war, no one should seek, accept, or be recommended for an appointment who is not prepared to endure hardness as a good soldier of Jesus Christ . . . None should go, then, who are influenced by either romantic or mercenary motives; who go for poetry or the pay; who wish to go South because they have failed at the North."

The American Missionary Association also had clear ideas about its teachers' "Personal Habits": "Marked singularities and idiosyncracies of character are specifically out of place here. Moroseness or perturbance, frivolity or undue fondness of society, are too incompatible with the benevolence, gravity, and earnestness of our work . . . Neither should any be commissioned who are addicted to the use of tobacco or opium, or are not pledged to total abstinence of intoxicating drinks."[38]

School supplies were difficult to obtain. The teachers were constantly begging the American Missionary Association's home office in New York to send necessities. Ellen Adlington, who wrote once to plead for a stove, wrote again from Berne, Georgia: "Please to send with the stove (if you should conclude to send it) a long pipe with 2 or 3 elbows, also a blackboard would be of great advantage to the school & I need very much some more first readers, those which begin 'girl, doll, boy . . . ' I want about ½ a doz very simple primary arithmetics, & one almanac for my own use . . . ."[39]

Supplies didn't always arrive in the shape in which they were sent. One teacher unpacked a box of staples and biblical tracts from the New York office to discover that rats had eaten the vegetables. A mixture of peppercorns and coffee grounds "made the Sermon on the Mount so pungent," she reported, "that we sneezed and wept alternately."[40]

The teachers who also frequently requested temperance pledges gave temperance lectures and formed societies of faithful members, with names like "Bands of Hope," "Vanguards of Freedom," "Lincoln Brigades," "Cold Water Societies," and "Excelsior Teetotalers."

One missionary had the task of explaining to the New York office a solicited gift, to somewhat humorous effect: "You have probably received from Albany a half barrel of ale directed to me— rather a curious package you may suppose. Let me explain. As I have stated we have had several cases of sickness among our teachers & they have requested they needed a little tonic. I have bought 2 bottles of ale, which is quite expensive . . . One of our young ladies was expecting a box from Albany & she remarked that her cousin was a brewer & a benevolent man & she had no doubt would be happy to send us some ale . . . I told her it might be best to pack in a half barrel the expected bottles with other things. He immediately replied to her, stating that he had sent a ? (barrel) of his choicest summer ale & hoped it would be of service. It is not of course in the form which would be convenient, & if tapped would sour before it could be disposed of, as a tonic, for those who from time to time might need a little, and had best not be forwarded. If it could be exchanged for bottled ale & kept on hand for the purpose intimated it might be well, but you of course are not prepared to go into the ale business. You may do what you think best."[41]

Purity and modesty were virtues among the AMA teachers. Superintendents reported on teachers caught playing cards, attending the theater, socializing too closely with army officers, or riding with men in open carriages. One Savannah superintendent revealed his anger and disgust when he returned to the mission home one night and found the hat rack bulging with the hats of gentlemen callers without "knowing where the heads were that belonged in them."[42]

Rev. L. A. Gaylor scandalized the association by advertising in a Baltimore newspaper for a woman teacher to accompany him to his post in Montgomery, Alabama, when his fiancée became too sick to travel. May Senderling responded to the ad. On the train ride south, "On waking up in the night, Miss Senderling was much frightened to find a man in the berth with her. She found it was Mr. Gaylor." She was very relieved to arrive at the mission home in Montgomery and "thankful to be saved from the snare of the fowler," according to the superintendent there. Mr. Gaylor, who was made most unwelcome, "stayed with us for two days, and left for parts unknown," according to the superintendent, who was "grieved that he should thus dishonor the cause of Christ and Christian ministry." Miss Senderling remained and became an outstanding teacher.[43]

During the war, American Missionary Association schoolteachers were paid ten dollars a month. After the war, undercutting its own ideals of equality, the AMA paid female and black male teachers fifteen dollars a month, while white males received twenty-five dollars. Superintendents—male only—were paid considerably more, though their work was far less demanding and exhausting than that of the teachers.[44]

A few teachers, who resented their lower salaries and the absence of leadership positions available to women, agitated unsuccessfully for change. Julia Shearman wrote frequent letters of complaint to the New York office, and Amy Williams penned that "the great disparity between the salaries and privileges of the men and women in the work is enough to arouse the indignation of any woman who has one particle of spirit or sense of justice about her."[45] Anna Snowden resigned over the issue in 1869. But the vast majority of the teachers accepted the sacrificial nature of their service and its low monetary reward without complaint.

Funds were often scarce, and many teachers who had the means to do so donated their time. J. K. Warner, superintendent of a Georgia school and mission home, who was responsible for feeding eleven teachers and family members, reported in December 1867 that he had only twenty cents in his possession. The previous month's rent was unpaid, he owed the local grocer five dollars for flour, and he had already borrowed all the money the teachers had. "Our dinner is purchased for today," he wrote. "Beyond that we know not."

Jonathan Cory wrote from South Carolina that his situation was improving: "I have ten cents, two postage stamps, 2 lbs of pork, 12 lbs of wheat flour, ? lb of coffee and 2 oz of tea." David Peebles reported that for months, nine-tenths of his diet was "batter-cakes—sometimes meal, sometimes buckwheat, sometimes flour." In 1875 Helen Leonard, in debt to local merchants, sent this appeal from Montgomery, Alabama: "Please send something to take away appetites or else money to buy food. Cash on hand seventy cents minus sixty-five dollars."[46]

In addition to physical hardships, the schoolteachers faced ostracism and harassment. Local whites often refused to give them lodging or sell them food, viewing them as hostile conquerors sent to further torment a defeated people after the war and recast the South in the image of the North. One teacher wrote, "We have so far, vainly endeavored to buy milk, one lady sending word she would not sell milk to Yankees to save her life, she hated the very ground they trod."[47]

Editorials in local papers described the teachers as "horse-faced" and "slab-sided old maids"; as "miserable wretches, imported scalawags, pale faced renegades and pensioned pimps"[48]; as "the scum of Northern society and of doubtful reputation."[49] A commissioner of the Freedmen's Bureau charged that all the AMA teachers in Augusta, Georgia, were "damned whores."[50] The teachers were accused of coming south to find black husbands and to "stir up strife and sow the tares of hate and evil in the minds of their pupils." A newspaper editor in Fayette, Mississippi, opined that white teachers in black schools should be hanged without benefit of judge or jury.[51]

"The refinement of torture" is how an editorial in the *Norfolk Virginian* described the coming of the Northern schoolteachers: "It did not draw our flesh off the bones as with hot pincers; nor did it stretch our muscles on the rack, and fill our whole physical system with aches and pinches; but it was the more refined torture of an insult to our pride of manhood and our feelings; it was heaping coals upon our mental anguish—to have sent among us a lot of ignorant, narrow-minded, bigoted fanatics, ostensibly for the purpose of propagating the gospel among the heathen."[52]

When local white churches shut their doors to the schoolteachers, they created their own worship. A visiting AMA officer reported the following poignant scene in a mission home in Virginia's Shenandoah Valley: "In a grand old room, defaced by war . . . I saw yesterday a scene not to be forgotten. A room full of youthful women, far from home and all its loves, sang the Lord's song in a strange land. (L)oving hearts trembled as they sang, 'Nearer, my God, to Thee, Nearer to Thee.'

"Here was the red-lipped school-girl, just from school; here the young widow, holding in tearful love the memory of buried husband and child . . . Such were the teachers of the freed slaves, who sat and knelt together; whose soft eyes dimmed with tears as they sang the hymns of home, and prayed for the blessing of God upon their work."[53]

Sometimes the threats against teachers were more than verbal. The Ku Klux Klan was founded in Augusta, Georgia, in 1868, with the express purpose of stopping the education of African Americans.[54] So threatening was the reading and recitation going on within school walls that angry whites determined to drive away the teachers and destroy the schools. Male teachers were most likely to be targets of beatings, and a few were grabbed by mobs and coated with tar and cotton. Arsonists burned schools across the South.After Straight School in New Orleans was destroyed by fire in 1877, the Continental Insurance Company of New York canceled its policies on all AMA schools, declaring the association's work "hazardous."[55]

"There is much opposition to the school," wrote a Georgia teacher in 1866. "Twice have I been shot at in my room. Some of my night scholars have been shot but none were killed. The nearest military protection is two hundred miles away."[56] In Austin, Texas, a military guard escorted the teacher to and from her school every day and stood watch over the classroom. Anne S. Dudley, teaching in Charlestown, West Virginia, said she felt obliged to keep "a good axe and six-shooter at the head of my bed at night."[57] A teacher in Patona, Alabama, was lynched. An AMA secretary traveling in Georgia in 1869 reported the following: "The Ku Klux Klan bands are active. When I reached Atlanta a few days ago, I found one of our male teachers here who had been warned to leave a town a few miles distant . . . The teacher went to the mayor for protection. That worthy officer was kind enough to say that he would not harm the teacher! but that he could not protect him, and would not be answerable for consequences! The man undoubtedly would have been lynched, or murdered, if he had remained.

"A day or two after this I was delayed at a station not far from that place, and saw a man who had been teaching a small colored school on his own account—on the plantation of his brother. He had been dragged from his bed a few nights before, severely whipped, hanged by the neck till almost dead, and warned to leave in five days . . .

"A (Freedmen's) Bureau officer has just told me of a colored man he had seen who had been shot through the face because he had taught a little school of negro children. Here were three cases within a short distance of each other, in less than a week."[58]

A teacher in Virginia wrote in 1870:

"We are in trouble. Five men, disguised in a Satanic garb, on the night of the 26th . . . dragged me from my bed, and bore me roughly in double-quick time one and a half miles to a thicket, whipped me unmercifully, and left me to die. They demanded of me that I should cease teaching 'niggers,' and leave in ten days, or be treated worse. I am not able to sit up yet. I shall never recover from all my injuries."[59]

Rev. H. W. Pierson, the AMA representative in Macon, Georgia, received the following letter printed on an image of a skull and crossbones: "Dr. Pierson (so called), . . . You have proved to be a scoundrel of the deepest dye, by maliciously interfering in matters which do not in the least concern you to the detriment of some of our citizens. This therefore is to warn you to leave this country forthwith, twenty four hours from the above date is the time allowed you to leave. If after the said time your devilish countenance is seen at this place or vicinity your worthless life will pay the forfeit. Congressional Reconstruction, the military, nor anything else under heaven, will prevent summary justice being meted out to such an incarnate fiend as yourself."[60]

Rev. Giles Pease wrote about the desolation that greeted him in Darien, Georgia, in March 1868. The coastal city had been deserted during the war and every building burned to the ground during General Sherman's March to the Sea. Pease described scores of blackened, stone chimneys standing alone, punctuating a charred and barren landscape, scattered with twisted rails and the bleached bones of cattle and horses. He observed that the souls of the city's returned inhabitants were equally scarred, by the war and by their own willing participation in the oppression of African Americans.

William S. Clark, a teacher in Albany, Georgia, offered similar reflections: "Some of the counties between here and the Gulf have not yet emerged from the shadow that slavery cast over them. For planting they clear land by cutting round the tree, through the bark only. The process is called 'deadening.' The tree dies and in the course of a few years drops most of its branches to the ground, leaving the straight trunk alone standing. As I rode along through miles of these ghostly pines, stretching their weird arms over the fields, white with cotton beneath, I could but think that as the axe had severed the principle that gave them life and strength and beauty, slavery was the instrument that had girdled all that was noble and worthy in the hearts of the people and left them deadened in body and soul."[61]

However difficult circumstances seemed for the teachers, the realities of life for their students and their families were often desperate. A teacher in Fortress Monroe, Virginia, wrote in 1867: "We have had continual snow and ice, making the roads almost impassable. The most destitute, who depend for fuel chiefly upon what they 'tote' two and three miles from the woods, have suffered extremely for the want of a fire. The day after New-Year's, I found . . . an old woman and her little grandchild lying in a bed, with the snow drifted in and lying about the neck and shoulders of the little boy . . . Some families, in their extreme suffering with cold, have burnt up their stools and even their bedsteads. One old woman, who had burnt up every article of furniture, began to take up the floor of her house, and while putting it upon the fire, she says this Scripture came to her mind: 'For we know that if our earthly house of this tabernacle were dissolved we have a building of God, a house not made with hands, eternal in the heavens,' and she sat down to think and praise God."[62]

Teachers making home visits were often appalled at what greeted them. One teacher, who found a family subsisting on potatoes, huddled around a dying fire, and shivering in miserable rags, wrote, "You have no idea what scenes of degradation we witness."[63] A Savannah teacher stood by the death beds of five persons in May 1867, including a child who starved to death, and another came across a child gnawing on the head of a rat.

A teacher in Cotton Valley, Alabama, wrote about her favorite student, a mischievous boy named Meredith. To get him to behave in her class, she had only to take away his "checker board," a simple game made from cardboard with eight wooden buttons that had arrived in a Christmas box from the North—the only toy he had ever owned. Meredith carried the treasure to school every day. He grew weak and thin the year the crops failed and food was scarce. When the teacher walked to his family's isolated cabin one night to check on him, she heard moans and weeping and strains of the spiritual "Swing Low, Sweet Chariot," and she knew that "another Comforter had already sent His messenger."[64]

Teacher M. L. Roth wrote from Andersonville, Georgia: "About one man in ten of their employers had dealt fairly & uprightly with them . . . Their patience under such injustice is most remarkable. One old Auntie after working all the season, nursing gently a crop of corn, doing the washing and ironing, was turned off with forty-five ears of corn. We asked her how she bore up under it. 'I asked the Lord to help me & keep me from starvin' & don' you see he has. He sent you ladies with the corn & clothes & I'se all right. Oh the Lord is mighty good to me . . . I'se sorry Massa John served his ole auntie so but I pray the Lord to forgive him.' . . .

"Two days since, a woman who had been turned off with nothing, came to us crying. About a week before while she & her child were at work in the field her house & everything it contained were burned, & since that time she slept under a few boards & without cover save an old quilt one of the blacks had given her. I was glad to have it in my power to help her. She has been a faithful scholar, since our coming here, walking three miles after a day of work to the night school. Her mistress' unfeeling heart grieved her sorely."[65]

"The white population is far from being re-constructed," stated an official of the Freedmen's Bureau.[66] Teachers struggled to match the forgiveness and lack of bitterness they found in their pupils. W. L. Eaton wrote from St. Simon's Island, Georgia, in 1865: "The planters along the shore counties kept their slaves until their crops for the season were made and then sent them away destitute of provisions, and almost of clothing. Some have landed upon our shores as destitute of clothing as our first parents before they used fig leaves, and not having tasted food for three days. And yet they came singing . . .

"I suppose I ought to be very patient towards those God tolerates but it cleans me out of that grace when I see their deep rascallity (sic) still at work. A repentant villain I can easily forgive, but were it not for the force of our military arm, we who are now engaged in the work of elevating the oppressed would lose our heads very soon!"[67]

The teachers were supported by churches and women's auxiliaries in the North, and they continually pestered their friends to send clothing and food for distribution, but there was never enough. Some learned to make dresses out of used tablecloths that arrived. Others had the unfortunate task of requesting cloth for shrouds to bury the many formerly enslaved people who died of disease, exposure, or starvation. Martha Ayres threatened to leave her mission field in the South, "as a knowledge of wretchedness I cannot relieve is a constant burden which I feel unequal to bear."[68]

Tugging most strongly at heartstrings, perhaps, were the thousands of emancipated children who lost their parents to war, dislocation, or disease. One teacher came across three small, starving, crying children, all suffering from small pox, the corpses of their parents and a sister still in the house. In response to appeals from its missionaries, the American Missionary Association opened orphanages in Wilmington, North Carolina, and Atlanta, Georgia, in 1866. The orphanages stayed in existence only a few years, as most children were reunited with long-lost relatives or adopted into other African American families. AMA teachers adopted a few older ones when other options failed to materialize.

Sarah Stansbury was among the most creative and committed American Missionary Association teachers. She wrote to AMA Secretary E. P. Smith in 1869 and informed him that Reuben Richards, an African American farmer in Cuthbert, Georgia, desired to open his own grocery store. She arranged for Mr. Richards to sell his cotton to a New York dealer and then give some of the proceeds to the AMA to purchase supplies and ship them south. His neighbors benefited from lower prices, and Sarah Stansbury facilitated the establishment of a black-owned business, a very rare phenomenon in Reconstruction Georgia, where exploitative sharecropping was the norm.

The education crusade was an effort of mutual sacrifice and courage by both teachers and students. Most pupils walked many miles to school every day, fitting their education around hard labor in the fields during planting and harvesting times; even the youngest were needed to scare away birds from seeds. The students often suffered harassment, sometimes physical abuse, from local citizens who hoped to shut down the educational effort. In Emily Hubbard's school in Petersburg, Georgia, "The pupils are almost every day stoned, and some of them beaten; and not infrequently stones are thrown into the schoolrooms."[69]

The students and their parents were remarkably persistent in the face of constant obstacles. They held bazaars and bake sales to raise money, scraped together pennies and produce to pay tuition. Squirrels were an acceptable form of tuition payment in

Alabama. The same Dorchester teacher continued: "(U)p North (tuition) means money; but down here it means eggs and chickens, and rice, and fish, and crabs, and blackberries, and sweet potatoes; and greens, and corns, and many other things . . . One morning after devotional exercises, as I was going to my office, one of the girls came from her school-room and pulled out a live chicken from under her shawl and asked: "Professor, do you take chickens for tuition?" . . . Again and again a little fellow has come to me and brought his little collection of one and two cent pieces and asked: "Professor, will that make up my tuition?"

There were always more eager pupils than the schools could hold, and many had to be turned away, often in tears. John W. Alvord, superintendent of schools for the Freedmen's Bureau, received a petition from plantations across Louisiana that was thirty feet in length, bearing ten thousand signatures—or X's from parents who were unable to write their names—pleading for schools for their children.[70] Two sisters in Alabama traded places every other day, between school and field work, teaching each other at night so that neither fell behind. One young man, who subsisted on meal and water, rose before dawn to attend school in Atlanta, taught in a country school many miles away, and guarded a building under construction until late at night to earn extra money. When a teacher urged him to pay a quarter to ride to his school so that he wouldn't become ill from overwork and lack of sleep, he replied, "O no! I must save every penny, for I want my sister here too."[71]

Margaret Thorpe wrote of an elderly man who walked six miles to get to her night school, who told her, "Isn't this a most blessed privilege? Many a time I have been whipped for being found with a book, for I always wanted to learn to read."[72] Teacher Clara Duncan had a student who was reported to be 108 years old and was only a few weeks out of slavery, who hunched over his lesson book and strained through dim eyesight to learn to read before he died.[73] "I have five now in spectacles and turbans," wrote another teacher. "It has been more of a pleasure than I can express to go with these old women over the precious truths of the Bible. I never can forget the tears that rolled down their faces as they read with their own lips of the Savior's sufferings and death."[74]

Emancipated citizens had a variety of reasons for wanting an education, including a desire to read the Bible for themselves. Some wanted to be able to understand labor contracts and avoid being exploited and cheated by white landowners and merchants, or to be prepared to read voting ballots when the opportunity arrived. Others longed to be able to write or read the many notices that appeared in newspapers and posted handbills that cropped up across the landscape, used to locate family members and friends who had been forcibly separated under slavery. Many saw the spelling book and primer as stronger weapons against re-enslavement than the gun and bayonet.

Ironically, through their fear of black literacy, whites impressed upon their slaves the import of reading and writing. Many of those who were formerly enslaved possessed an almost mystical awe regarding the power of knowledge and literacy, deemed so dangerous in their hands by whites. Teacher Harriet Ware came across a remarkable funeral on the sea islands: "As we drew near to the grave we heard all the children singing their A, B, Cs through and through again, as they stood waiting round the grave for the rest to assemble . . . Each child had his school book or picture book (that their teacher) had given him in his hand, another proof that they consider their lessons as some sort of religious exercise."[75]

"Families pinched with hunger asked more eagerly for learning than for food," wrote one historian.[76] A teacher in North Carolina observed children arriving at her classroom with tears streaming down their faces, "crying bitterly from the pain of frost bitten hands and feet," determined to get an education. In Beaufort, North Carolina, an enterprising teacher bought straw and taught her shivering, hungry students to make straw hats, using the profits to buy food and clothing for them.[77]

After a schoolhouse in Namsemond County, Virginia, was burned to the ground, forty-five African American men gathered amid the ashes and sent for the teacher. They told her that they would "build her a larger and better house of timber, *so green that it could not burn*, and would keep her supplied with green schoolhouses as long as she would stay."[78] The day after fire claimed a Norfolk, Virginia, school, a young student named Robert comforted his teacher by declaring, "Well, Miss Duncan, if they did burn our school-house, they can't burn what we've got in our heads, can they?"[79]

Many teachers stayed in the South for only a year or two, but some devoted their lives to the educational effort. Mary Frances Wells taught at Trinity School in Athens, Alabama, for almost thirty years. Rachel Crane Mather started a school in Beaufort, South Carolina, and stayed for thirty-six years. Esther Douglass taught for thirty years in four different states, from a Virginia lumber camp to a North Carolina confederate gun factory and a Georgia plantation, abandoning the work only when blindness compelled her to do so.

Though many other organizations responded to the crisis after the war, in 1867 almost a third of the teachers reported by the Freedmen's Bureau to be at work in the South were commissioned by the American Missionary Association. In the first decade of its work, the AMA commissioned 3,470 teachers and ministers, serving 321,099 students in its schools. It received more monetary support from the Freedmen's Bureau than any other organization. Of the $20 million the government and private sources spent to aid former slaves from 1861 to 1890, a third of that came from the AMA.[80]

Though united in a common cause, the benevolent groups often succumbed to jealousies and competed as rivals in fund-raising and controlling the mission field. One historian declared that "even the American Missionary Association, by far the most powerful and influential group in Georgia, suffered from a generous dose of cranky paranoia."[81] One AMA superintendent expressed fears that the Methodists and Old School Presbyterians would "gobble up" everything they could. "If we are going to hold our ground here in Atlanta," he wrote, "we have got to be wide awake. The Methodists are on the watch here, and will get all they can . . . "[82]

Early in the educational effort, the AMA's chief competition came from the American Freedmen's Union Commission (AFUC), which was formed when several smaller, mostly secular associations unified under its umbrella. The American Missionary Association refused an invitation to merge with the organization, which was critical of the AMA's blending of education with religion. As the AMA's more pietistic, evangelical approach came to dominate the work, the AFUC weakened, and it finally disbanded in 1869.

Like other missionary efforts of the late nineteenth century, the American Missionary Association educational campaign was too often marked by paternalism and cultural imperialism. Many of the teachers expressed surprise in their letters that their African American students could learn as well as whites. They arrived not only insensitive to the emotional wounds the war had created in the white Southern population, but also blind to the rich African American culture that existed in the sea islands and throughout the South. Much of what was rich and vibrant in black music, ritual, and faith they labeled "heathen." Critics have also suggested that the effort to educate freed African Americans drained energy from more critical struggles for land ownership and voting rights.

The AMA's self-description of its "invasion of light and love" reflects both what was noble and what was troubling about the missionary effort. Bringing "light and love" was a courageous calling, but too often the teachers did not understand that they were an invading force. They were entering vanquished territory, seen by Southern whites as from enemy ranks, and too often bringing the superior attitude of conquerors to their work.

Yet, the American Missionary Association distinguished itself in several respects. As early as 1865 the AMA issued a public call for the nation to grant African Americans suffrage and full citizenship, gaining it "a well deserved reputation for radicalism on the race issue."[83] That same year it also issued a call for universal education, an ideal that was revolutionary for its time. The AMA's unprecedented effort of sacrifice, courage, and empowerment laid the groundwork for a public school system in Southern states. AMA officials, believing that African Americans should ultimately be responsible for their own education as soon as possible, actively recruited black teachers both from the North and in the South. By 1870, one-fifth of the AMA's Southern personnel were African American.[84]

Historian Clara Merritt DeBoer observed that "African-Americans have done more for and through the AMA than any other predominantly white organization . . . [The AMA's] record in this regard was equaled by no other benevolent or abolitionist society."[85] When renowned abolitionist Frederick Douglass castigated other benevolent organizations for their paternalism in 1875, he described the American Missionary Association as an exception, calling it "a society honestly laboring to disseminate light and hope amongst us."[86]

About that time, a shift took place in the AMA's educational emphasis, with many of the elementary schools evolving into normal schools for the training of teachers. By 1888, the AMA had trained seven thousand black teachers, and these trained thousands more, their influence penetrating virtually every Southern black community.[87] Many of the AMA schools were turned over to their care.

That year, the work was aided considerably by Daniel Hand's donation of just over a million dollars to the American Missionary Association—the largest gift ever made by a living contributor to a charitable organization up to that time. Mr. Hand, who was eighty-eight years old and a widower of fifty years, had made his fortune as a merchant in the South. Bravery apparently ran in his blood: his Puritan ancestor John Hand had confronted injustice as a magistrate, refusing to pass judgment on "Goodwife Garlick," who was accused of witchcraft in Connecticut in 1658.[88]

Daniel Hand had consistently spoken out against slavery. On a visit to New Orleans, he was arrested as a "Lincoln spy," but he was soon released for lack of evidence. In Augusta, Georgia, an angry mob attacked the hotel where he was staying. Friends ushered him safely away, and he was carried in the mayor's carriage to the city jail, where he stayed a few days until he could leave safely.[89] His generous contribution to the American Missionary Association led to the establishment of many additional schools, which served elementary pupils and trained student teachers.

As the twentieth century approached, the nation was embroiled in a controversy about the nature of education for African Americans. The two principal spokespersons on opposing sides of the divide were both distinguished graduates of American Missionary Association schools. One was born enslaved, without a last name, on a plantation in Franklin County, Virginia. "I am not quite sure of the exact place or exact date of my birth," begins his autobiography, "but at any rate I suspect I must have been born somewhere and at some time."[90]

The young slave Booker's only brush with school was through carrying the books of his master's daughters. After emancipation, his family moved to West Virginia, where he worked in a salt furnace and later a coal mine, learning to read at night, getting to his classes on time by secretly moving up the hands of the boss's clock. When a teacher asked him his last name, Booker promptly replied "Washington," claiming for himself a proud heritage. He later added the middle name "Taliaferro."

Booker T. Washington overheard two miners talking about the school founded by Mary Peake, then known as the Hampton Normal and Agricultural Institute, and he determined to find his way there. Friends gave him nickels and quarters, and he departed with a small satchel from his ailing mother, covering the five hundred miles to Hampton walking and begging rides in wagons and cars. He arrived, dirty and disheveled, with fifty cents in his pocket. The head teacher, unimpressed by his appearance, handed him a broom and told him to sweep a recitation room. He swept it three times and dusted it four. When her inspection failed to produce a speck of dust, she said quietly, "I guess you will do to enter this institution."[91]

Upon his graduation in 1875, Washington became an instructor at the school. In 1881 he was tapped to become the principal of the newly forming Tuskegee Institute, whose only tangible asset at its founding was an old, blind horse. Under Washington's direction, students built their own classrooms and dormitories, made mattresses stuffed with pine needles, and tended crops. Tuskegee soon became renowned as a school devoted to industrial education for the sons and daughters of slavery.

On February 23, 1868, a boy was born in Great Barrington, Massachusetts, and endowed with four names. William Edward Burghardt DuBois grew up the son of a domestic servant and an absent father. Working his way through school shoveling coal and splitting wood, he edited for a brief time his short-lived high school newspaper, *The Howler*—a sign of things to come. With the aid of the Great Barrington Sunday school and three Connecticut Congregational churches where his minister had connections, W. E. B. DuBois went off to AMA-founded Fisk University in Nashville, Tennessee.

Upon graduation, DuBois attended Harvard University. He was rejected from the glee club for what he believes was racism, but he excelled in oration and published several essays in *The Courant*, a weekly African American newspaper. He received a masters degree in history from Harvard, and he eventually earned his PhD from the university in 1895—the first African American to do so.

DuBois studied in Germany and Paris. He turned down two offers from Booker T. Washington to teach at Tuskegee and instead taught the classics at Wilberforce University in Ohio and at Atlanta University. In April 1899, while DuBois was living in Atlanta, Sam Hose was lynched and burned in that city. A mob of two thousand fought over his flesh. While hand-carrying a letter of protest to Joel Chandler Harris, then editor of the *Atlanta Constitution*, DuBois discovered that Hose's charred knuckles were on display in a downtown shop window. That same year, DuBois's two-year-old son died of diphtheria while DuBois was vainly searching for an African American doctor to treat him. DuBois was "shattered" by these events, and determined to dedicate himself to the fight for racial equality.[92]

Growing in reputation as an orator and essayist on the issue of race in America, he wrote *The Souls of Black Folk* in 1903, which rocketed him to national prominence. In 1905 DuBois organized the meeting that led to the founding of the Niagara Movement, dedicated to the uncompromising pursuit of political and economic rights for African Americans. In 1910 he was hired as director of publications and research for the NAACP (National Association for the Advancement of Colored People), founding, editing, and writing for its weekly magazine, *The Crisis*.

Booker T. Washington embraced the philosophical position of his mentor at Hampton, Samuel C. Armstrong, who believed that agitating for economic and political rights was counterproductive, and that the best education for African Americans was industrial in nature. In his controversial address to the 1895 Atlanta Exposition, which came to be known to many as "The Atlanta Compromise," Mr. Washington declared: "Our greatest danger is that in the leap from slavery to freedom we may overlook the fact that the masses of us are to live by the production of our hands, and fail to keep in mind that we shall prosper in proportion as we learn to dignify and glorify common labour and put brains and skill into the common occupations of life . . . No race can prosper till it learns that there is as much dignity in tilling a field as in writing a poem. It is at the bottom of life we must begin, and not at the top . . . The wisest among my race understand that the agitation of questions of social equality is the extremest folly . . . The opportunity to earn a dollar just now in a factory is worth infinitely more than the opportunity to spend a dollar in an opera-house."[93]

Proponents of equality accused him of accommodating a plantation mentality and accepting the alleged inferiority of African Americans, of advocating silence and submission in the face of injustice, and of promoting a form of education that mirrored the second-class status of slavery and consigned blacks to a future of perpetual menial labor. DuBois, who fervently agitated for the pursuit of civil rights and the development of a "talented tenth" among African Americans, was chief among Washington's critics. Following one exchange of insults, DuBois referred to Washington as "the Arch Tempter," a synonym for Satan.[94]

Both Southern whites and Northern philanthropists found a friend in Booker T. Washington. As increasing amounts of money were channeled into industrial schools, the American Missionary Association held steadfastly to its commitment to liberal education. Though industrial education was rarely absent from AMA schools, it never formed the heart of the AMA's effort. "There has been a good deal of zigzagging in dealing with the American Negro," wrote a son of an ex-slave. "Such, however, has not been the case of the American Missionary Association. It has moved straight ahead with conviction and courage . . . It holds the place of paramount importance among the agencies responsible for the establishment and development of those schools in the South which have become the outstanding institutions of higher learning for Negroes."[95]

In a conversation about African American education between Wallace Buttrick, then president of the General Education Board, and Theodore Roosevelt, president of the United States, Mr. Roosevelt is reported to have said, "I suppose a primary education is about all that a Negro needs."

Mr. Buttrick replied, "Granted, but what about their teachers?"

"I suppose they ought to have a high school education," answered Roosevelt.

"What about the high school teachers?" asked Buttrick.

"Well!" declared Mr. Roosevelt, "I suppose they ought to go to college. Really, there's no end to the thing, is there?"[96]

The American Missionary Association indeed believed there was "no end to the thing." Having expanded many of its schools from basic literacy into teacher training, the AMA went a step further and put many of its resources into liberal arts education at the university level. Several of its schools developed into outstanding colleges and universities: Fisk University, Talladega College, Tougaloo College, Dillard University (formerly Straight University), LeMoyne-Owen College, Huston-Tillotson College, Berea College, Hampton University, and Atlanta University. By 1890, more than one-third of all Southern African American college graduates came through AMA institutions.[97]

One Fisk University graduate gave truth to President Roosevelt's observation. As superintendent at the J. K. Brick Industrial School in Enfield, North Carolina, he oversaw innovative feats of rural engineering on the school's 1,100 acres, and the engines he designed for the shops were the envy of the surrounding white neighborhood. When one neighbor asked where he had learned to do all that, he replied, "Oh, studying Greek at Fisk."[98]

W. E. B. DuBois believed that, without the normal schools and colleges for emancipated citizens, they would "to all intents and purposes . . . have been driven back to slavery."[99] In *The Souls of Black Folk*, DuBois wrote of the educational crusade of the 1860s in the most glowing terms: "Behind the mists of ruin and rapine waved the calico dresses of women who dared, and after the hoarse mouthings of the field guns rang the rhythm of the alphabet. Rich and poor they were, serious and curious . . . They did their work well. In that first year they taught one hundred thousand souls, and more . . .

"This was the gift of New England to the freed Negro: not alms, but a friend; not cash, but character. It was not and is not money these seething millions want, but love and sympathy, the pulse of hearts beating with red blood—a gift which to-day only their own kindred and race can bring to the masses, but which once saintly souls brought to their favored children in the crusade of the sixties, that finest thing in American history, and one of the few things untainted by sordid greed and cheap vainglory. The teachers in these institutions came not to keep the Negroes in their place, but to raise them out of the defilement of the places where slavery had wallowed them . . . In actual formal content their curriculum was doubtless old-fashioned, but in educational power it was supreme, for it was the contact of living souls."[100]

The power of the American Missionary Association endeavor perhaps can be seen most poignantly in its transformation of two dominant symbols of suffering. Both were places of untold grief. And both became havens of hope.

The stockade at Andersonville, Georgia—where thirteen thousand Union prisoners of war had died from overcrowding, malnutrition, poor sanitation, disease, or exposure, and thirty-two thousand more had survived in wretched misery—became a lightning rod for Northern anger and anguish about the Civil War. In a July 9, 1864, entry in his diary, prisoner of war Sergeant David Kennedy of the Ninth Ohio Cavalry called the twenty-six-acre camp a "hell on Earth where it takes 7 of its occupants to make a Shadow."[101] Civil War nurse Clara Barton had led efforts to get medical supplies and aid for the imprisoned troops, and after the war, President Lincoln authorized her to gather information on missing soldiers and identify and mark the graves of the dead. Captain Henry Wirz, the stockade commander, was found guilty of conspiracy and murder in a federal military tribunal and hanged in Washington, D.C., on November 10, 1865.

In the spring of 1867, AMA teacher Julia A. Shearman traveled throughout Georgia, visiting AMA schools. Two young women from the North had established a school in the former Andersonville stockade. On May 13, Ms. Shearman wrote a letter to AMA officials in New York about her experience in Andersonville: "As I stepped out from the nightschool at half past ten o'clock, & stood with the ladies in the exquisite moonlight, watching the patient, plodding men & women disperse to their homes, how many thoughts crowded my mind! Did they ever imagine, those rebel officers, who used our poor boys, to erect their buildings—buildings put up to enable them to hold 30,000 prisoners in unheard of tortures—did they ever imagine to what use those buildings were to be applied, and so soon? Did they dream that the wail of the captive would scarcely be hushed, & the last victim laid to sleep his long sleep in those awful witness bearing trenches, before two angels of mercy should take up their abode there, transforming that hell upon earth into a little earthly heaven?

"Yes, Andersonville has been cleansed & sanctified, & thank God by the purity, the presence, the labor & the love of woman! Where the rebel soldier's jeer & oath used to be heard, now daily ascends the sweet sound of prayer & praise. For the howl of the hungry hound, eager to chase the perishing Union fugitive, you may now hear the sweet voices of the children blending in songs. The jailer has fled haunted by the memory of his crimes . . . & two gentle women have taken possession of this deserted dwelling; the persecuted slave has found a shelter in the huts erected by his persecutors, & the Freedman's corn is growing in the now empty stockade!"[102]

Ms. Shearman, whose letter was circulated widely through the AMA, went on to exhort "Ye who dwell in luxurious houses, who rest on cushioned chairs and elastic mattresses," to think of their sisters at Andersonville. She wrote that the teachers were threatened by enemies, and that they sat up one entire night expecting their dwelling to be set on fire. She then quoted one of the devoted Andersonville teachers. "Andersonville will ever be to me a memory of suffering, a home of dead heroes, a planting of Freedom's seed . . . It is germinating; already the mellow soil is breaking from the struggles of the embryo which wants the light and air. We have but to lay our ear to the earth, to hear the swelling and the struggle of the new life beneath. A few more rains of love, a few more dews of mercy, a few more suns of grace and the blade will appear. After that the going on from strength to strength till the harvest time shall come."

As dreaded as Andersonville was to the Union soldier, so was the slave market to the African American, with its auction blocks, dehumanizing scrutiny, and wrenching separation of families. Savannah's Joseph Bryan, who auctioned off Pierce Butler's slaves in 1857, was notorious among slave marketers in the South. But with all its tragedy and sorrow, the Savannah chapter also contained one of the clearest and strongest images of hope in the entire American Missionary Association story, a symbol of the transforming power of the educational effort. Rev. William T. Richardson ended his January 1865 letter to AMA officials, which spoke of the commitment of Savannah's parents to their children's education and the grand march of students through the city, with this observation: "One of the buildings now used for colored schools was used as 'Bryans Slave Mart' (as the sign over the door indicates) until the taking of the city by the Union forces. It is a three story brick building fronting on Market Square and contains two large rooms on the second and third floors, about thirty by fifty feet. The upper one has strongly grated windows in which the poor slaves have often been confined there to be bought and sold, as the beasts of the field. These halls in which the poor slave mother has often groaned in the anguish of her soul, as she has seen her darling babies one after another torn from her embrace and sold forever from her sight—are now resounding with the merry shouts of happy school children."[103]

All across the South, AMA teachers sowed seeds of hope, waiting for "a few more rains of love, a few more dews of mercy, a few more suns of grace" to bring them to fruition. In unexpected corners, amid carnage and despair, against all odds, their patience and perseverance paid off. The harvest, as the years would show, turned out to be abundant.

6

"The Torch of Enlightenment Burns Brightly"

The Courageous Witness of Talladega College

The note, sorrowful and poignant, was found lodged under a sliver of a rail fence near Patona, Alabama, on the afternoon of July 12, 1870: "My Dear Wife: I die to-night. It has been so determined by those who think I deserve it. God knows I feel myself innocent. I have only sought to educate the negro. I little thought when leaving you so far away, that we should then part forever. God's will be done. He will be to you a better husband than I have been, and a father to our six little ones . . . God of mercy bless and keep you, my dear, dear wife and children. —Your William"[1]

The lynching of William C. Luke in 1870 was one tragic episode in a sustained campaign by some of Alabama's whites to keep education from its emancipated population. One white resident lamented that blacks, "little and big, have all gone crazy about schools."[2] Five years before Mr. Luke was murdered, in November 1865, fifty-six African American men had met in Mobile, declaring to their fellow citizens, "(W)e regard the education of our children and youths as vital to the preservation of our liberties, and true religion as the foundation of all real virtue, and shall use our utmost endeavors to promote these blessings in our common country."[3]

Among those men were William Savery and Thomas Tarrant, former slaves from Talladega who, upon emancipation, had organized a rudimentary school for African American children. Inspired by the meeting and a visit to a school in Mobile sponsored by the American Missionary Association, the two men began to expand their dream. When they returned to Talladega, they enlisted several neighbors and established an educational society to plan and supervise a school.

The new school was opened in a two-room home, which was immediately overcrowded with students. The educational society then purchased an old carpentry shop, which it dismantled and rebuilt as a school on a more favorable site. But William Savery had bigger dreams yet. In 1851, as a young slave and an accomplished carpenter, Savery had helped to build a Baptist academy in Talladega for white boys. During the Civil War, the building was used as a prison for captured Union officers, one of them having etched the words "prisoner of war" into a windowpane. When Mr. Savery learned in 1866 that the three-story brick building and surrounding thirty-four acres were for sale for eight thousand dollars, he contacted General Wager Swayne of the Freedmen's Bureau and convinced him that Talladega was an excellent location for a black college.

General Swayne proposed the idea to American Missionary Association officials. Pointing out successes farther south in Alabama, Swayne argued that Talladega was healthier in climate and that a school in the grain-growing center of the state was more affordable than one in the cotton belt. After considerable hesitation, the AMA agreed to advance four thousand dollars for the purchase, if the Freedmen's Bureau would contribute the other four thousand plus two thousand for repairs. Through this partnership between a visionary and dedicated local African American community, the American Missionary Association, and the Freedmen's Bureau, Talladega College was born.

While negotiations for purchasing the building were still under way, the AMA sent twenty-eight-year-old Henry E. Brown to Talladega. Rev. Brown had been a student at Oberlin College in 1865 when Abraham Lincoln's funeral train passed through, and he had listened carefully as Rev. Charles G. Finney, renowned abolitionist preacher and president of the college, had offered an impassioned prayer for Southern blacks. That night Brown fell to his knees and dedicated himself to Christian service on their behalf. He arrived in Talladega in October 1867 with his pregnant wife and three-year-old daughter.

As the principal of the only school for blacks in nine adjoining counties, Rev. Brown journeyed to the many small log churches scattered around the region, entreating the congregations: "Pick out the best specimen of a young man you have for a teacher, and bring to church with you next Sunday all the corn and bacon you can spare for his living. I will take him into my school and make a teacher of him." His plea was eagerly followed. In one church, people "brought their corn, from a handful to four quarts—more often a handful—in the pocket, or tied in a handkerchief, and laid it on the altar in front of the pulpit, singing as they marched around the aisle."[4]

Students walked ten, twenty, even thirty miles to Talladega with sacks of corn and bacon on their backs. No accommodations existed for them, so they were "obliged to sleep on the floors of such cabins as could receive them and give them a chance to bake their corn bread by the fire."[5] Some boarded in the unheated attic of Swayne Hall, the renamed school building, so overcrowded that they had to sleep two to a bed.

The school opened in November 1867 with three teachers and 140 pupils. Though Talladega didn't introduce a full college curriculum until more than twenty years later, it was incorporated as a college in February 1869—the first school in Alabama with an interracial charter. The incorporators included William Savery and Henry Brown, both of whom also served on the first board of trustees, along with AMA officials Edwin P. Smith and George Whipple, as well as Ambrose Headen.

Mr. Headen, like Mr. Savery a carpenter and former slave, had worked alongside him to construct the school building as a Baptist academy, which the sons of his former owner attended. Headen spoke of the hardship of building a school for other children, when he had no hope of educating his own. "But God has turned things about so," he marveled. "I was building a college for myself and my family."[6] All four of his children enrolled as students at Talladega. In 1873 he wrote that it seemed like a dream: "I rub my eyes and try to wake myself. When my boys and girls come home from school with their algebras, Greek and Latin books . . . I say to myself, are these my children that were slaves a few years ago, counted no more than cattle? Yet it is not a dream but the blessed truth."[7]

From the moment he arrived in Talladega, Rev. Brown began besieging AMA officials in New York for money and approval to build a dormitory. A year after the school opened, the AMA sent a steam engine and a sawmill. During the summer of 1869, students studied half days and sawed logs, made bricks, and built a drying kiln the remainder of the time, working alongside local volunteers. The immense forests around the school provided an ample supply of wood. On August 7, 1869, with great fanfare, the cornerstone was laid to Foster Hall, named for Rev. Lemuel Foster of Illinois, who had made a generous donation toward its construction. It included a kitchen, a dining room, and sleeping space for fifty female students and faculty.

Early on, the Talladega school was committed to training teachers, and it boasted a normal department "second to none in the South."[8] Its normal school students had to be at least twelve years old, pass a qualifying exam, and possess good moral character. Potential applicants were warned that "those who have not a fixed purpose to improve their time, and an earnest desire to fit themselves for usefulness, should not seek admission, as the presence of such is not tolerated."[9] In the summers, many students, some having advanced only to second- and third-grade readers themselves, went home to teach in "bush schools" that they conjured wherever they could find pupils, passing on the basics of education and earning money to further their own.

The school had industrial and agricultural components as well, including training in carpentry, needlework, and the use of a printing press, and a 159-acre farm that sustained livestock, oats, and 6,500 strawberry plants. It hosted agricultural institutes, which emphasized proper care of livestock and crops, and the importance of owning land. But industrial education was never the school's main focus. When Talladega, despite being outsized, defeated Tuskegee Institute 28-0 in a Thanksgiving Day football encounter one year, Talladega chemistry professor Clara M. Standish declared that it was "a decided victory for higher as compared with industrial education."[10]

Students arriving at Talladega without money were permitted to work on the farm or in the college laundry until they earned enough credits to enroll, attending night classes in the meantime and participating in the college community. When students were unable to keep up their fees, they also worked on the farm or in the laundry, taking a break from the classroom until their fees were paid. Ethel Kiel, who arrived at Talladega in 1891 penniless but dedicated, took nine years to attain her normal diploma, alternating study and work in this manner.[11]

Rigorous discipline marked student life at Talladega. Attendance in classes and church services was mandatory, as was adherence to daily study hours. Dress had to be "plain and simple." Travel was prohibited on the Sabbath, incoming and outgoing mail was censored, nightly curfews were enforced, and use of tobacco and alcohol was expressly forbidden.

The school's main mission was to endow its students with "a trained mind and a devoted heart."[12] H. M. Bush, superintendent of education for the Freedmen's Bureau in Alabama, credited Talladega with having "collected the best class of minds to be found in any of his schools."[13] AMA official Augustus Field Beard applauded the "religious zeal and consecration" that were integral to the school, creating "an atmosphere so surcharged with power and love that the teachers thought of little else than their mission."[14]

The school's success evoked the wrath of those who were threatened by it. Members of the Ku Klux Klan drove two normal students, Irving Jenkins and Dallas McClellan, from their posts and burned their schools. In the presence of his students, five Klansmen seized Jenkins; he escaped from their grasp in a hail of rifle fire. Fire destroyed the sawmill at the college. One night approximately fifty Klansmen began marching from the town's courthouse to the campus, intent on wreaking havoc. They desisted only when several prominent citizens of the town intervened.

The atmosphere of constant threat and fear pushed several faculty members to request that the American Missionary Association send rifles and ammunition, which arrived from New York packed in a consignment of blankets. Both male and female teachers learned to shoot the weapons, and male students stood nightly guard around the campus during the 1870-71 school year. They shot at a man attempting to burn the campus in 1871, but he escaped on horseback.

The lynching of William Luke was among the most traumatizing of the violent events that affected the Talladega teachers and students. Mr. Luke was born in Ireland in 1831, moved to Canada, and as a young man became a teacher and minister. While returning home from a trip in the summer of 1868, Henry Brown met Luke at the American Missionary Association office in Cincinnati, where Luke was applying for a commission as a teacher in the South. Brown was immediately impressed with Luke and persuaded him to come to Talladega.

Luke supervised the workers who built Foster Hall, then he responded to an invitation to start a school a few miles away in Patona, near a new railway line, with an emphasis on training railroad telegraphers. His advocacy of racial equality and fair wages for railroad workers earned him the enmity of local whites and made him the target of constant threats, as well as a volley of Ku Klux Klan rifle fire. He wrote to Rev. Brown after the shooting, "You may yet have to write my obituary," signing his prophetic letter, "Yours from the Lion's den."[15]

The Klan reportedly chose a twelve-man execution squad to make another attempt on Luke's life. Their opportunity came with an incident at the railroad station. The owner of a mule kicked and beat a young African American boy, who was holding the mule when it became frightened by an approaching train and ran off. Several black men who witnessed the abuse got off the train, and shots were exchanged between some of them and a group of white men who had gathered.

A former Confederate major led a white posse in pursuit of the blacks who were accused of participating in the exchange. Luke claimed that they were acting in self-defense and was seized along with the others. They were turned over to the sheriff and put in jail.

More than sixty Klan members, armed and dressed in full regalia, met at the Baptist Church at eleven o'clock that night. They marched to the jail and past the sheriff, seized four of the African American men and Luke, and took them about a mile away to Cross Plains. Luke pleaded for time to write a letter to his wife and to pray. The mob had only three ropes, so they hanged three of the men first on trees by the roadside, then cut down two and used the ropes to hang Luke and the other man.

News of the tragedy reached Henry Brown the following morning. Accompanied by William Savery, who considered Luke a close friend, and a sympathetic circuit court judge, who Brown hoped would offer some protection, Brown boarded a train to undertake the dangerous mission of retrieving Luke's body. On the trip, they overheard a man say, "Yes, we got Luke, Brown's satellite. We'd rather had had Brown."[16]

In Patona, locals refused to lend or rent them a carriage. After some effort, they found a man who agreed to let them use his oxcart and helped them make a crude coffin. They discovered the five bodies side by side in a makeshift pen. Henry Brown spied Luke's last letter to his wife nearby.

Rev. Brown presided at Luke's large funeral at Talladega College the next day, amid threats and taunts from some local whites. The lynching had a chilling effect on the campus, sending a clear message that some Alabama whites saw teaching African Americans as grounds for murder. A newspaper in Marion, Alabama, declared that Luke's lynching had served the public good.

But Talladega College survived, and thrived, thanks to the courage and dedication of those who refused to be cowed by the threats and violence. On June 22, 1876, the inaugural class of the normal department, composed of eight students, was honored at Talladega's first graduation exercises. The college extended its commitment to its graduates, hosting annual teachers' institutes, which were open to all teachers in the surrounding counties.

The school's determination to train excellent teachers was equaled by its commitment to prepare outstanding ministers. In 1872 the American Missionary Association established theological departments in several of its institutions, including Talladega. Student ministers spread throughout the neighboring counties, holding "precious ingatherings," or Congregational revivals, preaching by the light of burning torches in "brush arbors" hastily constructed from pine branches.

In the summer of 1873, Rev. Brown and his four theological students carried a large tent to a wooded area outside nearby Kingston. They held a revival at night, built a church by day, and then moved on to repeat the exercise several times more, using land and hardware purchased by the American Missionary Association. One of the student ministers later reflected, "It must have been a novel sight to see the professor and his pupils in the piney woods during the long, hot summer months, with their great gospel tent, holding evangelistic meetings at night, and by day felling and hewing the tall pines with which to erect a house for school and church purposes."[17] Another reported fondly on those evenings when people came from all around to sing and pray: "After meeting they lit their 'fat pine' torches and went in all directions down the hill through the pine woods towards their little cabins, one, two, or three miles away. Then we prepared our beds by turning one seat around so as to face another and spread our blankets on the two together."[18]

By 1879 the AMA had sponsored fifteen Congregational churches in Alabama, eight of them within forty miles of Talladega. Theological students pastored the new churches in order to gain experience and help with school expenses—though the congregations had little money and often paid them in game, vegetables, and eggs. One church dubbed a row of their potato crop "the Lord's row" and gave those potatoes to their minister for his services.

For many years at Talladega, theology was the "high water mark of scholarship."[19] Under the leadership of Rev. George W. Andrews, who had grown up in a home that served as a station on the Underground Railroad, the theology department blossomed into a full-fledged seminary by 1891. Admission had been opened to women in 1886, and a decade later ten women had been trained as pastors. By that time only Howard University, whose theology department was also founded by the American Missionary Association, could boast more theological graduates than Talladega.[20] As it did for teachers and farmers, the college hosted institutes for pastors as part of their ongoing education.

Talladega underwent radical changes through the years, but some challenges persisted through generations. Albert A. Safford, a former Union captain who succeeded Henry Brown and led the school for several years before being stricken with recurrent attacks of malaria, moved the school toward being a college in more than name only. Like Brown, he persistently begged the AMA for money, claiming in May 1876 that the college had only five dollars and an unpaid bill of thirty dollars for the previous month's food expenses. Soap was in short supply. The roof of Swayne Hall, the only building in Talladega where the town's African Americans could gather for social and political functions, had a severe leak, letting in rain that occasionally gushed through bedrooms, halls, and classrooms.

One New York official, tired of Mr. Safford's pleadings, suggested that he needed to hear a good sermon based on James 1:4— "But let patience have her perfect work, that ye may be perfect and entire, wanting nothing." Safford retorted that he would listen to such a sermon if AMA officials would consent to hear one from Proverbs 13:12—"Hope deferred maketh the heart sick: but when the desire cometh, it is a tree of life."[21]

Safford's departure in 1876 opened the door for personality conflicts and tension between his replacements, G. Stanley Pope and Edward P. Lord, and other leaders at the school, which were somewhat resolved when Lord left. Lord was accused of bringing a spirit of "unrest and anarchy" to the school. He publicly humiliated James F. Childs, a prominent African American from Marion, denying him a seat for a concert in what Lord deemed the reserved "white section" of the chapel during 1877 commencement exercises. The following year brought the discovery that Mr. Lord was concurrently engaged to marry six different AMA teachers, with wedding dates set from two months to two years into the future. The American Missionary Association removed him in 1879.[22]

Lord was replaced by Henry S. DeForest, an inspiring and gifted president known for the alliterative mottoes he shared with students: "Push, Pluck and Perseverance"; "Grit, Grace and Greenbacks"; "Dirt, Debt and the Devil."[23] Under his seventeen-year tenure at Talladega, the standard of scholarship was raised, student enrollment almost tripled, and the faculty, library, and physical plant were greatly expanded. A nursing program was launched, and Cassedy School, an elementary school that reached local children and provided training for normal students, was built on the campus in 1887.

DeForest oversaw the repair and renovation of school buildings, as well as the construction of Stone Hall, a dormitory for males named after benefactor Valeria G. Stone of Malden, Massachusetts. James McCann, a brick contractor and former slave, received the bid to erect the building. On May 13, 1881, abolitionist Lewis Tappan's Bible was placed with several other articles in the cornerstone at a celebration of the hall's completion.

DeForest and college treasurer Edwin C. Silsby challenged the state's tax assessment against Talladega, the only Alabama college required to pay property taxes, and also successfully contested a county law that for years had required male students to work on public roads. He aroused the rage of some white Talladega citizens when he told a Northern audience that the walls of Swayne Hall "went up with whips and groans" and that three slaves had died during its construction. Mayor W. H. Skaggs, who had once called Talladega College "an eyesore," accused DeForest of slander and declared that the college had been "treated with great kindness and charity by this people, notwithstanding it has been little more than a public harem, a place of refuge for Northern reprobates, thieves and incendiaries."[24]

DeForest's tenure came to an abrupt end in 1896 when he died after suffering a massive stroke and falling down a flight of stairs.

He was buried under elm trees along a river in New Berlin, New York. He told a friend shortly before he died that, though his life had been devoted to African Americans in the South, when he got through he "did not want any confed(erate)s to tramp over his head."[25] In 1903 DeForest Chapel was built in his memory, as a tribute to his lasting legacy.

In addition to being college treasurer, Edwin Silsby was a beloved dean, professor, and administrator. Known as someone who was trusted by all, he served as a bridge between the local white community, the local black community, and the college. After his death, the college built the Silsby Science Hall, with modern biology and physics laboratories, as a tribute to this man who had lavished love and devotion on Talladega for more than thirty-five years.

Rev. Frederick Azel Sumner, a Congregational minister who had graduated from Oberlin College and Yale Divinity School and began his tenure at Talladega in 1916, is credited with "fulfilling the dreams of its founders and ardent supporters."[26] He was a warm and popular president with students, faculty, and supporters alike. He helped the college rebound from a 1912 tornado that did extensive damage and a 1913 smallpox epidemic and typhoid outbreak, the latter the result of contaminated well water.

Rev. Sumner, along with James Cater, the school's first African American dean, moved the school away from what AMA Secretary Augustus F. Beard called "scatteration" toward a solid college curriculum.[27] These two men ushered Talladega into a new era, bringing an explosion of activities, including theater, debate, literary societies, and intercollegiate sports—and the first swimming pool at a black college. Student enrollment increased steadily, and the number of black faculty increased from 16 percent in 1910 to 66 percent in 1925.[28] Representatives of the U.S. Bureau of Education visited Talladega in 1927 and "pronounced it the best college which they had surveyed."[29] Two years later, Jane E. McAllister became the first Talladega graduate to earn a doctorate, at Columbia University.

Through the years Talladega students, who were being trained to be independent and free thinkers, agitated for a relaxation of some of the school's most rigid rules. Following a wave of student resistance, mixed card playing and dancing were finally allowed in 1928—but then only "under strict and adequate supervision" and with six inches between male and female dancing partners. A writer in the student newspaper declared in 1929 that "we really often wonder whether we are attending one of America's leading colleges for Negroes or a reform school."[30] In response, school officials suspended the dress code and permitted men to visit women on the first Saturday of each month from 3:30 to 5:00 p.m.

At age twenty-nine, Buell G. Gallagher became the college's sixth president, declaring that accepting the post was moving him "one step nearer to the firing line in the struggle for Christian brotherhood."[31] Gallagher, who believed in the "essential oneness of (hu)mankind," achieved a national reputation as a staunch opponent of segregation.[32] The school continued to grow and thrive, even through the years of the Great Depression. In 1938 Talladega was the only black college out of twenty-two schools selected by the American Council on Education for a three-year study of general education.[33] The college extended its service to its neighbors with a community library and a bookmobile, a half-ton panel truck that hauled seven hundred books around to the county's forty, mostly one-room, rural schools.

In 1933 the campus hosted the first of its annual conferences for YMCA and YWCA delegates. The American Missionary Association declared that it was the first time in Alabama that black students and white students lived together on the same campus. Talladega faculty and students chartered a campus chapter of the NAACP and helped to form the Talladega Civic League, which aided voter registration and worked to overthrow the poll tax; supported the Scottsboro boys, nine black teenagers unjustly convicted of raping two white women near Scottsboro, Alabama; publicly condemned lynching; and joined female sewing-machine operators in their campaign for fair wages.

One visitor, referring to Alabama towns that had exploded with racial violence, said that though Talladega belonged to the segregated South, "the presence of a college there so many years kept it from being a Marion, a Selma, or an Anniston."[34] In 1943 Enoc P. Waters, a correspondent for the *Chicago Defender*, visited the campus and wrote afterward that Talladega was "an oasis of racial democracy in a desert of racial segregation and prejudice. Despite dark surroundings, the torch of enlightenment burns brightly here."[35]

Talladega College President Adam D. Beittel, who declared in 1949 that the college "exists in a small Alabama community as a living protest against segregation," continued and escalated the legacy of campus activism.[36] A few local whites commented that he served the roles of "needler," "agitator," "radical," and "dangerous man" more ardently than any previous president.[37] President Beittel urged the mayor to form an interracial commission and hire African American police officers, agitated for an end to segregation in the local hospital, encouraged organization of an interracial ministerial alliance, railed against segregated education and protested the low salaries of black public school teachers, and supported students in forming the Alabama Student Conference on Civil Rights. He complained to the notoriously brutal Eugene "Bull" Connor, Birmingham's commissioner of public safety, when Talladega students were barred from that city's cultural events. In response, the Ku Klux Klan burned a cross at the college in 1948 and returned the following year to parade through the campus.

Arthur Douglass Gray, a 1929 graduate and the grandson of a slave, became Talladega's first African American president. At his inauguration in 1953, eighty-five years after William Savery and his colleagues founded the school, Gray bowed his head and wept as the chair of the board of trustees placed the gold chain signifying the presidency around his neck. Gray boldly asserted that "segregation in any form is harmful to the growth of personality and is a violation of the spirit of Christianity and democracy." At commencement ceremonies in 1956, he declared, "The South must integrate or perish."[38]

The college continued to grow and mature under President Gray's leadership. From 1950 to 1959, Talladega was first among black colleges in the percentage of its graduates who went on to earn PhDs, with outstanding recognition in the sciences and medicine. Talladega ranked thirteenth among colleges in producing physicians. Eighty-nine percent of its male graduates and 78 percent of female graduates had pursued graduate work; 60 percent had earned advanced degrees.[39]

But the sweep of the civil rights movement was beginning to overshadow all else. Students escalated their protests, refusing to run the ads of segregated businesses in the school paper, taking individual stands on buses and in segregated facilities. In 1956 the campus provided safe haven for Autherine Lucy, the first African American admitted to the University of Alabama, who was expelled when whites violently protested her presence. Talladega graduate Arthur Shores served as Ms. Lucy's legal counsel, and President Gray issued the invitation for her to come to Talladega for seclusion, rest, and recovery after her ordeal.

The Southern Christian Leadership Conference (SCLC), one of the primary organizations that provided direction for the civil rights movement throughout the South, was founded in 1957. That was the year that Dr. Martin Luther King Jr. and Rev. Andrew Young met at Talladega College, when both young men were invited as speakers for an event there. They would emerge as principal leaders in the SCLC and become recognized heroes of the civil rights movement.

In 1961 Talladega senior Arthur Bacon and college staff member Moses Lawler were beaten, almost to the point of death, by men with blackjacks and sawed-off baseball bats in the "whites-only" waiting room of the railway station in Anniston. Talladega students voted to march in protest. When rented buses failed to arrive, they piled into campus and community cars and taxis and headed to Anniston, where they marched through downtown under a hail of insults, curses, and spit. A few onlookers threw heavy chains at them.

A Social Action Committee was organized, and workshops on nonviolent resistance began in March 1962. Representatives from CORE (Congress on Racial Equality) and SNCC (Student Nonviolent Coordinating Committee) visited the campus and offered support. On April 9, after negotiations with the owners failed, eighteen students and college chaplain Everett MacNair visited the soda fountains of three drugstores, demanding to be served, and were arrested and jailed. That week shots were fired at the campus from passing cars, bottles were thrown at students, and windows were broken on campus. In partnership with the town's Talladega Improvement Association, the student Social Action Committee planned an Easter boycott of stores, encouraging sympathizers to "wear old clothes for freedom at Eastertime,"[40] and attempted to integrate six white churches on Easter Sunday.

The following Tuesday a tear-gas bomb was hurled at students protesting at a local theater. The next day city police, reinforced with highway patrol and county officers, prodded and shoved students back within the campus borders. Two days later, on April 28, a circuit court judge issued a temporary injunction prohibiting demonstrations, sit-ins, and boycotts in Talladega. Attorney General MacDonald Gallion, who had obtained the injunction, charged that the college was "a boarding house for out of state agitators" and "a hot-spot for left wing activity." Mayor J. L. Hardwick claimed that the injunction would provide an opportunity "to let things simmer down and let the people revert to their normal way of life."[41]

But things never really became "normal" at Talladega in the way the mayor hoped. A century of courage and perseverance became context for further agitation for civil rights, forays into Black Nationalism, and escalating activism on the campus. In 1967, in an attempt to cultivate better relations with students, the college administration engaged Milton S. Hurst, a Talladega graduate who had facilitated negotiations between the mayor and the college during earlier protests, as director of student activities.

Today, Rev. Hurst serves as the pastor of Talladega's First Congregational United Church of Christ, a New England-style, white clapboard church on the edge of the campus. Founded in 1868 by Rev. Henry Brown, it was the first Congregational church in Alabama. Hurst joined while attending Talladega in 1958. A namesake of the great poet Oliver Wendell Holmes was pastor at the time. The pastor had spearheaded an effort to integrate Atlanta's golf courses and was beginning to talk of a boycott of Talladega businesses, the first whisper of civil rights activity in the town. At a community meeting, he was impressed with the articulate and passionate young Hurst, and told him he belonged in his church.

Hurst, who was raised in the Missionary Baptist tradition and wasn't very familiar with Congregationalism at the time, attended a few times and concluded, "He was right. I wasn't going to be happy in any church not committed to social justice." From that time he became very involved in civil rights activities, learning from the movement's leaders. "I did what they told me to do, what they prayed for me to do," Hurst said.

Milton Hurst spent thirteen more years at Talladega, filling several positions, including professor of social sciences and dean of students. His first job was assistant to the president. "This being Talladega, I had about fifteen 'hats' that I wore," he said. He proudly had a business card printed up with about six of his titles on it, prompting a former roommate to exclaim, "If you're doing all that, what in the world is the president doing?"

Hurst worked closely with the student Social Action Committee and a church-funded summer program that set out to integrate Talladega. He became the executive secretary of the Talladega Improvement Association. Strategy meetings took place at First Congregational Church. Other congregations, fearing white retaliation, had refused their space, saying, "No, they will bomb our churches," according to Hurst. "We felt that we were under the umbrella of the church and could make decisions regarding social justice that other churches could not."

Older members of First Congregational Church have vivid memories of those days. Mable C. Moore remembered the first march by Talladega students, when fire hoses were turned on them. Her daughter was a high school student who wanted to participate in the civil rights movement. As word circulated around her school about a march, the principal announced that any students caught marching would be put out of school. Ms. Moore told her daughter, "If you want to march, you march. If he puts you out, you come on home." It was a glorious moment, according to Ms. Moore—who spent that day organizing caravans of cars to bring children home from jail—when the Talladega students marched by the school and all the children ran out and got in step with them. The first person her daughter picked out in the watching crowd was the principal, "standing there and grinning at her."

Lillian W. Duncan recalled the important role the college played in confronting racial discrimination and violence in the town. One night several Talladega students were in line for a midnight movie at a downtown theater. A police officer, claiming they were being disorderly, knocked a young woman down. On returning to the campus, a few of the other students reported what had happened to the president. "President Gray called down to the chief of police," according to Ms. Duncan, "and he said, 'If you don't fire (the police officer), we will keep every student on the campus out of town. I will open up a commissary right here, and they won't buy even a toothpick in town.' The next morning that guy was fired, and he never got on the police force again."

Through the years Talladega faculty often pastored First Congregational Church. In the early days, according to Rev. Hurst, "the minister would offer a prayer, read the scripture, get down and play the piano, get back up and read another scripture, preach the sermon, and deliver the benediction." Members have taken pride in their clergy's education and the quiet nature of their worship. Ms. Duncan explained that she became a Congregationalist as a young woman after feeling unsatisfied in another church: "I sat next to a sister, and when the preacher started preaching, she'd throw her hands up and knock my hat off. I was just fit to be tied." When a friend took her to a Congregational church, she said, "I was hooked for life. Once you get hooked in this denomination, there's no leaving it."

Loyalty to the church is strong. Even people who have left the area send money back regularly. "They don't forget about the church they grew up in," said Reginald Brasher. "When I can't attend church, I'm lost all week," added Willie Brown. "When I come to church, I get that spiritual food that I can feast on throughout the week."

The church that came to birth in a tent outside Kingston in the summer of 1873, the first one planted outside Talladega by Henry Brown and his students, exists now as King's Chapel United Church of Christ in the town of Alpine. In this flat stretch of Alabama, the seemingly misnamed Alpine (changed from Kingston) reflects not topography but the European chalet-style architecture of a building that one of the town's leading citizens constructed.

The church, known by its members as "the little church with a big heart," started with thirteen members. It was named for King Solomon Calhoun, a former slave of U.S. Vice President John C. Calhoun, who moved from South Carolina to Alpine and was instrumental in its founding. Also for a Mrs. King of Cincinnati, Ohio, who had raised Samuel B. White, the founding teacher of the AMA school in Alpine, and had donated forty dollars to start construction of the church. Like many other Congregational churches in the area, the theology department of Talladega College supplied most of its pastors.

A worn, handwritten journal, with fading ink, frayed pages, and entries dating back to September 1879, is the original record of the church. According to Ovell B. Calhoun, great-grandson of King Solomon Calhoun, the journal was discovered by chance at the location of an old outhouse when a church member was hauling trash away from the site. Its black covers bear tables chock full of intriguing (and presumably helpful in its era) information— "Carrying Capacity of a Ten-Ton Freight Car" (seventy barrels of salt, fifty to sixty hogs, eighty to one hundred sheep, sixty barrels of whiskey, or twenty thousand pounds of butter); "Weight per Bushel" of barley, buckwheat, potatoes, turnips, clover, and coal; and "Quantity of Seed Required to Plant an Acre" (three pounds of lettuce, two bushels of oats, or eight thousand asparagus plants).

The journal details names of members, numbers of baptisms, and every penny spent on nails and lumber in the construction of the church building. Members covenanted to support the church with their time, money, and prayers; to submit to the authority of its leaders; and to "abstain from all the useless practices that waste money, or time, or injure body, or soul." Presumably several failed at the last, as entire pages are dedicated to lists of members who were excommunicated, often restored to membership, only to be excommunicated again. In 1896, states the record, fourteen of the church's eighty-one members were excommunicated or dismissed.

In the days before the civil rights movement, according to Mr. Calhoun, the Ku Klux Klan "had a heyday" in this part of rural Alabama and lynchings were common: "If you said anything contrary to [law enforcement officers], they wouldn't get to jail with you, they'd get you to the biggest tree they could find." Mr. Calhoun said that he had one of his worst experiences when he was in the U.S. Navy during World War II and got news that his sister had passed away. He left Japan, made his way to Birmingham, Alabama, and was on a bus on the way to her funeral in Childersburg. Despite the fact that he was wearing his uniform and had been risking his life in the Pacific theater of the war, he was forced to stand for the duration of the bus ride. "I felt safer out there on the Islands with the [Japanese] than I did in Alabama with other Americans."

Mildred Wheeler, who joined the church when she was ten years old, remembered that she was first sprinkled in the church and later immersed in a nearby pond at her baptism. She had to walk several miles with her sisters to school, while white children rode in a bus. "In the winter time, the ice would be on the ground, and our shoes weren't that good, and we were cold. The bus driver would stop and say to us, 'Hey, y'all want a ride?' and I'd take off. By the time I'd get there, he'd slam the door in my face." Her older sisters counseled her to stop running to the bus, but, she said, "Every day I'd take off knowing he wasn't going to let me on, but that's just how cold and tired I was."

Church member Josie Calhoun added, "When I was walking, and the white children on the bus were throwing spitballs at us, I was just wondering, is there a God? Because if there's a God, He doesn't care anything about us. It used to bother me. I'd go to the Woolworth's up in Talladega, and I'd see the 'white' fountain, and I wondered, what does 'white water' taste like? But they told me I couldn't drink that. I really thought there wasn't a God."

Harvey Calhoun, the son of Ovell and Josie Calhoun, spoke of Talladega's founding: "Blacks and whites started a college. Whites came down, and these people actually cared. When you could know that these people weren't bad, you couldn't say that all white people are bad—or all black people—because they're not." Mr. Calhoun commented that prejudice and violence in the world are "coming from that one four-letter word, *fear*, and the strongest fear is coming from within . . . Even right here in the heart of Jim Crow, there were some whites who cared, but they were as fearful as we were to speak out. The Ku Klux Klan operate out of fear, (believing that if they) can plant the fear of God in you, then they can control you . . . This is fear taking over their souls and their bodies. But when you grasp Jesus Christ, you begin to lose the fear."

Ovell Calhoun spoke of the lessons he learned from the scriptures and the people who taught them to him: "They didn't teach hate. They didn't teach against the whites. They taught us love, and I guess that's why we survived. Love was the only reason we survived."

First Congregational Christian United Church of Christ in Birmingham, Alabama, was founded and opened in a vacant store in 1882. As with most of the Congregational churches in the South, this one grew up close to an AMA school and was supported by the American Missionary Association for years.

Odessa Woolfolk, president emeritus of the renowned Birmingham Civil Rights Institute, is one of several Talladega graduates who have found a church home at First Congregational

Christian Church. She was a college student in the 1950s and a participant in a Race Relations Institute at Fisk University. She is one of many civic leaders who speak with pride about their years at AMA schools and credit that experience with forming their commitments to service and justice, as well as preparing them for the work of leadership and social transformation: "I think that Talladega inspired me to think about liberty in a very progressive, activist manner . . . By the grace of God, we are equal; we come on this earth as equal beings . . . That means that no human-made institution should create a set of circumstances that proscribe one person to do something because he or she is black or white or male or female . . . And any institution that tries to restrict this equality is itself ungodly and ought therefore to be railed against . . .

"Talladega was the only school in Alabama that did not have in its charter segregated living. Everybody was open to everybody . . . It bred a sense of being one. Education was very important. We were sitting at Talladega thinking we were at Harvard or one of those schools, because that was the mindset. A lot of whites who got involved (in the civil rights movement) started paying attention to blacks then, and they assumed that that was the period at which blacks started going to college. I find myself a lot of times reminding them that Talladega College was founded in 1867—and surely people were there."

June Fox Davis, also a member of the Birmingham church, spoke fondly of her years at Talladega: "(The college) had copies of paintings by the Masters, in a sort of gallery in the library. When you first got there, you could go and pick two for your room. You would have these all year long, and then the next year you could go pick two more.

"Our advisers would have small-group sessions with us. They'd have us over to their apartment and have ice cream sundaes or something in the afternoon, and go over things with you. They kept up with you. The idea was, nobody was going to fail. If you got (to Talladega College) in the first place, you had the ability to do the work, but everybody didn't come there with the same skills . . .

"The first two years everybody took the same classes: humanities, science, physical education, social studies, and a language. And everybody had to take swimming. We learned about music, theater, visual arts. I remember them teaching us even how to clap—how to applaud at a concert, how to stand and go out. We were a little oasis in a small, segregated town.

"When we came, we had to bring a napkin ring with us for our table. We had assigned places, and we dressed for the evening meals. So we learned a lot about social living, and all that of course instilled in us a sense of pride. I've never felt inferior . . . We knew there were problems in the world, but it had nothing to do with you as a person.

"The teachers always called us Miss Fox, Mr. Davis—never by our first names. They were never superior to us. We related person to person. It was that way in the classroom; it was that way when you saw each other on the street. They participated with us on the same level.

Several Southern states, determined to keep their graduate schools for whites only, refused to admit African American students and paid for them to attend Northern graduate institutions. According to Ms. Davis: "Black people could leave the state and go to better schools. They could go to Yale, Harvard, anywhere they got accepted. And the state was paying for them to go, just to keep their University of Alabama, and Auburn, white. . . . And that's the reason the state's so poor—because they spent all this money on segregation."

As in other Southern states, Alabama officials tried to keep African Americans from registering to vote. Talladega graduate J. Mason Davis, Jr. shared his experience of registering: "I was in law school, at the end of my second year, and I had done an entire year of Constitutional law. . . . I went down to register—this was in 1957. There were three members of the Board of Registrars, a woman and two men—all white. So they asked me—this was in the county courthouse—they asked me to interpret the Fourteenth Amendment. Now they had to have been totally stupid, or they hadn't read the application. It said I was in law school at the University of Buffalo.

"So I started talking, and I regaled those people . . . They didn't have a clue what I was talking about—you could just see it on their faces . . . When I finished, this woman looked at me, her eyes wide. She said, "How do you know so much?"

"I said, 'Ma'am, if you look at the application, it will show you that I am a rising third-year senior in the University of Buffalo, and I'm on the Law Review.'

"She said, 'What's that?'

"I said, 'That's for the top fifteen people in the class. We write all the articles.'

"And so she said, 'Well, if you know so much, I bet you don't know who's the only woman in the United States Senate.'

"I said, 'Ma'am, her name is Mrs. Margaret Chase Smith, and she's the senior senator from Maine.'

"That woman slammed her hand down on that counter and said, 'Aw, just let this nigger vote.'"

A few years later, Mr. Davis was filing court petitions and arguing cases against discrimination in voter registration practices and jury selection, as well as leading a campaign in the courts to desegregate lunch counters, elevators, and schools in Huntsville, Alabama. For twenty-five years he taught at the University of Alabama Law School—the same school that had once refused to consider him as a student. "The majority of the lawyers and judges in this state are my students," he said, and many still come back to thank him.

Mr. Davis comes from a long line of courageous leaders. His grandfather was a pioneer in education. The abolitionist Republican Party in Alabama came to birth in the home of his great-great-grandfather. Between them, Mr. and Ms. Davis can count twenty-two relatives who have graduated from Talladega College, including their son.

Many social observers considered Birmingham to be the South's most segregated city. Its infamous racial segregation ordinances made it illegal for whites and blacks to play cards or checkers, football or baseball, together. They could not sit in a restaurant together unless "separated by a solid partition extending from the floor upward to a distance of seven feet or higher," and then only if separate entrances were available.[42]

During the civil rights era, "The Magic City," which was a boomtown under the steel industry, became known as "The Tragic City." Some referred to it as "Bombingham." With the city's law enforcement in the grip of the rabidly segregationist Bull Connor, dozens of bombings went uninvestigated, including the Sunday-morning blast at Sixteenth Street Baptist Church in September 1963 that claimed the lives of four young girls.

When asked if First Congregational Christian Church provided its members a safe haven during the civil rights violence, Marilyn Jones replied at once, "It was a target." Arthur Shores, the renowned civil rights attorney who served as legal counsel to Dr. Martin Luther King during the Montgomery bus boycott, was a prominent member. Radical activist Angela Davis, who grew up in the church, was on the FBI's Ten Most Wanted list. Ruth Barefield-Pendleton spoke of her role: "I was the secretary of the Central Committee. That's the committee of local citizens who met in Room 10 at the A. G. Gaston Motel with Dr. King and his lieutenants . . . Each morning after I got my children off to school, I would go down and sit in on the meetings. They would talk about the mass meetings which had occurred the night before, and what stores they planned to (boycott) that day."

Ms. Barefield-Pendleton recalled that First Congregational Christian Church hosted many mass meetings during the civil rights era. "I live up the hill, and you could pass by and you'd find policemen in the parking lot taking license tag numbers. That was their way of identifying who was in the church and who was breaking the law of segregation." She said of the meetings, "There were times when you felt very timid and sometimes very frightened, because there were always policemen present. But then somebody would start humming, and somebody else would pick it up, and before you know it, the entire church would be engulfed with music and you'd just feel lifted up."

Ms. Jones remembered counsel she was given when she was looking for a position as a chemistry teacher: "I was told when I interviewed for a job that I was not to say that I was a member of the Congregational church." At her first interview, she was asked about her church affiliation. Ms. Jones answered, "I'm a Baptist," justifying her answer to herself because she had been raised Baptist. "I felt very bad about that," she confessed, "but at the same time, I needed a job. When your parents struggle to send you to school, you need a job."

Ms. Jones once "got in trouble for bringing a newspaper to school." She explained: "The *Montgomery Advertiser* would come once a week. This was during the time that the bus boycott was going on, and (school officials) were just trying to keep that away from the people. I was sent down to the superintendent for having a newspaper at school, and he wanted me to explain, how did that interconnect with chemistry?"

Threats and harassment also visited Ms. Jones and her neighbors at their homes. "Our husbands stood guard around our houses, because people walked or drove by and threw bottles and that kind of thing. So the men took turns standing guard, and that was the time we had to discontinue Halloween."

Beverly Richardson added that during this "very frightening time" people also took shifts guarding the church through the night. She remembered the impact of the bombings. So frequent were they, the neighborhood around First Congregational Christian Church was renamed.

Ruth Barefield-Pendleton reflected, "Every time the bombs went off, my house shook—I mean literally. The Sunday of the Sixteenth Street (Baptist Church) bombing, I was getting my kids ready for Sunday school when I heard the blast . . . Of course we knew the families that lost the kids (Cynthia Wesley, Carole Robertson, Addie Mae Collins, and Denise McNair were killed in the bombing). I was around the Wesley house when this big white tank came up the hill. They said, 'You niggers get back in the house.' We were standing there, all gathered in front of the Wesleys' house, there to show our condolence—tears running down—and we did not move . . . Those were terrible times, terrible times."

In Birmingham, children were an integral part of the civil rights struggle. The sight of water cannons knocking over children marching for freedom in Kelly Ingram Park, and police dogs attacking them, riveted the world on the civil rights movement and helped to turn the tide of public opinion away from legalized segregation.

Odessa Woolfolk was a teacher in a public high school in 1963 when marches were called in protest of the Sixteenth Street Baptist Church bombing. The Birmingham Board of Education declared that any children who marched would be marked absent, and eventually expelled if they persisted. Ms. Woolfolk described the situation: "Some teachers were supporting the movement, though not publicly identified with it, because jobs were lost . . . I was teaching American government, and it was clear that (our textbooks) had one model of what freedom was, that was different from what was practiced in Birmingham, Alabama. It was pretty easy for the kids and the teachers to see this gap between promise and practice . . .

"Some of the kids hopped fences, in schools where there were fences. In Auburn High School, they would sneak out behind the old band room and run down the street so nobody would see them leave. A lot of the kids left.

"I remember telling some of my kids that I could not say to them whether they should go march, go down and face Bull Connor's fire hoses and volleys of water—but that it was almost like you flunked government class if you showed up when everybody else was out there . . . They didn't show up . . .

"I remember when some of those kids left and got arrested and came back. Some had been incarcerated for several days—out at the fairgrounds or in the Birmingham City Jail—and they came back to class with little American flags . . . And the kids who hadn't marched and the teacher all sat in the back of the room and had the kids teach the class that day. It was very, very special to see how those kids felt that they had done something very significant."

The members of First Congregational Christian Church in Birmingham speak of their church as a family and as place of spiritual support, nurture, and empowerment. As in the Talladega church—and many United Church of Christ congregations from the Congregational tradition—worship typically has been quiet and reserved. Beverly Richardson reflected with a smile, "I mean, if somebody said Amen, everybody in the church turned around. We used to make a joke: 'If you shout, you'll be on your own, because there's nobody to catch you.'" But that's changing somewhat under the leadership of Rev. Rodney Franklin, a young pastor who has encouraged community involvement, a vibrant choir and music ministry, and free expression in worship. Grinning across the table at choir member Kathryn Robinson, Ms. Richardson elicited a wave of laughter when she declared, "Why, Kathryn and them sometimes sway when they sing!"

The Talladega legacy lives on. It is vibrantly alive in the courageous lives of the school's graduates and lingers in the churches it planted generations ago. And it is memorialized in the campus's two outstanding landmarks.

In 1996, due in large part to a generous donation from comedian Bill Cosby and his wife Camille, sixty-five stained-glass windows were designed for DeForest Chapel by Dr. David Driskell—a renowned artist and art historian whose first teaching job was at the college in 1955—with the assistance of painter, poet, and provost Dr. Arthur Bacon—the same Arthur Bacon who almost lost his life as a student in the beating in Anniston. The east wall of "Heroes and Heroines" includes striking stained-glass portraits of Rosa Parks, Dr. Martin Luther King Jr., W.E.B. Dubois, Jackie Robinson, Harriet Tubman, Booker T. Washington, and others. The north windows focus on "Ancestry and Heritage," with each depicting the language and native products of an African nation, and the west windows symbolize "Liberal Arts Curricula."

In 1939, seventy years after former slave William Savery founded his school, the new library at Talledega College was consecrated Savery Library. The imposing building was completed on the one hundredth anniversary of the mutiny on the *Amistad*, and it contains inspiring tributes to that momentous event. Inlaid in the lobby's terrazzo floor, in multiple hues of marble, is a five-foot-tall depiction of the ship. Students have decreed that it shall never be stepped on, as it symbolizes the circumstances that gave birth to the American Missionary Association and Talladega College. Hale Woodruff, then chair of Atlanta University's art department, was commissioned to paint vivid and vibrant murals of the mutiny, court trials, and return to Africa, as well as a portrayal of the Underground Railroad and scenes from Talladega's history, on the walls that ring the lobby.

Four of the children of the man for whom the library is named graduated from Talladega's normal department, and three of them taught at the college. Cicely Savery, who received her normal diploma in 1887, was invited to address a gathering of the American Missionary Association. She told the crowd that initially she was tempted to decline. "But," she added, "having been trained in an American Missionary Association school all my life, I have at least learned the art of obedience, and so I concluded to put that art into practice."

Ms. Savery recounted in her address how in the "strange, dark and dangerous days of 1865," her father and two other men "bought an old kitchen and moved it down near a place called the Branch," starting a school there. When her father set his sights on the former Baptist academy, the building "was expected to fall at any time," she recalled. So he and Henry Brown took a light with them late one night and examined the building. To their surprise, they found only one support decayed. The building was purchased. "Thus," declared Ms. Savery, "the little seed, planted by three colored men and watered by benevolence of our Northern white friends, through the American Missionary Association, has continued to grow until it is now one of the best schools in the South, Talladega College."

Ms. Savery recalled her first teaching experience, at the age of fourteen. Her family had grown to number eight children, so it was necessary for her to contribute something toward her own support. She persuaded her parents to allow her to teach a summer school. After "a dreary ride of fifty miles," she came to the one-room, sixteen-by-twenty-foot log cabin that she would share with a family of seven: "They gave me a hearty welcome, took several of their prettiest quilts, tied them up around the best bed in the house, and gave me my 'room' . . . My host owned a good cob pipe, and every night perfumed the house with the dreadful odor that can only come from home-raised tobacco; my hostess had a stout snuff stick which was her constant companion. I did my first real missionary work trying to get them to give up these habits, and succeeded."

Her oldest pupil was fifty-four, the youngest six. Four mothers came to school with their infants. "The books brought were anything the pupils could get. Some brought Bibles, others old newspapers, and anything that had 'reading in it' they thought would do." At the end of three weeks, she had 105 students "and as heavy a heart and long face as you would care to see." She sent home for books and charts, made great progress, and regretted the day she had to leave. "One widow came to me the last day of school, and with tears in her eyes, said she intended to educate her daughter if it 'took the last shuck out of the corn crib.'" Ms. Savery learned years later that the daughter went on to be a fine teacher.

Cicely Savery had begun her remarks by declaring, "For all that I am I owe to the benevolence of the American Missionary

Association, and I am continually giving thanks to God that this Society has not only administered to my necessities, but to those of so many of my people, who without this aid, would even now be in utter darkness." She ended on a similar note of thanksgiving and hope, lavishing on the AMA and Talladega as fine a tribute as they ever received: "We are better and the Southland is better for your noble efforts . . . Truer living will stand out clearly and firmly against the ruins of the past. These teachings will endure through all ages, transmitted from generation to generation, and the great pulsing heart of humanity will feel them forever."[43]

7

Reverberations of Hope

Singing the Praises and Troubles of Fisk University

The churning waters of Tennessee's Cumberland River rushed past Sarah Sheppard as she stood on its bank, clutching her helpless young daughter in her arms, preparing to slip over the edge and end her unbearable anguish. Ella Sheppard was just three years old, and already her mistress had begun training her to spy on her mother. The practice was not uncommon under slavery. Young children were often easily bribed with buttered biscuits and sweet cakes to inform on parents whose owners suspected them of shirking at their labor or plotting an escape. Stories even circulated of owners posting parrots in their fields to serve as spies—or so they told their slaves.[1]

The mistress had relayed young Ella's first report to Sarah, greatly exaggerated and accompanied with threats, sending Sarah into deep despair. Imagining the future of deception and cruelty that awaited her daughter, she decided to end both their lives. But Sarah was reportedly overtaken at the water's edge by an elderly enslaved woman named Mammy Viney, who cried out to her, "Don't you do it, Honey. Don't you take that that you cannot give back." Then she gazed toward the heavens and said, "Look, Honey, don't you see the clouds of the Lord as they pass by? The Lord has got need of this child."[2]

Another version names the old woman Aunt Cherry and claims that her prophecy was more explicit: "God's got great work for this baby to do. She's going to stand before kings and queens."[3] And still another says that she cried out, "Wait! Let the chariot of the Lord swing low and let me take one of the Lord's scrolls and read it to you." The woman then made the motion of unfurling an imaginary scroll from God and convinced Sarah not to drown herself and her daughter, claiming a great future for the child.[4] Whichever riverside version is true, Sarah, cradling Ella closely, walked back into slavery and waited on God to reveal a plan.

Later that same year, 1854, Sarah's owners, Harper and Phereby Sheppard, decided to move to Mississippi. Sarah's husband, Simon, had earned enough money as a liveryman to buy his own freedom for $1,800 and was working to save an additional $1,300 to buy Sarah's. But her mistress, declaring, "She is *mine* and she shall *die* mine," refused to sell Sarah. Determined not to allow her daughter to be enslaved, Sarah made a deal with Phereby: if she would allow Simon to buy Ella, Sarah would remain Phereby's faithful servant; but if she refused, Sarah would kill both herself and her daughter.[5]

Simon Sheppard bought his daughter for $350 and kept her with him in Nashville, while Sarah was taken away to Mississippi. Ella Sheppard would see her mother only once more before the outbreak of the Civil War. When Ella was six years old, Sarah visited her in Nashville with Harper Sheppard. When it came time for her to leave her daughter, Sarah's screams were so loud and long that her master determined that she should never see Ella again.

Not until she was fourteen did Ella see her mother again, after Sarah's owners had brought her back to Nashville. Ella sadly recalled later, "I did not even know her face." Her mother anguished to her daughter, "My back was never struck, but my heart is like a checkerboard with its stripes of sorrow."[6] During their three-month visit, Sarah told Ella about her Cherokee great-grandmother, Rosa, who had borne fourteen children and lived to the age of 109; about the old woman's prophecy by the river when Ella was three years old; and about the deal Sarah had made for Ella's freedom. Though the exact words proclaimed over Ella Sheppard by the old seer by the river are lost to history, the following years revealed that she would grow up to fulfill every prediction.

In 1871 Nashville's Fisk University was in desperate condition. The school had opened in January 1866 in a complex of former Union hospital barracks, designed as temporary shelter on a "damp and pestilential site."[7] Fisk legend would speak proudly of the school being established where once soldiers had recovered from the wounds they suffered fighting to free the enslaved. But in truth, a high proportion of the hospital's patients had been victims not of warfare but of venereal disease, contracted from Nashville's plentiful prostitutes.[8]

The way had been opened for the school in December 1864 when Nashville fell into Union hands, the first rebel capital to be captured. Confederate General John Bell Hood had recklessly led his ragged, barefoot Army of the Tennessee into battle near the statehouse. General Hood had had one arm maimed at Gettysburg and a leg amputated at Chickamauga, and had to be hoisted into his saddle and strapped onto his horse for the disastrous encounter that led to the decimation of his troops.

As in Savannah and the South's other urban centers, thousands of bereft former slaves crowded into Nashville after the Union victory. Wrote John Eaton, the Union Army's Superintendent of Contrabands: "Their arrival among us of these hordes was like the oncoming of cities. There was no plan in this exodus, no Moses to lead it . . . A blind terror stung them, an equally blind terror allured them, and to us they came. There were men, women and children in every stage of disease or decrepitude, often nearly naked, with flesh torn by the terrible experiences of their escapes."[9]

Nashville's camp for refugees teemed with desperation, destitution, and disease. "This is hell, isn't it?" newcomer George L. Knox asked his brother as they sought refuge there. His brother agreed but encouraged Knox to hang on until things got better. The brother died a few weeks later. In the first winter, more than a thousand African Americans would succumb to exposure, starvation, or disease.[10]

Three men—John Ogden of the Freedmen's Bureau and Erastus M. Cravath and Edward P. Smith of the American Missionary Association—had been searching in vain after the Union victory for a site for a school in Nashville. Ogden, who served as a second lieutenant in the cavalry during the war, had spent several months in a Confederate prison camp. He brought experience as a normal school principal in the Midwest to his post as Tennessee's superintendent of education with the Freedmen's Bureau.

Cravath, who grew up in a New York home that was a station on the Underground Railroad, remembered the escapees from slavery huddled in the family's root cellar, their feet "swollen, shapeless masses from sleeping in the woods in the dead of a northern winter, when to have kindled a fire would have brought upon them the slave hunter and the bloodhounds."[11] His father risked ruinous fines of a thousand dollars per fugitive to take them in his sleigh to a local black stationmaster for the trip across the border to Canada. Cravath attended abolitionist Oberlin College, was ordained a Congregational minister, and served as a chaplain during the war. Smith, also a minister, was part of a movement that placed destitute and vagrant children with adoptive farm families in the West. He held the post of district secretary for the AMA.[12]

The men were convinced that Nashville was an ideal location for a school that could serve both the border states and the deep South. They shared a visitor's assessment that the city was a "nostril" through which Tennessee had "long breathed the Northern air of free institutions."[13] But they quickly discovered that no local whites were willing to sell them land or property. When the federal government put up for sale the land on which the former hospital barracks stood, the three men handed over four thousand dollars in personal money for the down payment. The AMA, the Freedmen's Bureau, and the Western Freedmen's Aid Commission made future payments.

General Clinton B. Fisk, assistant commissioner of the Freedmen's Bureau for Tennessee and Kentucky, assisted heavily in the purchase of the buildings on the land. A committed teetotaler who would receive a quarter of a million votes in the 1898 election as the Prohibitionist Party's presidential candidate, Fisk was a champion of black education. The school, originally known as the Fisk Free Colored School, was named after him.

Within a month of opening, Fisk's enrollment soared from two hundred to six hundred students. Within six months, it had reached its self-imposed maximum of a thousand scholars. It underwent several name changes: from Fisk Free Colored School to Fisk Academy, then Fisk School, Fisk High School, and finally Fisk University.

As with other AMA schools, Fisk held its students to a rigid discipline. Piety was valued as highly as education. Early school officials kept a monthly scorecard of Christian conversions and sent a regular report to the AMA offices in New York.

John Ogden, who assumed the position of principal at Fisk, refused to include agricultural and industrial training at the school. He believed that what African Americans needed most were teachers and other professionals. The normal department was established in the fall of 1867, and the first college students were enrolled in 1871.

By then, the buildings at Fisk were rotting and crumbling. The teachers had gone unpaid for months at a time. One had written to the AMA pleading for the back salary due her, as it was cold and she had no shoes. Provided little else by the school, teachers slept on horsehair mattresses. Several suffered from the variety of illnesses that plagued Nashville. Precarious finances, overwork, undernourishment, social ostracism and threats, and a lack of privacy led to an abundance of "shattered nerves and short tempers."[14]

One teacher claimed that "half our quarrels and troubles arise from sour stomachs."[15] Facing tight finances in 1869, the faculty had voted to reduce the serving of dessert in the dining room to once a week. Teachers put up hundreds of jars of preserves in an effort to feed the students, many of whom survived on one meal a day of soup and cornbread provided by Nashville's shelter for the indigent. The American Missionary Association—overextended, seventy-eight thousand dollars in debt, and having to make difficult decisions about which schools it could afford to sustain—seemed ready to abandon Fisk for seemingly more viable institutions.

A group of students excavating the grounds of the school one day made a gruesome discovery. Buried just beneath the surface were piles of rusted manacles and chains, leftovers from the days before the war when Porter's Slave Yard occupied the site. The students dug up these artifacts of enslavement and sold them for scrap metal, using the money to buy Bibles and spelling books, turning instruments of bondage into tools of liberation, and thus keeping their school and their dreams alive a bit longer.

But Fisk continued to teeter on the edge of insolvency. Letters from creditors and parents begging for more time to pay their children's tuition piled up on the desk of Treasurer George L. White. Taller than Abraham Lincoln, with a thick beard, a tempestuous brow, and steely eyes, White had once joined the "Squirrel Hunters," a ragtag group of men who had rushed to the defense of Cincinnati, Ohio, during the war. Dressed in his black schoolmaster's clothes, carrying a rifle and his ever-present Bible, this empathetic schoolteacher and fiddle player appeared to be a misplaced warrior among his buckskinned comrades. He had organized a Sunday school for African American children in the woods outside Cincinnati, using rails for seats, and had likely joined the campaign to defend the city in order to keep the children he taught from being enslaved. White served in the infantry and later blamed his permanently compromised health on a week of futilely trying to cross Virginia's Rappahannock River during severe winter storms and a grueling charge up Tennessee's Lookout Mountain that immobilized him for two months.

At Fisk, George White was beginning to feel that his dream of educating Nashville's African Americans was crumbling along with the school's walls. He consoled himself by inviting students to his apartment every evening for group sings. He drew upon his ad hoc training as a choir director and military band leader as he conducted the students in singing a variety of hymns, temperance and folk songs, and patriotic tunes.

Some of the students began gathering in private to sing their own songs, often behind locked doors, with window curtains drawn, sitting on the floor in whatever isolated corner they could find. The melodies, passed on from parents and grandparents, were at once melancholy, joyful, drenched in sorrow or exploding with hope. Ella Sheppard, by then a Fisk student, wrote in her diary that "every phase of human experience save those of hatred and revenge" is expressed in the songs her ancestors referred to as "crystallized tears."[16]

A Connecticut man who had once heard enslaved men and women singing at daybreak on their way to a tobacco field wrote: "They were singing; not in joy, for the song was too sadly plaintive for that; not in despair for the hopeless do not sing . . . [W]ave on wave of wild, weird melody, that told what no language can tell, came rolling over us, as the ghostly shadows of the night . . . were flying before the beautiful morning . . . Their song was at once a burden of woe and a glad prophecy. Wrongs which another race would have avenged with bloody knife and flaming torch uttered themselves in plaintive murmur."[17]

Ms. Sheppard reflected, "The slave songs were never used by us then in public. They were associated with slavery and the dark past, and represented the things to be forgotten. Then, too, they were sacred to our parents."[18] But over time the songs known then as "plantation melodies," "slave hymns," "cabin songs," and "sorrow songs" came to George White's attention. He began to collect them, with the assistance of Sheppard and others.

Eventually introduced to the world as Negro spirituals, these hymns "not only declared faith but carried news, raised protests, expressed grief, asked questions, made jokes, lubricated a slave's never ending toil."[19] Many of the songs' words carried multiple meanings, always lost on the masters and overseers who heard enslaved people singing day in and day out. "Canaan," "the Promised Land," and "Paradise" could all point to heaven, the North, Canada, or emancipation. "Follow the Drinking Gourd" referred to escaping slaves following the Big Dipper and the North Star to freedom, and "The Day of Jubilee," about Moses leading the Israelites out of bondage, reflected the slaves' hope for their own liberation. "Steal Away to Jesus" announced a secret meeting at night, and "Go Down Moses" was often sung to signal the presence of Underground Railroad conductor Harriet Tubman in a neighborhood.

With deep appreciation for the mystery and stubborn hope of the spirituals, George White viewed them as a gift from his students. And they in turn began to feel that White's talent for eliciting harmony and polish from their untrained voices was God-given. He drove them to perfection, often pacing fervently, with his fiddle ready to check their pitch, making them sing a song over and over until it was just right.

Early in 1871, Mr. White proposed to Erastus Cravath that student singers go on a Northern tour to raise money to save Fisk. AMA officials and General Fisk were unconvinced of the merit of the project and refused to endorse it, calling it a "wild goose chase."[20] Outraged, White telegraphed the AMA board, "I'm depending on God, not you."[21] Fisk's trustees encouraged White to pick a dozen singers and drill them over the summer in preparation for a fall tour. He spent much of the summer pleading with parents—who opposed the disruption of their children's education, feared that they would be targets of violence, and had learned during slavery to equate travel with permanent separation—to allow their daughters and sons to be part of the troupe.

All of the singers came from circumstances of extreme hardship; six had been enslaved. Jennie Jackson, who was the granddaughter of former U.S. President Andrew Jackson's personal servant, helped her ailing mother scrub clothes in Nashville's infamous Smoky Row, a desperate collection of teeming shanties, tenements, and brothels. America Robinson was eight years old when Union and Confederate troops clashed in her master's yard. She watched the wounded and dying soldiers writhing and screaming in pain before she and her father hid in an army wagon and escaped to Union lines in Nashville. Eliza Walker's father ran an ice house in the city after emancipation.

Thomas Rutling's earliest memory was the sale of his mother— who frequently ran away and was regularly whipped—when he was about two years old. His mother wept as she was dragged away, and Rutling remembered the feel of the whip striking his young arm as they lashed her for clinging to him. She was handcuffed, tied behind her owner's buggy, and driven away, leaving Rutling wailing alone in their cabin. The last word Rutling ever heard about her was that she had been whipped nearly to death.

Isaac Dickerson, who was orphaned by the age of five, was captured during the war and forced to march seventy-five miles. He eventually wound up working for a Jewish shopkeeper in Chattanooga, whose son taught him to read and write. Georgia Gordon taught herself to read the Bible, and Minnie Tate, the youngest singer, was taught by her mother, who received her freedom just before her master's death.

Benjamin Holmes, a tailor's apprentice who was sold to a trader who fed him on "cow's head, boiled grits, and rice," worked after emancipation as a store clerk and barber. He taught himself to read and write by studying the letters on signs and in his first master's measuring books. While he was being held in a pen at a slave market, Holmes discovered a copy of the Emancipation Proclamation, which he read aloud. "Such rejoicing as there was then!" he recalled. "One old man held a prayer meeting right there in the mart."[22]

For several years during the war, Greene Evans was on the run with his master, all across the South. Both he and Isaac Dickerson were among the early students at the American Missionary Association's Lincoln Chapel in Memphis, which was among twelve schools burned down during that city's May 1866 riot. The riot was likely sparked by an incident with black troops, but the Southern press blamed a by then familiar scapegoat: "the teachings of Northern 'school marms' in the nigger schools."[23] A rampaging mob armed with knives and guns murdered African Americans on sight in broad daylight, according to the AMA's Rev. E. O. Tade, and raging fires burned for two days, claiming, in addition to the schools, four African American churches and ninety homes.

Surely the Memphis riot had made Greene Evans aware of the risks of teaching. But he, like many Fisk students, taught school during the summers. Deployed near the Mississippi border, he gleaned timber from the surrounding woods to build his own desks, benches, and schoolhouse, which "did not lack for ventilation, for a bird could fly through anywhere."[24]

On her way to and from Fisk every day, Maggie Porter passed by the train depot, where she intently scanned the throng of incoming refugees for her long-lost sister, sold away from her family many years before. Porter missed out on a reunion with her one day, because the whites who owned the house where her mother was a servant told her never to allow in a stranger. Porter began teaching in Bellevue, Tennessee, when she was just fifteen years old, and she returned from spending Christmas with her family in Nashville to find her school burned to the ground. A powerful soprano, Porter had sat on the steps outside churches as a young girl, uplifted by the music. Her greatest singing ambition, she said, was "to get the people to cry."[25]

The troupe members were given a glimpse of both the dangers of their venture and the power of their singing after a trial concert in Memphis in June 1871. The concert itself was disappointing, the turnout small. On the ride back to Nashville, the singers got stranded between trains in a small town. A mob of drunken whites began hurling insults and threats at them. The singers retreated into the train station to pray.

George White stood between them and the disorderly crowd and led them in singing some hymns. Slowly, one by one, the rioters hushed and then drifted away, until only the leader stood next to White. He removed his hat and stood quietly as they sang "Home Sweet Home," riveted by the music. "Our hearts were fearful and tender," recorded Ella Sheppard in her diary, "and darkness was falling." The troupe was just finishing the last verse when, according to Ms. Sheppard, "we saw the bull's eye of the coming engine and knew that we were saved. The leader begged us with tears falling to sing the hymn again, which we did. As the train passed slowly by I heard him repeating, 'Love, rest and home, sweet, sweet home.'"[26]

Witnessing the potent soothing effect of the music on southern hostility, George White was even more determined to take the troupe on tour. But he had many detractors, including some people who thought the singers were no better than the traveling minstrel groups so popular at the time, composed of whites who used burnt cork to blacken their faces, mocking African Americans. Some feared the singers would bring shame on Fisk.

Adam K. Spence, who replaced John Ogden when he resigned in 1870 and was a rival of White, feared that the tour would exploit the singers and expose them to the "wickedness" of the theater. He asked critically if the tour was truly godly. White shot back, "Of course it is of the Lord. It's as plain as day."[27]

George White and his new wife, Laura, sold their jewelry, wedding presents, and many other personal belongings to raise money. Mr. White added every cent he could borrow and all but one dollar of Fisk's institutional funds to the account for the tour. No one seemed optimistic. Even White, recognizing the burden he and the singers were shouldering and believing them to be Fisk's last hope, confessed, "I have less courage than I have ever had before in regard to our future." Mr. Spence declared, "If they fail they get home if they can."[28]

On the eve of their departure, George White and ten singers gathered in Fisk's chapel to pray for their mission. "We were nothing but a bunch of kids," wrote singer Maggie Porter later. "All we wanted was for Fisk to stand."[29]

The courageous little band of singers headed out on October 6, 1871, sent off at the train station by a chorus of wailing parents. Teachers lent clothes to the ragged troupe, none of whom had a coat or heavy garments for weathering the bitter cold of a northern winter. Their itinerary followed the route of the Underground Railroad, along which George White found sympathetic churches to host them, and their repertoire was largely the folk songs and hymns White had taught them.

In Chillicothe, Ohio, they held their first concert, which was rea-
sonably well attended and produced a collection of almost fifty
dollars. That night the great fire swept through Chicago, consum-
ing a major portion of the city, killing 250 people and leaving a
hundred thousand homeless. Despite the precariousness of their
own situation, the singers decided to donate all their proceeds to
the Chicago relief fund.

No hotel in Chillicothe would take them in. Throughout the tour
they were refused lodging, ejected from trains, barraged with
insults and threats. On one occasion, a boardinghouse proprietor
felt compelled to tie up his wife with a clothesline to prevent her
from pushing them out.[30] The money they earned barely covered
their expenses. Mr. White occasionally had to plead with scant
audiences at the conclusion of a concert for enough money to
make train fare to the next town. Food was scarce, and sleet and
snow were plentiful. One observer reflected, "A more poverty
stricken company was never out on a more noble mission."[31]

A Springfield, Ohio, concert had to be canceled when only twenty tickets were sold. In Akron, Thomas Rutling tried to accompany
himself on the piano: "In his fright, he played in one key and sang
in another—an experiment he found unsuccessful."[32] Singer Phebe
Anderson, the daughter of a Methodist pastor who was alarmed at
reports of the singers' travails, was summoned home to her
father's deathbed, where she promised him never to tour again.
Ella Sheppard wrote in her diary, "Our strength was failing under
the ill treatment at hotels, on railroads, poorly attended concerts,
and ridicule."[33]

George White served as musical director, general manager,
advance agent, ticket seller, and porter. Ms. Sheppard, his assistant and the group's pianist, often directed rehearsals and per-
formances. She wrote that despite the seemingly insurmountable
obstacles, Mr. White "depended wholly on God and trusted him literally. He used to say that if the Lord told him to jump through a
wall, it was his part to jump and the Lord's to put him through."[34]

On November 16, the troupe was scheduled to sing for the
meeting of the National Congregational Council at Oberlin College.
They expected a warm welcome at the abolitionist institution that
provided many of Fisk's teachers, but their presence seemed an
embarrassment to the college. Oberlin was attempting to de-
emphasize its radical past in a bid for respectability among
Northern whites who were beginning to grow weary of the needs of
the nation's emancipated citizens.

The singers "sat through the council's dreary proceedings in a miasma of mildewed hymnals, musty wool, wet boots, and surreptitious

doses of cough syrup." The chairman called for a recess, then appealed to the milling delegates to listen, please, to "the colored youngsters of Fisk University."[35] At first, no one did. George White whispered to the singers, gathered at the back of the chapel, to start singing very softly "Steal Away to Jesus." A hush slowly overtook the crowd. One attendee said that the "soft, hauntingly beautiful music seemed to come from nowhere; it filled the church and seemed to fall gently on us all."[36]

An eyewitness reported that Oberlin's dark, cloudy skies opened at the moment the troupe began singing, and sunlight streamed through the windows and lit with a stunning radiance the singers' faces.[37] Another observed of the audience, "That dignified body, taken by surprise, was now melted to tears and now lifted to jubilation."[38] As the singers' voices swelled to the concluding line—"The trumpet sounds within my soul, I ain't got long to stay here"—they were met with a rapt silence, followed by thunderous applause. The audience clamored for more—that day and the next.

In the crowd was Tom Beecher, brother of Henry Ward Beecher, Congregational pastor of Brooklyn's prestigious Plymouth Church, considered by many the best preacher in America at the time. Tom contacted his brother, and arrangements were made for the troupe to perform at Plymouth.

George White decided that the group couldn't go forward to New York without a name. He spent a long night petitioning God in prayer and received a vision of Moses and the children of Israel being led out of bondage in Egypt. The next morning he appeared with a radiant glow on his face and announced to the troupe that they were now the Jubilee Singers. The name reflected the biblical year of Jubilee, a time in ancient Israel when debts were forgiven and slaves were set free. The troupe rejoiced and heartily embraced the name.

But the hardships continued. Ella Sheppard, who had worn out her shoes and had nothing to wear on her feet except a pair of cloth slippers, developed bronchitis. All the singers were suffering from exhaustion and exposure to the cold. They spent one terrible, sleepless night in a rickety room infested with insects. Offerings still barely covered expenses. Erastus Cravath wrote Mr. White a letter accusing him of recklessly endangering Fisk's survival. But, lacking all else, George White and the Jubilee Singers still had faith.

Very late on the night of December 14, they arrived in New York City, an unlikely venue for a change of fortune. Four days of rioting in 1863 had led to the destruction of the Colored Orphan Asylum and the murder of hundreds of African Americans, many of whom were hanged from lampposts and set on fire. Almost every policeman in the city was killed, and ten thousand Union troops had to be summoned from their recent victory at Gettysburg to restore order. In 1871, corruption, anger, and racism still boiled in the big city.

Though the American Missionary Association was still withholding its official endorsement of the tour, three of its secretaries—Erastus Cravath, George Whipple, and Michael Strieby—provided the singers with warm clothing and took them into their homes. They were also welcomed by the controversial Henry Ward Beecher. At the height of his fame, the jowly, lion-like Rev. Beecher was at the center of a scandal regarding a female parishioner, about whom he admitted only to a "paroxysmal kiss." On Friday nights he sat in an enormous armchair in the church, "sniffing adorably at a bouquet of roses or violets provided by the ladies of the church and dilating on all sorts of subjects."[39]

From this royal throne, he invited his congregation to listen to "the songs that have been sung by generations of benighted souls; . . . songs that have enabled the captive to endure his chains, the mother to hope against hope and keep her soul up when all looked black and dark; when she had parted from all she loved, and the iron had entered into her soul."[40] The Jubilee Singers had snuck into the choir loft and hidden behind a curtain. George White bent his tall frame and crawled on his knees to give the pitch. Once more, the hushed, haunting strains of "Steal Away to Jesus" filled a church and transfixed all hearers. Many wept; others waved handkerchiefs in appreciation and tribute. After several spirituals, Rev. Beecher, visibly moved, stepped forward, emptied his pockets into the offering plate, and commanded his congregation, "Do likewise." The collection came to $1,300.[41]

Beecher invited the Jubilee Singers back for a public concert, and afterward White proudly sent a pile of money to an astonished Adam Spence back at Fisk. "Success is sure," declared White. "It is only a matter of time."[42] Indeed, the tide had turned in New York. Seeing the truth of White's prediction, the AMA finally got on board with its endorsement, challenging patrons to raise twenty thousand dollars to save Fisk.

William H. Goodrich, a minister in Binghamton, proclaimed the Jubilees' spirituals "the only style of music characteristically American." Upon hearing them, he wrote, "Your eyes fill and your heart is heaving with a true devotional feeling. You see clearly that these songs have been, in their untaught years, a real liturgy, a cry of the soul."[43] Rev. Theodore Ledyard Cutler was equally lavish in his praise, stating that the songs were sung "with a power and pathos never surpassed . . . I never saw a cultivated Brooklyn assemblage so moved and melted under the magnetism of music before."[44]

No longer did hymns and folk songs anchor the Jubilee concerts, as spirituals took center stage. Sold-out, standing-room-only concerts became the norm. Henry Ward Beecher had to cancel a lecture scheduled at the same time as a Jubilee concert, due to lack of interest. He cheerfully went to the concert instead, calling forth from the floor a deluge of cash, checks, and jewelry for the Jubilees.

Other contributions poured in for Jubilee Hall, the imposing building that George White now had in mind as a tribute to the singers' dedication, to be built as a centerpiece of Fisk. A Bristol, Connecticut clock manufacturer promised a supply of clocks; the Meriden Britannia Company invited the singers to its factory to gather up as much silverware as the university might need; Parker Brothers supplied pens. A group of Winsted businessmen pledged a great bell inscribed with the Jubilees' names.[45]

In New Haven, reported Gustavus Pike of the AMA, who dedicated himself to their tours, the singers "were almost obliged to march on the heads of the people to reach the pulpit; and so deep was the interest, that persons who entered the church long before time for the service, remained standing till the last song was sung." In some New England cities that hosted them, additional trains had to be run on concert evenings to carry all their patrons, and tickets were auctioned off because of the overwhelming demand. Ella Sheppard wrote in her diary: "In the midst of applause and flattery, I often wish to be back in some little secluded spot where I can be (away) from every eye—in the presence of my God and pour out my soul in thanksgiving."[46]

The Jubilee Singers were not only raising money to save Fisk, they were raising consciousness about racial segregation. When influential citizens in Newark, New Jersey, discovered that the troupe had been refused lodging at its Continental Hotel, they passed a resolution condemning the hotel's proprietor. The next night, the Board of Education in nearby Jersey City voted to integrate its schools.[47] On a later tour, Erastus Cravath extracted from railroad giant George Pullman a private car for the Jubilees' return home and a pledge that all Pullman cars would be integrated from then on.[48]

The Jubilees insisted at many of their venues that the African American cooks, maids, waiters, launderers, and bellboys who served their patrons be given reserved seats in the front rows to hear them sing. "By their sweet songs and simple ways," wrote an editor in the New Jersey *Journal*, the singers were "moulding and manufacturing public sentiment."[49] A concertgoer reflected, "The ideas of many with regard to the race seem entirely revolutionized."[50]

When the Jubilee Singers concluded their first tour on May 2, 1872, they had raised twenty thousand dollars toward the purchase of a new site and building for their school. A throng of relieved parents and grateful admirers met them at Nashville's train station and paraded them through the streets, with drums beating and banners flying.

Julia Jackson, Edmund Watkins, and Mabel Lewis—courageous souls all—joined the troupe on its return. As a young girl, Ms. Jackson had carried meals and smuggled money to her aunt, who was kept imprisoned in a slave pen. Jackson scouted out breaks in the fence to help her escape, then kept showing up daily with meals long after she was gone, so that no one would sound an alarm and search for her. Jackson survived what was likely a brutal sexual assault by her employer, saved money for her schooling, and while at Fisk taught in a country school, building her pupils' benches herself out of planks and stones.

Edmund Watkins picked two hundred pounds of cotton every day as a child in slavery. He escaped as a young man and eluded six men sent to capture him, but he was caught when he sneaked onto his former master's plantation to visit his mother and sister, then taken into the woods and whipped. He spent two years at Talladega College before finding his way to Fisk.

Mabel Lewis, daughter of a Frenchman and a New Orleans slave, was spirited off to a convent when she was a child, where she was punished for singing a Protestant hymn she learned from a chimney sweep. Like Maggie Porter, Lewis was inspired by the story of Jenny Lind, the "Swedish Nightingale," who as a young girl was discovered when she was singing to her cat. Given shelter by a judge in New Bedford, Massachusetts, Lewis borrowed his accordion and walked up and down the town's streets, singing and taking in pennies, hoping to be discovered.[51]

Invitations for concerts poured in to the Jubilee Singers, and famous fans lined up. The troupe entertained President Ulysses S. Grant in the White House and exchanged songs with Frederick Douglass in his home over tea. Abolitionists William Lloyd Garrison and Wendell Phillips welcomed them. Phillips applauded them for "laying one of the main cornerstones toward removing prejudice," penning in their autograph book: "Peace if possible, liberty at any rate."[52] Poet John Greenleaf Whittier invited them to his New Hampshire home, writing to them: "Voice of a ransomed race: sing on/ 'Til Freedom's every right is won/ And slavery's every wrong undone."[53]

At the World's Peace Jubilee in Boston in June 1872, waltz composer Johann Strauss reportedly waved his violin in excitement after hearing them sing. Mark Twain, among their most ardent fans, reflected, "I do not know when anything has moved me as did the plaintive melodies of the Jubilee Singers . . . I have heard them sing once, and I would walk seven miles to hear them sing again. You will recognize that this is strong language for me to use, when you remember that I was never fond of pedestrianism."[54] Twain believed that "in the Jubilees and their songs, America has produced the perfectest flower of the ages."[55]

On a European tour in the spring of 1873, the singers so inspired England's Queen Victoria that she ordered her royal portrait painter to make a large oil painting of them. At Prime Minister William Gladstone's home, they entertained the princess of Wales, the czarina of Russia, and Jenny Lind; in gratitude, the prime minister sent a book collection to Fisk. The Jubilees sang in Westminster Abbey and accepted an invitation from famed evangelist Dwight L. Moody to perform at a revival. After stops in Scotland, Ireland, and Wales, they returned to Fisk with another fifty thousand dollars for the construction of Jubilee Hall.

Two years later, the Jubilee Singers returned to England, where, in addition to the usual concerts, they sang free of charge at churches, orphanages, soup kitchens, and asylums. A hotel proprietor in Ireland sprayed a hose to drive away curious fans gathered in trees to get a glimpse of the famous singers. In Switzerland they performed for their first non-English-speaking audiences, who wept and applauded like any other. When George White asked through an interpreter how they could be so moved by the songs when they didn't know the meaning of the words, one listener replied, "We cannot understand them, but we can feel them."[56]

The singers entertained the king and queen of the Netherlands, where throngs of children in wooden shoes followed them everywhere and no cathedral was large enough to hold their concerts. The crown princess of Germany was so moved by their music that she could not sleep at night. The Jubilees traveled on, even farther from home. "Steal Away to Jesus" brought tears and looks of wonder to the eyes of aboriginals in Australia and charmed the native Maori of New Zealand.

Frederick Loudin, a booming bass who joined the Jubilees and later organized his own troupe when George White's health failed, wrote of their concert in India's Taj Mahal: "As the tones of that beautiful slave song, 'Steal Away to Jesus,' which we had sung before emperors, presidents, kings, and queens, awoke the stillness of that most wonderful of temples, we were so much overcome by the unique circumstances that it was with the utmost difficulty we could sing at all."[57] The troupe went on to Burma, Hong Kong, and Japan, where schoolgirls ran after them as they were carried away in rickshaws. Back home, Loudin built himself a stunning house from rare wood he had shipped back from all over the world.

The grueling schedule and months away from home took their toll. Quarrels began to increase among the singers. They were plagued by persistent coughs and exhaustion. America Robinson contracted bronchitis, and Julia Jackson suffered a paralyzing stroke. Doctors, declaring Ella Sheppard's nerves shattered, told her that only complete rest would bring recovery.

Mabel Lewis became so weak she had to be sent home. Replacement Lucinda Vance was so incapable of performing that Mrs. Swart, hired by White as an assistant in case Sheppard collapsed, had to crouch behind her and sing the alto part while Vance mouthed the words. George White, suffering from tuberculosis and grief after his wife's death, had to be carried on a mattress onto a ship for his last voyage home.

By the summer of 1873, Jubilee Hall was still only a gaping hole in the ground. The American Missionary Association, with funds drying up in the midst of a national depression, had borrowed money from the Jubilee Fund—which by then was larger than the AMA's entire income—to keep itself solvent. A cholera epidemic claimed one of every forty Nashville residents that summer, most of them African Americans. Hundreds of barrels of tar were set on fire around the city to try to smoke out the miasma that was believed to be the cause of the disease. Morale among Fisk's faculty had reached an all-time low.

A year later, Congress passed a Civil Rights bill, which precipitated massive Ku Klux Klan rallies in Nashville and a decline in Fisk's enrollment. Adam Spence reported "a reign of blood and terror" in Tennessee. Fear of lynching was so intense that male students didn't go out at night. Work continued to creep along on Jubilee Hall, with cadres of eight students at a time, armed with a hundred rounds of ammunition, keeping watch over the construction site at night in response to Klan threats to destroy the building.[58]

Finally, on January 1, 1876, while the Jubilee Singers performed in far-off Newcastle, England, General Fisk presided over the dedication of the imposing Jubilee Hall. Elegant wood sent by an alumnus from the Mendi mission in Sierra Leone graced its entrance halls and stairways. Flying from its grand turret—which both announced the educational beacon Fisk intended to become and provided a watchtower where armed students continued to keep an eye out for arsonists—were both an American and a British flag, acknowledging the generosity of patrons across the ocean toward the edifice's construction. An Army band played, and letters from dignitaries around the country were read.

At the end of seven years, the Jubilee Singers had raised $150,000 for Fisk—worth about $2.5 million today—and made it the most well-known black university in the world.[59] They brought the spirituals out from closets of obscurity and entered them into the universal liturgy of musical lament and celebration all across the globe. Henry Ward Beecher wrote glowingly of the Jubilees, "The work done by this group of singers is without a parallel. It leaves the Old Testament hopelessly in the distance, for Joshua's army only sang down the walls of Jericho—while the Jubilee choir have sung up the walls of a great university."[60]

Ironically, not one of the original Jubilee Singers graduated from the school their voices built; they were too busy touring and singing. Benjamin Holmes died of tuberculosis at the age of twenty-eight in the dank former hospital barracks while the construction of Jubilee Hall crawled toward completion. He left behind words encouraging parents to "kindle in the bosom of your children a flame of love of God and their race which will radiate as they grow," and to young African Americans to "strike out boldly and fearlessly" to please God and serve humanity.[61]

Soon after the dedication of Jubilee Hall, rumors circulated that Fisk's trustees couldn't possibly intend to devote such a grand building to black education. In part to stifle such charges, Adam Spence hired James Burrus, the university's first African American professor, to teach mathematics. Burrus and his two brothers had made it through elementary school by taking turns wearing the same pair of trousers, which their mother, a cook at Fisk, patched over and over. Burrus and his brother John had been half of Fisk's first graduating class in 1875.

James Burrus went on to Dartmouth, where he became the first African American to receive a master's degree from an accredited university. After an outstanding career in academia, Burrus moved on to further success in real estate and pharmaceuticals. He died of a heart attack in the black section of a Nashville streetcar in 1928, leaving his entire estate, which included eighty-five houses and more than $120,000 in stocks and bonds, to Fisk University.[62]

Erastus Cravath became Fisk's president in 1875. In 1878 the university sent several of its most promising students, led by Albert P. Miller, to the Mendi mission in Africa. Rev. Miller, who had received his freedom at the age of fourteen, presided at the funeral of Sengbe, the leader of the *Amistad* mutiny, whose courage had set in motion the events that made the dream of Fisk University and Miller's education possible.

In 1855 a white reporter in Nashville described Fisk as "the most important and influential institution of its kind in the United States."[63] The university continued to expand its programs. In 1895 it added a Daniel Hand Training School to the campus to enhance teacher training.

Fisk men reportedly organized the first black collegiate football team, calling themselves "the Sons of Milo," in honor of President Erastus Milo Cravath.[64] Between 1899 and 1904, playing without a coach, the team lost only one game. John W. Work, a Latin professor and leader of the Jubilee Singers who was named coach in 1907, took the football team on a two-week tour; they played four games and sang over a dozen concerts.[65]

Both Cravath and Adam Spence died in 1900, ending an era at Fisk. Together the two men had devoted sixty-five years to black education. Mr. Spence was best remembered for sitting in the black galleries of Nashville theaters with Fisk students when segregation forced them to sit there. Mr. Cravath was succeeded by James G. Merrill, who had served several Congregational churches and edited a Congregational magazine before taking the post as Fisk's president.

Rev. Merrill was followed by Rev. George A. Gates in 1908. On the day of his inauguration at Fisk, the Nashville Board of Education had to declare a holiday in public schools, because half of the state's teachers were Fisk graduates and wanted to attend. Gates added the sociology department to Fisk's curriculum, for which the university would become internationally renowned.

By the turn of the century, the popularity of industrial education was on the rise in the nation, with a corresponding lack of interest in liberal arts education for African Americans. President Gates discovered that Tuskegee and Hampton institutes had cornered the philanthropic market for black education in New York and the Midwest, largely through the influence of Booker T. Washington. Washington's wife, Margaret Murray Washington, was a Fisk graduate who had taught at Tuskegee Institute. Despite his many public proclamations in support of industrial education, Mr. Washington agreed to send their son, Booker Jr., to Fisk.

In 1909 Washington was elected to the Fisk Board of Trustees, in the hope that his influence with several foundations would aid the school, which was once again facing dire financial straits. President Gates felt it necessary to make a public announcement that the selection did not indicate that Fisk was going to abandon its liberal arts curriculum for industrial education. Fisk eventually received support from several philanthropic organizations, including the Carnegie Foundation, Anna T. Jeanes Foundation, Phelps-Stokes Fund, and Julius Rosenwald Fund, which together would within a decade give Fisk a million-dollar endowment.[66]

On his way to meet with trustees in New York in 1912, President Gates suffered a massive brain concussion in a train accident. The concussion created such serious mental disturbances that his wife had to write his letter of resignation without his knowledge or consent. He died soon after.

Dr. Fayette Avery McKenzie succeeded Gates in 1915. In his inaugural address, he proclaimed, "Fifty years of idealization and effort, of sacrifice and devotion, of conscience and intelligence, have made Fisk University the symbol, the corporate realization, of education and culture for the Negro in the South."[67] Dr. McKenzie emphasized the importance of service to the community, vowed to develop a school of religion at Fisk, and expanded the music and science departments. With Professor George E. Haynes, he increased the university's work in the local black community, launching such innovative services as Bethlehem House, a settlement house that trained students in the social sciences, and pioneering the organization of the Tennessee Colored Anti-Tuberculosis Society. In 1917 a government study concluded that, among African American schools, Fisk and Howard were best suited to be developed into full-fledged universities. By 1922, more than one-third of all black college students were enrolled at the two schools.[68]

As the memory of Reconstruction dimmed, racial violence still continued to explode across the South. More than 2,500 lynchings were carried out in the last sixteen years of the nineteenth century, and a thousand more between 1900 and the beginning of the First World War. More than three thousand people responded to a newspaper invitation in Tennessee to watch a black man be burned alive. In the summer of 1919, dozens of blacks were killed in twenty-five riots around the country.[69] President McKenzie called publicly for calm, a gesture that many people considered too accommodating to the white-dominated status quo, and criticism of his administration began to grow.

Money continued to be an issue at Fisk, without enough to make critically needed repairs and expansion. Water soaked through the walls of some of its buildings, and toilet facilities were woefully inadequate. The heating system was so inefficient that both faculty and students had to heat and carry bricks to keep warm in winter. More than three hundred women had to be turned away in 1919 because of lack of dormitory space. Similar situations prevailed at other black institutions. By contrast, during the

1920s income from endowments at Harvard, Yale, and Columbia universities was one and a half million times greater than the combined income of all private institutions for African Americans in the United States.[70]

Student unrest was escalating. President McKenzie disbanded the student government association, forbade student dissent, and suspended publication of the *Fisk Herald*, the oldest student newspaper among black colleges. Fraternities and sororities were disallowed; card playing, alcohol, and tobacco were prohibited; and dancing was considered "a trap of the devil." Ragtime music was banned from university pianos, mail was censored, attendance at daily chapel was required, and women were not allowed out after dark.

Dress regulations for women filled three pages of the college catalog: no lace or embroidery, only three ruffles per skirt, "strong shoes with sensible heels" required. Arcane dating rules dictated that if a young man escorted a young woman twice, he had to ask out another woman before dating the first again. Most unusual of all, perhaps, President McKenzie had declared some students who killed and cooked chickens that had wandered onto the campus guilty on three counts: illegal killing, nonessential expenditure of heat for cooking, and holding "irregular parties without very special reason and permission."[71] Fisk at that time reflected poet Langston Hughes's observation, made after visiting more than fifty African American schools and colleges, that walking the campuses was "like going back to mid-Victorian England, or Massachusetts in the days of witch-burning Puritans."[72]

Fisk's most distinguished alumnus weighed in. W. E. B. Dubois had attended Fisk from 1885 to 1888. During one summer, he taught in a small, isolated, country school, after which he announced that he "would not take $200 for his experience and would not go through it again for $300."[73] It was at Fisk that the nation's foremost spokesperson for racial equality at the turn of the century began his acclaimed public speaking, and here that he launched his public writing career as editor of the *Fisk Herald*.

Mr. DuBois had spoken of his years at the university as "splendid inspiration," the teaching "excellent and earnest." He gave his alma mater high praise for tackling the race issue: "At Fisk the problem of race was faced openly and essential racial equality asserted and natural inferiority strenuously denied."[74] He credited the university's environment with helping shape his own views at a formative time in his life.

DuBois appeared back at Fisk in June 1924 to deliver the alumni address. Attacking President McKenzie as an overbearing patriarch who was too accommodating to racist Southern whites and Northern industrial philanthropists, DuBois announced that he had come to Fisk to say openly to McKenzie what many graduates were saying behind his back. He called for an alumni boycott until the school was reorganized. In the next issue of the NAACP's *Crisis*, he wrote that Fisk had become "a place of sorrow, of infinite regret; a place where the dreams of great souls lay dusty and forgotten."[75]

The November meeting of Fisk trustees was disrupted by students banging loudly on tin pans and presenting demands, which were largely disregarded. In February 1925 the campus erupted. Forty-two panes of glass were broken in one dormitory, the chapel was ransacked, and shots were fired into the air. Students chanted, "DuBois! DuBois!" Seven were arrested for inciting a riot. Three-fourths of the student body went on strike, refusing to attend classes. President McKenzie submitted his resignation on April 16, 1925, effective at the end of the academic year.

Thomas Elsa Jones, a Quaker, assumed the presidency in September 1926. He announced upon his arrival, "I am here to build a college that is second to none in the United States and my whole being is in the task." He believed himself to be "right in the center of one of the most important developments not only in America but in the world."[76] President Jones oversaw an era of unprecedented growth at Fisk. He dramatically increased African American faculty, named the first black dean, added alumni trustees, and initiated a student council. He relaxed some rules, allowing students more freedoms, fraternities and sororities, and such perks as dances and unchaperoned walks to the nearby Chocolate Shop.

Mr. Jones launched an ambitious funding campaign, prompting W. E. B. DuBois to call on Fiskites in the March 1927 issue of *Crisis* to give "till it hurts" to the plans of the new, progressive president. That year the high school program was abandoned and emphasis was placed on graduate work. In 1933, on Jubilee Day—observed every October 6 on the anniversary of the launch of the first tour of the Jubilee Singers—renowned poet and composer James Weldon Johnson called Fisk University "a leader among the schools that have made progress of the Negro in America possible," which, he said, "would have been impossible without such schools as Fisk."[77]

The Great Depression hit hard, at Fisk and elsewhere. Money for such simple necessities as curtains was nonexistent, and women students took to changing their clothes in closets when neighbors complained about being able to see in the windows of Jubilee Hall.

The Jubilee Singers went Christmas caroling to raise money for Bethlehem House, whose patrons' suffering far surpassed a lack of curtains, and Fisk faculty trained fifty recreation teachers to work in city parks. The university organized a community training center for religious workers, where ministers and lay leaders from several denominations came to study missions, evangelism, and Christian education.

In 1937, Professor Charles S. Johnson founded the Fisk University Social Settlement, which offered a People's College providing practical education in such areas as business, civics, economics, history, literature, and dramatics for adults, and a Children's Institute that offered prenatal health care to mothers and preschool education for their children. The social science department studied the system of Southern sharecropping, aided the improvement of housing projects in several states, and initiated a training program for rural leaders and an Urban Life Studies program in cooperation with the American Missionary Association and the Julius Rosenwald Fund.

When President Jones moved on to a position with the American Friends Service Committee in June 1946, he left a much better school than he had found. The proportion of African Americans on the faculty had reached more than one-half by 1936, and about two-thirds by 1945. Under Jones's administration, Fisk became the first African American institution to be awarded a Class A rating by the Southern Association of Colleges and Secondary Schools, and it was the first black university to be placed on the approved list of the Association of American Universities.[78]

In October 1946, the trustees announced the appointment of Fisk's first African American president, Charles S. Johnson, whose vast credentials and accomplishments as chair of the university's social science department were unequaled. Dr. Johnson was an eminent teacher and an internationally acclaimed scholar, who had served as editor of three magazines and as U.S. delegate to the United Nations Educational, Scientific, and Cultural Organization. Instrumental in identifying and encouraging young African American writers, he was known as the "godfather to the Harlem Renaissance."[79] Dr. Johnson was director of the Chicago Urban League, overseeing a study of the Chicago race riot of 1919, and later the National Urban League. He served on President Herbert Hoover's Housing Commission and on the Committee on Farm Tenancy under President Franklin D. Roosevelt.

Under Dr. Johnson's presidency, Fisk became renowned for its pioneering research on race relations. In 1942 the American

Missionary Association established a Race Relations Department at Fisk, under Johnson's direction. After the Second World War, demand for workers precipitated a massive migration to urban industrial centers, raising racial tensions throughout the nation. Riots erupted in the spring of 1943, and staff members from the department were deployed as widely as Mobile, Detroit, and San Francisco to help citizens work toward constructive social change.

In 1944, in partnership with the American Missionary Association, Fisk hosted its first of twenty-six annual Institutes on Race Relations. The inaugural institute drew 137 educators, religious workers, journalists, and labor and civic leaders from around the country for three weeks of intensive study regarding racism and discrimination. Over the years the institutes drew more than three thousand participants, including an impressive array of prominent historians, writers, judges, and Civil Rights activists—a sort of "Who's Who" in social change—including Martin Luther King Jr., Julian Bond, Constance Baker Motley, James Lawson, Bayard Rustin, Vernon Jordan, James Farmer, A. Philip Randolph, Roy Wilkins, Thurgood Marshall, Vincent Harding, and Lillian Smith.

Other notables passed through the doors of Fisk as students and faculty: historian John Hope Franklin, poet and novelist Arna Bontemps, poet Nikki Giovanni. James Weldon Johnson resigned as secretary of the NAACP in 1931 to accept the newly created Adam K. Spence Chair of Creative Literature and Writing. He said that "on this favorable ground" he would be able to help in "developing additional racial strength and fitness and in shaping fresh forces against bigotry and racial wrong."[80]

As early as the 1930s, Fisk was known not only as a hub for scholarship and research, but also as a center of African American culture. An annual Festival of Music and Fine Arts was inaugurated in 1928, and Fisk's reputation was further enhanced when it received the George Gershwin Collection of Music and Music Literature. Fisk students excelled at debate and staged one of the top African American little theaters in the nation.

The university also became home to one of the nation's premier collections of African American art. And in 1949, artist Georgia O'Keeffe presented Fisk with the modern art collection of her late photographer husband, Alfred Stieglitz. The collection of more than one hundred works by Cezanne, Picasso, Renoir, Toulouse-Lautrec, O'Keeffe, and other acclaimed painters was considered the outstanding display of its kind in the South.

The lynching in late 1933 of Cordie Cheek, who was seized at the edge of Fisk's campus, inaugurated civil rights activism at the university that spanned several decades. Students protested the murder vigorously and pushed for a trial of the killers. They also added their voices to protests about the case of the Scottsboro boys and other racially motivated violence and discrimination.

John Lewis, now a member of the U.S. Congress from Georgia, reflected on the crucial role that Fisk played in the civil rights movement during the 1950s and '60s, when he was a college student at the American Baptist Theological Seminary in Nashville and a leader in SNCC (Student Nonviolent Coordinating Committee). Lewis drove to Fisk frequently to hear the many civil rights leaders invited to address the university community—Thurgood Marshall, Fred Shuttlesworth, Roy Wilkins, Martin Luther King—and confessed to being "awed" and "dumbstruck" when he met W. E. B. DuBois walking across campus one day.[81]

Lewis, Fisk students Diane Nash and Marion Barry, and others put Nashville on the map as a center of the student sit-in movement. Mass meetings to strategize and train in nonviolence took place in Fisk's chemistry building auditorium. After their first arrest while attempting to desegregate a downtown lunch counter, Lewis and eighty-one others were released into the custody of Fisk President Stephen J. Wright. The next day more than a thousand students from across Nashville jammed into Fisk Memorial Chapel to hear Dr. Wright give his wholehearted blessing to the student movement, making him the first African American college president in the nation to take such a stand.[82]

Soon after Easter in 1960, a bomb went off at the home of civil rights attorney Z. Alexander Looby, who had represented the students. The blast blew away the front of the house and shattered 147 windows at Hubbard Hospital, related to Meharry Medical College, a block away. Miraculously, no one was injured or killed. Close to five thousand students, teachers, and citizens marched on city hall that day, the first mass march of its kind in the country, according to Mr. Lewis.[83] At the front of the march, Diane Nash confronted Nashville Mayor Ben West about racial segregation. Despite his attempt to dismiss her with the patronizing address "little lady," Ms. Nash refused to back down. The next morning's banner headline in the *Nashville Tennessean* read: "Integrate Counters—Mayor."

That night people packed into Fisk's gymnasium to hear Martin Luther King Jr. Loudspeakers had to be set up outside for the hundreds who could not get in. After clearing the building in response to a bomb threat, the throng returned and heard Dr. King proclaim, "I came to Nashville not to bring inspiration, but to gain inspiration from the great movement that has taken place in this community."

The crowd erupted with cheers and applause. King ended his speech with this challenge: "No lie can live forever. Let us not despair. The universe is with us. Walk together, children. Don't get weary." Three weeks later, at 3:15 on the afternoon of May 10, 1960, six downtown stores served food to African American customers for the first time in Nashville's history.[84]

Through the civil rights era and beyond, Fisk continued to excel as a university, preparing its students for careers in science and social work, education and engineering, medicine and ministry, law and literature, architecture and the arts. A recent Fisk admissions brochure states proudly that one of every six of the nation's African American doctors, lawyers, and dentists is a Fisk graduate; more than 60 percent of the most recent graduating class attended graduate or professional schools; and Fisk has the highest per capita number of alumni Ph.D.s among all U.S. educational institutions and is second only to Columbia University in proportion of graduates admitted to law schools.[85]

Newton Holiday Jr., whose parents and siblings all attended Fisk, shared the honor with a fellow student of being the first graduates from the university's art department. His father once told him that he didn't know how his son got through Fisk, to which Mr. Holiday replied, "Well, some of the nights I told you I was in the library, I was." Mr. Holiday said, "If you're from Fisk, you're supposed to be capable of doing anything, so that's the way a lot of people look at us." He spoke of the intense loyalty and gratitude of its graduates: "If we hit the sweepstakes, Fisk would get a good part of it."

Jean Welch-Wilson, whose father Wilson Q. Welch Jr. was a Fisk professor and then pastor of Nashville's Howard Congregational United Church of Christ, was raised on the Fisk campus. "Being a part of this kind of environment was phenomenal," she said. "The spiritual life, the education, the social life—it was all just one marvelous world."

Despite the fact that, according to Ms. Welch-Wilson, "there was nothing I could do in my community that my mother and father would not find out about," her fondest memories are of being a child on the campus. She remembered the joy and pride of watching her father and his colleagues march in, dressed in full academic regalia, during Fisk graduations. She and her friend Beth Howse often showed up after college receptions at the back door of the president's house, where the cooks gave them all the leftover finger sandwiches and mints. And Marie Johnson, wife of Fisk President Charles Johnson, invited the girls and their dolls over for teas on Sunday afternoons.

The civil rights era was particularly inspiring for Ms. Welch-Wilson. "Langston Hughes was always on campus, and Andrew Young, and Martin Luther King, and Thurgood Marshall. There was always somebody from the Civil Rights movement." She spoke of the challenge of growing up as part of such a racially integrated and multinational community, then having to face a segregated and prejudiced world. "But for those of us who went other places, we carried the memory."

Cheryl Hamberg graduated from Fisk in 1962. She remembered her parents dropping her in front of Jubilee Hall on her arrival. "When my feet touched the Jubilee Oval, I knew I was in the right place. It was spiritual . . . We were surrounded by intellectuals and people who were role models . . . We were taught to stand up for what's right, no matter what the consequences are."

Though President Thomas Jones had relaxed some of Fisk's most stringent rules decades before, the university still had dress codes and curfews in the 1960s. "If you were caught breaking a serious rule, you were on the train the next day, going home," said Ms. Hamberg. "If it hadn't been for Beth (Howse)'s grandmother, I wouldn't have graduated." Ms. Hamberg had a boyfriend in the city with a car during her first year of college. "When you were a freshman, you weren't allowed to ride in cars or drive," she said. "And one day Mother Moore, as we called her, said, 'Cheryl, let me talk to you for a minute . . . If you're going to sneak into that young man's car, it might be a good idea if you didn't do it in front of my house.'"

Beth Howse serves as archivist at Fisk's library, whose rare treasures include the famous Lincoln Bible. The Bible, which Abraham Lincoln's son, Robert Todd Lincoln, gave to Fisk in 1916, bears the inscription: "To Abraham Lincoln, President of the United States, the friend of Universal Freedom. From the loyal Colored people of Baltimore, July 4, 1864." First presented at the White House by representatives of Baltimore's recently freed population, the Bible is a large, purple-velvet pulpit edition, with bands of solid gold at the corners. On the left cover is an image of Abraham Lincoln standing in a cornfield, knocking the shackles off the wrists of a man whose hand is raised in blessing over the president. At his feet is a scroll inscribed "Emancipation."[86]

Perhaps most treasured by Ms. Howse are the diaries of her great-grandmother, Ella Sheppard. She remembered as a child being pulled out of school every October 6, Jubilee Day, to visit the gravesite of her beloved ancestor. But, she said, the importance of Ella Sheppard's story didn't strike her until she started working in the library in 1970 and came across the Jubilee Singers' letters, diaries, and artifacts.

Sheppard's diaries, which were discovered in an old trunk at Fisk, remain the clearest record of the singers' travails and triumphs. "Imagine the excitement," said Ms. Howse, "of opening up her diaries and reading the actual words that she had written while they were on tours of the United States and abroad . . . Sometimes when I think about working here, I realize that if they had not gone out to sing, I might not even have a job; I wouldn't even be here."

Indeed, much of the credit for the Jubilee Singers' success, and Fisk's early survival, goes to Ella Sheppard, whose tireless dedication inspired the troupe to persevere against all odds. "It's really an honor to be associated with Ella Sheppard," said Ms. Howse. "I've worked here over thirty years, and I always feel like I was put here to uncover the many aspects of my family's history. It's all right here at my fingertips."

After her work with the Jubilee Singers, Ms. Sheppard married George Washington Moore, whose tinsmith father had made buckets, ladles, gutters, and dustbins for Fisk. As a child, Moore had been content to spend his time on the streets smoking cigarettes, selling tinware, and carrying market baskets for the prostitutes of Smoky Row. Worried about his son's future, the father took him on a walk that covered thousands of miles through eight states—the same path he had walked while a fugitive fleeing for freedom. The grueling journey changed young Moore's life, and upon his return to Nashville, he entered Fisk and decided to become a minister.

Rev. Moore's career included teaching theology at Howard University and serving as field superintendent for Southern Church Work for the American Missionary Association. Forty-five years after the end of the Civil War, as he was completing his seventeenth year of service with the AMA, he wrote an article praising the association and its work: "We shall always be grateful to the missionary for coming to our relief in our hour of need. The American Missionary Association, as the channel through which our needs were met, has always stood for all that was best for our elevation. Its first efforts in our behalf were in preparing the race for its freedom, and it has done more to help the Negro to help himself than any other agency since Emancipation . . . The growth of the colored people during the past forty-five years can be largely measured by the growth of the educational work of the A.M.A."[87]

In 1876, Rev. Moore was appointed co-pastor of Howard Chapel, located on the Fisk campus and named for General Oliver O. Howard of the Freedmen's Bureau, who had been instrumental in raising funds for its construction. The congregation worshiping in the chapel moved off campus after the construction of Jubilee Hall and eventually became Howard Congregational United Church of

Christ. The unique building in which the congregation worships now was designed by church member Newton Holiday Jr., who learned architectural design from Calvin McKissack, a Fisk graduate considered by many to be Nashville's most gifted architect. Mr. Holiday, who taught art classes at a local high school, made the church's elegantly graceful altar, constructed of oak and walnut inlaid with mosaic tiles, and he supervised some of his students in creating the sanctuary's exquisite chancel cross. Annie Neal, a dean at Meharry Medical College, who remembers the sting of racial discrimination as a child, says of Howard, "The church has always been the place where you gathered and you knew you were special . . . Regardless of what happened to you out there in the world, at the church you felt that you were somebody."

After her marriage to Rev. Moore, Ella Sheppard served as president of the Tennessee Women's Missionary Union. Through her writing and public speaking, she became a strong and eloquent advocate for African American women. She died in 1914 from an infection following appendicitis, just days after delivering the commencement address at the American Missionary Association's Trinity School in Athens, Alabama. A Fisk teacher said of her, "In intellect, in spirit and in musical attainment she was one of the gifted women of the world."[88]

The oil painting of Ella Sheppard and the other original Jubilee Singers commissioned by Queen Victoria hangs today in the Appleton Room of Jubilee Hall, covering an entire wall. The Fisk admissions brochure calls Jubilee Hall "probably the most famous college residence hall in the world."[89] Almost 130 years after its dedication, the grand edifice—the South's first permanent structure built for the education of African Americans—still remains the centerpiece of the Fisk University campus, which was placed on the National Registry of Historic Landmarks in 1978.

On the Jubilee Singers' first European tour, the queen had been particularly moved by their rendition of the spiritual "Swing Low, Sweet Chariot." When she asked where it originated, she was told of a desperate young slave mother clutching her daughter on the bank of the Cumberland River and an old woman's vision about the chariot of the Lord swinging low to save the child for greatness. Just hours before her death in 1912, Sarah Sheppard joined her daughter at the piano in her home to sing one last time the lullaby with which she had secretly serenaded Ella in their days of bondage.

Indeed, all prophecies proclaimed over Ella Sheppard as a young child at the riverbank were fulfilled. She entertained kings and queens and, in the process, served God and saved a university. She was instrumental in introducing to the world the music that, according to W. E. B. DuBois, "still remains the most original and beautiful expression of human life and longing yet born on American soil."[90]

In a letter of introduction addressed to British friends before the Jubilee Singers' first European tour, Henry Ward Beecher penned, "Their music will strike a chord which will vibrate long after their songs shall cease."[91] Indeed, the persistent hope and undying faith that saved Fisk still reverberate through the great university's halls. And generations of students, who have picked up the song, continue to find themselves equipped to make their mark in the world, joining the bold chorus of voices past and present proclaiming freedom.

8

Rearing the Altars of Freedom

Tougaloo College Offers a Refuge from Racism and Brutality

Early in 1869, the American Missionary Association commissioned former Union officer Allen P. Huggins to find suitable land for a normal and agricultural school in Mississippi. Seven miles north of Jackson—forty minutes through dense pine woods by wood-stoked locomotive—he found the two thousand-acre former Boddie plantation. It sat at the convergence of two brooks, on a spot that Native Americans had called Tougaloo, meaning "at the fork of the stream."[1]

John Boddie's fiancée, for whom the plantation's spacious antebellum mansion was built, had requested that it be topped with a cupola from which she could view the city of Jackson. But before the mansion was complete, she married another suitor. Some people accused her of being fickle; others said she was repulsed by Boddie's harsh treatment of his slaves.

Disappointed by love, Mr. Boddie used the mansion to store his cotton and the cupola to observe his field hands. After his fiancée's departure, he had the work on the building completed as cheaply as possible. When H. S. Beals of Angelica, New York, arrived in October 1869 to take charge of the AMA's project in Tougaloo, he found evidence of Boddie's change of heart. The mansion's glass, he declared, was fit for a palace, while the brick hearths were scarcely suitable for a cabin.

By April 1870, Mr. Beals had begun repair work on the house, acquired an AMA teacher, and surveyed 160 acres into homesites, the sale of which generated money for the school and attracted stable families to the community from which students could be drawn. He reported that "a steady work of grace" had been following the school since the first scholars "began spelling out the divine messages of the New Testament."[2] Student enrollment steadily increased at the school, and every communion service brought additions to the Congregational church that was established nearby.

Mr. Beals was unrelenting in his appeals to Northerners to support the AMA's work at Tougaloo, requesting money and prayers to "rear the altars and light the fires of freedom and righteousness."[3] Two African Americans were killed near the school soon after Beals's arrival, and he wrote to officials in the AMA's New York office that it would cost more to rouse the people in Mississippi to sympathy for their cause than elsewhere. He observed that white Mississippians "acted as though they were just awakening from a Rip Van Winkle sleep," as if unaware of the tumultuous sea change that had just taken place in the nation. They were "uninspired," he said, with no apparent ambition but to raise more cotton. To them, cotton was "more than King—it was Lord."[4]

Many people scoffed when Tougaloo University received its charter in May 1871. Captain H. R. Pease, who served as superintendent of education for the Freedmen's Bureau and then as Mississippi's first state superintendent of public education, believed the name to be less than lovely. Others felt the title "university" was a sham. AMA Secretary Augustus Field Beard responded by declaring that when parents name a baby they give it an adult name, and he charged school officials at Tougaloo and elsewhere, "The universities were named all right. Now you bring them up."[5]

But the first bachelor's degree wasn't conferred at Tougaloo until 1901, and then to only one student, who comprised the college program's first graduating class. Subsequent administrations were more realistic than Mr. Beard about the school's aspirations. The name was officially changed to Tougaloo College in 1916.

The American Missionary Association chose Rev. J. K. Nutting of Glenwood, Iowa, to be Tougaloo's first president. A month after his arrival in April 1873, the Tougaloo family was besieged by fifteen cases of measles, twenty of diphtheria, and several of pneumonia. One student died, and several parents withdrew their children from the school. Cotton prices dropped, undercutting profit from the school's large crop, and the cotton gin was destroyed by a fire.

S. C. Osborn, Tougaloo's farm superintendent, wrote to Erastus Cravath in New York, declaring that the school had only a two-day supply of food, had exhausted its credit, and was unable to buy a barrel of flour or a pound of meat. Days passed. The school went to half rations of food, and Osborn went to his knees and prayed for a special blessing. The next morning, he received a check from the AMA for five hundred dollars, and another soon followed.

Nutting and Osborn instituted changes to ensure Tougaloo's financial stability. They moved the school away from dependence on cotton, which was always vulnerable to unpredictable weather and fluctuating prices, as well as to the loss of labor every summer when students were absent. They rented out tracts of land to local farmers and focused their own acreage on an orchard, poultry, and livestock. Nutting invented several devices designed to cut down on labor costs, including a rudimentary washing machine that cleaned 1,700 pieces of clothing between breakfast and supper. When some white neighbors got wind of it, they asked the school to do their laundry for a fair price. Under Nutting's direction, students began making furniture for sale.

But still money was scarce, and the buildings fell into disrepair. Tarpaper that had been laid over the mansion's original roof was torn, and every wind blew ten to forty more feet of it to the ground, while every rain flooded the upper floor. The classrooms were so cold in winter that one elementary teacher wrote that she was asked to work "with her lips blue and her teeth chattering and her pupils' ditto."[6]

The original cistern went dry, and an additional one was begun, but it was never bricked for lack of funds. It had begun to cave in and was endangering the foundation of the young men's dormitory. The only other source of water was Molasses Lake, which received its name because of its dark, murky appearance; or perhaps because mansion residents had dumped molasses in the lake during the Civil War to keep Union soldiers from benefiting from either it or the water; or because it was surrounded by sugar cane. When volunteers from the community cleaned the lake, they were paid in molasses the school made from the cane.[7]

Several teachers and staff members resigned under the hardships. Ten students who couldn't afford tuition were sent home, in great despair at losing their only chance at an education, and applicants were turned away daily because they couldn't pay. Still, the buildings were crowded, and the boys were sleeping three to a bed. Nutting went on a speaking tour to raise money to renovate the former slave pen behind the mansion, where disobedient plantation workers had been punished and manacled at night, into a dormitory for boys.

Despite the best efforts of Nutting and Osborn, the school continued to decline. It owned four pairs of mules and horses and a pair of oxen, but it did not have a wagon to transport needed supplies. Teachers and students were reduced to a diet of bacon and bread. Repairs went unfinished.

On the last day of 1873, the AMA deployed James F. Claflin, a lawyer from Chicago, to serve as Tougaloo's superintendent. After surviving a life-threatening illness, Mr. Claflin had pledged to devote the rest of his life to God and humanity. A longtime admirer of the American Missionary Association, he offered his services without salary. When he saw the desperation that greeted him upon his arrival, he vowed to sell his watch and his clothes if necessary to keep Tougaloo afloat.

Claflin immediately procured a wagon for bringing supplies from Jackson. He focused on improving and expanding the school's buildings. He was so busy, he said, that he "had not even time to trim his corns."[8] He fenced the livestock and improved the agricultural program's efficiency. "If system could accomplish it," he declared proudly, "the very pigs would lay eggs and the rooster give milk."[9]

Claflin instituted regular Bible readings in the former slave quarters. He assigned students to work teams for chopping wood to satisfy the voracious appetites of the school's fourteen fireplaces. Anyone who "counts his hours of work," he wrote, "will never build up this school; a person must come here . . . (to) work for one greater than the A.M.A. and be willing to work till the blood comes without whining."[10]

Mr. Claflin expended great energy on getting ten thousand dollars in state appropriations for Tougaloo, spending six days in Jackson to guide the appropriation bills through the Mississippi legislature. The AMA secretaries in New York were less than pleased with what appeared to be Claflin's political manipulation of the process. The legislature, feeling pressured, eventually rescinded its decision, but it gave annual appropriations from $1,500 to $4,500 to Tougaloo through 1877.

The state's withdrawal of funds in 1877 appears to be motivated by both a general waning of enthusiasm for African American schools and the AMA's violation of Tougaloo's charter. The AMA continued to hire and fire faculty and staff, though the school's charter stated that these tasks were the responsibility of the board of trustees. After two years, the funds were reinstated, until Mississippi's 1890 constitution banned state appropriations to schools that charged tuition or were privately run. The governor expressed public regret in his 1892 address to the state legislature that the constitution forbade funding Tougaloo, which at that time emphasized industrial education more than most AMA schools, stating that "no appropriation ever made for the education of the colored race has yielded as good returns."[11]

Contributions to Tougaloo also flooded in from individuals. One donor gave the AMA two thousand dollars for "a normal school which did not teach a dead language"; Tougaloo qualified.[12] Others sent seeds for the garden. A dollar arrived, with an apology for the small sum, from a contributor who described herself as "an aged and feeble woman with a small income."[13] Another donor, who obviously lacked the education he desired for others, wrote, "Pleas find two Dollars for Freedmen it is not so much as usealy (but it is according to my means at presant)."[14] A reused envelope, with a dollar tucked inside and "For Christ's cause" written on the outside, reflected the motivation of most of the contributors to Tougaloo and other AMA schools.

At Tougaloo, the tensions with AMA officials that plagued many other schools seemed particularly acute. The New York officials exercised a centralized control, generally refusing to delegate authority commensurate with responsibility to administrators in the field. They were often out of touch with the real needs of the schools, causing unnecessary delays in making improvements. Tougaloo's isolation and character as a former plantation added to the usual complications.

G. Stanley Pope, an Oberlin graduate and Congregational minister from an abolitionist family, assumed the presidency of Tougaloo in 1877. He immediately turned his attention to the deteriorating mansion, adding a coat of paint, exterminating rats that had taken up residence, and replacing the straw matting on its floors with twenty-eight yards of carpet from the Misfit Carpet Store, at a cost of a dollar per yard.[15] Pope worked to strengthen the basic elementary and normal courses, stating, "We are willing to take the rough stone from a quarry and put on the heavy, telling strokes of the builder and leave the most artistic strokes of the sculptor to be given by some of our sister institutions."[16]

Systematic Bible study was added to every grade, and industrial education was expanded to include blacksmithing, carpentry, shoe repair, wheelwrighting, and tinsmithing. D. I. Miner, the new farm superintendent, implemented scientific farming to improve the soil and crop yield. He planted thirty thousand strawberry plants, shipping the berries from Tougaloo's railway station directly to markets in Chicago on the Illinois Central Railway. He purchased a high-quality Ayrshire cow and calf from Talladega.

In January 1881 the young men's dormitory went up in flames. Bereft of their quarters, the displaced students moved into the nearly completed barn before the cattle could take possession;

they dubbed it Ayrshire Hall. Tougaloo students began making brick from the clay found in nearby creek bottoms, and over the summer students from other AMA schools arrived to help construct Strieby Hall, named after AMA Secretary Michael E. Strieby, who presided at its dedication on Thanksgiving Day. It served as the young men's dormitory and included classrooms, science laboratories, and a reference library.

In 1886, uniform state teacher examinations were required, and teachers' certificates were issued for the first time. While 70 percent of the examinees across the state failed the first year, those who had been trained at Tougaloo did very well. The school developed a reputation for thorough training, and its students were in high demand by superintendents across Mississippi, as well as in Arkansas and Louisiana.[17]

Frank G. Woodworth gave twenty-five years of his life as president of Tougaloo, beginning his tenure in 1887. Committed to preparing leaders equipped with "the wider, nobler visions seen from the loftier heights," Woodworth expanded the liberal arts curriculum and instituted the college program in 1897. The music department flourished, and its choral groups were in demand around the state. Mr. Woodworth's goal was for each student to leave Tougaloo with "a mind well stored with philosophy, science, history, literature, art, and in communings with the intellectual aristocracy of the past."[18]

The majority of students, many of them from sharecropping families, had to supplement their tuition costs with work. The May 1891 edition of *The American Missionary* described a daily routine that began at 4:00 a.m., when several boys arose and went to the barn to milk cows, while the student baker began preparing up to fifty three-pound loaves of bread for the day's use. A second group awoke at 5:00 a.m. to kindle fires and clean the schoolrooms.

At 6:00 a.m. a large triangle bell was rung outside the kitchen, which was answered by a larger bell in Strieby Hall, followed by the howl of the campus dog. After daily room inspection, boys and girls marched in blue uniforms to the dining hall, while the farm boys rushed milk to the milk room, where girls strained it. Breakfast began with the singing of "The Doxology."

Music practice and other assignments followed. At 8:45 a.m. a march was struck on the piano in the music hall, and all students filed upstairs for devotions. Classes began at 9:00 with Bible study. Normal students took their turns at observation or practice teaching at the Daniel Hand Primary School, which was built on the campus to serve community children and aid teacher training.

Students enjoyed a free hour before afternoon classes, which emphasized the industrial arts and homemaking for girls. More chores followed. Boys plowed, planted, and fenced the campus's corn fields—which fed faculty, students, and several teams of mules—while girls made small brushes and brooms from the special broom corn that was planted on several acres every year. Reading, recreation, and music practice were allowed before dinner, which was followed by evening devotions and study hours. Calisthenics took place at 9:00 p.m. before lights out at 10:00.

As at other AMA schools, social engagements among older students were strictly controlled. If a young man desired to escort a young woman, he was required to send her a written invitation, via the matron, who considered not only the substance of his request but also its grammatical construction and spelling. The young woman's response underwent the same scrutiny. "Mail call" took place at the foot of a stairway in Beard Hall, where inviters and invitees waited anxiously. At socials, students were allowed to march side by side but not to dance. Students mingled at football games—popular at Tougaloo, which claims to have introduced the sport to southern African American colleges.[19]

Students were not allowed to receive food from home. Parents sometimes tried to hide their children's favorite foods inside shoes or the pockets of clothing they sent. One matron kept a Persian cat that sniffed all incoming packages and showed special interest in those that contained edibles.[20]

Mosquitoes were "so numerous and hungry" at Tougaloo, wrote one teacher, "that we all look as if we had the small pox."[21] The school's annual opening was delayed by several weeks at least five times between 1887 and 1899, until fall frosts eliminated the danger of yellow fever.[22] When epidemics overtook Jackson, supplies from the city were dropped off near campus at what came to be known as "Quarantine Oaks." Tougaloo's carpentry shop had the grim task of making coffins in large quantities for local children who were claimed by disease.

Health principles were strictly adhered to at the school, including such admonitions as, "Under no circumstances should a child be put to bed with cold feet."[23] Local sharecroppers and tenant farmers and their families used Tougaloo's infirmary for primary health care. Children were transported there from around the county for immunization campaigns. The infirmary nurse made visits in the community, often uncovering dire situations such as that of an elderly, near-blind couple who lived in a cold, damp storage building that leaked. Tougaloo's president paid for bedding for the couple, students cut firewood and prepared meals for them, and a staff member gave them a small country house, which student members of the YMCA repaired and the school's home economics class furnished.

A small hospital was erected on campus in 1901 to serve students and facilitate the training of nurses. The county's thirty-eight thousand residents, thirty thousand of whom were African Americans, had just one public health nurse until 1939, when a second one was added. That year public health services were expanded to include preschool clinics and school health programs for white children, but black children received only immunizations to prevent the spread of communicable diseases.

The following year, a fire caused the loss of more than two hundred lives in an African American section of Natchez, Mississippi. Ms. E. F. Scott, the college's registered nurse, was released to work with the Red Cross, marking the first time the organization accepted African American nurses. On her first day of service, Ms. Scott officiated at forty-three funerals, making sure that the graves were the appropriate depth and attending to sixty-eight people who fainted graveside. Her days of devotion during the emergency won many friends around the state for Tougaloo.

Tougaloo's buildings, resting on Mississippi's three hundred-foot-deep, shifting alluvial plain, sank and settled irregularly. Strieby Hall had to be reinforced in 1888 with twelve anchors running lengthwise and ten running crosswise through the building. In 1890 its foundation had to be entirely redone and its walls replastered. Contractors advised that Ladies' Hall be razed. Instead, during vacation, students remained to do the work of reinforcing its foundation, lifting the building section by section, adding concrete footings, brick piers, and heavy timbering.

Ten years later, the day before Thanksgiving, Ladies' Hall went up in smoke. The dining room and a summer's worth of canned goods were lost; the smokehouse, hen house, and windmill were all destroyed. The mansion next door was threatened; had it caught fire, the blaze likely would have destroyed the entire campus. One teacher stood on its roof, in heat so intense that her hairpins burned her head, shouting out instructions to students who worked to keep the mansion walls watered down.

Beard Hall, named for AMA Secretary Augustus Field Beard, was constructed in 1898. In 1901 Woodworth Chapel was built, largely with student labor. Furniture for the chapel was made in the school's shops. A patron donated a two-manual organ, thought to be the first of its kind in the South. Since neither electric nor water power was available, a student had to work the pumps to keep air flowing over the organ's pipes.

The school continued to be overcrowded. At the turn of the century, among AMA colleges, only Fisk boarded more students than Tougaloo.[24] In 1906, the U.S. Department of Agriculture named Tougaloo one of its demonstration centers. Under its supervision, the farm averaged two bales of cotton to the acre, compared to the state average of only half a bale, and sixty-four and a half bushels of corn per acre when the state average was less than twenty. The farm, which kept eighty to a hundred cattle, as well as swine, sheep, horses, mules, and poultry, was virtually self-sufficient for meat, milk, butter, and eggs. Its prize bull was made available to local farmers. Tougaloo instructors patterned the college's industrial courses after the curriculum at the Massachusetts Institute of Technology, where most of them had been trained.[25]

The Congregational church at Tougaloo was organized almost simultaneously with the school, and its early presidents were as much pastors as school administrators. Some four thousand children were reached every summer by students who stayed and conducted a Sunday School Institute. Mr. Woodworth convened night classes for ministers in the field. When an avowed atheist renowned for his blasphemy died, his distraught daughter told Tougaloo's chaplain that he had made her promise to keep his body out of church. So the chaplain conducted a Christian funeral, with many people in attendance and the man's body in the hearse outside.[26]

An active Temperance Society discouraged use of profanity, tobacco, and "ardent spirits."[27] During the summer, students spread out across Mississippi, collecting signatures on temperance pledges—a risky endeavor in a state whose liquor interests were known to have a stranglehold on party politics. The White Cross Society for men included a pledge to treat all women with respect, to refrain from coarse and indecent language, and to embrace purity as a virtue as necessary for men as for women. The White Shield Society for women encouraged virtue and modesty.

A Missouri newspaper correspondent visiting Mississippi early in the century wrote that he found it incredible that, in a state so blemished by racism, white Mississippians so heartily praised Tougaloo.[28] During one of the school's popular commencement celebrations, which drew people from across the state to their gala picnics, speeches, and exhibits, J. R. Dobyne, superintendent of the state school for the deaf, declared, "You have the growing sympathy and respect of the best people of the state."[29] At that time, Tougaloo's administrators were urging students to educate themselves for intelligent citizenship, stay out of politics, and accept realities that, in their view, could not be remedied, including Jim

Crow segregation. Tougaloo could be praised easily by whites because the school wasn't making any social or political waves that rocked the status quo.

In 1913 William Trumbull Holmes took up residence in the president's mansion for a twenty-year tenure. By his own description, he moved Tougaloo from a manual training high school with a college addendum to a fine liberal arts college with a feeder high school. He brought to the campus a variety of speakers, including George Washington Carver, who showed the school how to save money during World War I by baking sweet potato bread and extracting "milk" from soybeans. Mr. Holmes was renowned for his midnight patrols of the campus, one night discovering a young man descending a ladder from a young woman's dormitory room. The next morning he drove the two of them to the courthouse, procured a license, married them, and dismissed them from school.[30]

Holmes focused much of his energy on fund-raising, making frequent trips to the North and personally pecking out with two fingers on his typewriter thank-you notes to donors. One of his favorite fund-raising ploys was offering Spanish moss plucked from the branches of Tougaloo's large live oak trees to Northern churches. One pound could decorate a parlor, three a small sanctuary, and ten a large church. The moss looked especially nice, Holmes wrote, hanging from chandeliers. He shipped it without charge, accompanied with a description of Tougaloo's mission and the notation that a year of tuition, room, board, and books for a student cost $155.

In 1922 Holmes announced a campaign to bring electricity to the campus. Northern contributors helped, but students raised money by putting on plays and cooking food for sale. In 1926 Holmes oversaw the construction of Holmes Hall, the first building in an expansion effort that eventually included a girls' dormitory, a laundry, an addition to the dining hall, seven teachers' residences, and a practice housekeeping bungalow. On the eve of the dedication of Holmes Hall, the school's hospital caught fire. Young students threw bowls and pitchers of water at the blaze, doing little to put out the flames but breaking most of the dining room crockery. The hospital was destroyed.

To replace the loss, the American Missionary Association donated funds to build the Sarah A. Dickey Hospital, named for a woman who had struggled as a young orphan to get an education and then dedicated her life to teaching African American girls. The Rosenwald Fund—which Julius Rosenwald of Sears, Roebuck, and Company established in 1917, with the bulk of its $22 million endowment going to building elementary schools for African

American children in the South—proclaimed Tougaloo one of the outstanding institutions of its kind. It contributed eight thousand dollars to Tougaloo for teacher training, after a plea from Holmes, who informed the fund that fewer than six thousand teachers existed in Mississippi for almost half a million black children.[31]

An explosion of cultural and literary activities took place at Tougaloo. One of the most prominent organizations, the Cheeseman Literary Society for young men, gave instruction in parliamentary procedure, debate, and political campaigning. The annual inauguration of its incoming president involved him dressing up in a formal suit, pleated shirt, black tie, and stovepipe hat nearly two feet high, being led through campus on the most decrepit animal in the barn—mule, horse, or cow—to the mansion, where the college president gave a speech and everyone cheered. The Paul Robeson Dramatic Club produced stunning plays, and Scribia encouraged students to write poetry and sponsored campus visits from such literary dignitaries as Countee Cullen, Langston Hughes, and James Weldon Johnson.

In 1931 the Association of Colleges and Secondary Schools fully accredited Tougaloo's high school, making it the first African American school in Mississippi to receive this affirmation.[32] With the help of another Rosenwald grant, the library was improved and faculty members received scholarships to upgrade their degrees, leading to Tougaloo College receiving standing with the Southern Association of Colleges and Secondary Schools.

When William Trumbull Holmes became too ill in 1933 to continue serving as Tougaloo's president, Charles B. Austin, president of Straight University in New Orleans, took over. He regularly rode the two hundred miles between the two schools on the Illinois Central Railroad, boarding at 11 o'clock at night at one point and arriving at the other in time for breakfast. His absences increased the burdens on Tougaloo faculty and staff, and the arrival of the Great Depression brought further hardship and a precipitous drop in enrollment at the school. Its survival became tenuous. Students had to depend on clothing donations from the North, which they could buy at little expense in an industrial shop on campus that they dubbed The Emporium—the name of an upscale department store in Jackson.

Rev. Judson L. Cross became president in 1935. His tireless fund-raising helped to keep morale high during unusual financial stress. He built Cross Hall with donations from the American Missionary Association and the Women's Home Missionary Union of the Congregational Churches of Massachusetts. He acquired a movie projector, providing weekly entertainment for the school and the local African American community, which faced difficulties getting to Jackson theaters and suffered discrimination in them.

In 1940, 92 percent of Mississippi's African American children of high-school age were not in school. The average expenditure for education for a white child averaged ten times higher than that for a black child, with the disparity as high as forty times more in some counties.[33] White children had a nine-month school year.

"We had only four months of school," said Henry Thornton Drake, "and very little of the basics, none of the sciences, and very little English." Mr. Drake, a member of Union United Church of Christ, the congregation that worships in Tougaloo's Woodworth Chapel, arrived at Tougaloo as a freshman in 1947. School for black children "was scheduled for four months," says Drake, "but chances are you didn't get but two months, because you had to stop maybe in the middle of four months to chop cotton, pick the cotton, or whatever. Those four months were broken into parts until you finished."

After a stint in the Navy, Mr. Drake worked in a sawmill at night and earned his high-school equivalency degree. "I made up my mind that I was not college material," he said. His wife was expecting their first child, and he tried to convince her and her doctor that he needed to be home for the delivery. But the doctor retorted sharply, "Me and your wife's having this baby, so you get you on down to Tougaloo."

Mr. Drake said, "I came here very frightened, (with) very little background in academics. But the class saw something in me and elected me president." Beverly Williams had a similarly empowering experience at Tougaloo. "There was something (here) that said, 'You can make it,'" she explained. She used to sit often in Woodworth Chapel and just "breathe in the peace."

Lillie McKinney Cooley's mother graduated from Tougaloo High School in 1929. "She came to Tougaloo," said Ms. Cooley, "because my grandfather, who was a butcher, said that if it took nine months to educate a white child, it took nine months to educate his children." In 1939 Ms. Cooley and her brother, who suffered from asthma, were the first children from Jackson to ride the Tougaloo bus to the Daniel Hand School on the campus. They had to wait up to three hours every day after school, under the supervision of the college bus driver and groundskeeper, for the college students to finish before returning home.

Annie Smith said, "Tougaloo was the place that every child in the community heard about and wanted to come to." She and her sister, Sarah Douglas, who started school as a six-year-old in 1938, made a six-mile roundtrip on foot every day. Though they lived three miles from the campus, they could hear Tougaloo's bell from their home, and as very young children they longed to respond to that bell.

Ms. Smith, who still lives in a place where she can hear the bell, remembered the joy of commencement days: "When I was a small girl, people would come from all over Mississippi in wagons, buggies, walking. And they would sell fish, and hot dogs. You could get a whole cone of ice cream for a nickel. They would make and sell candy, and peanuts. You didn't need but a quarter to get a whole meal. And there was the man who had a hood over his big camera, and he would take the pictures. It was just a glorious day. Everybody would come to Tougaloo on that day."

Ms. Smith knew about the AMA because "at Christmas time they would send a box of toys, and all of us got a toy at Christmas time from the American Missionary Association . . . And after that the boys always had to climb up the trees to get the 'mistletoe' (Spanish moss)," which was sent north to AMA donors in large boxes.

As White Citizens Councils began to be organized across the state, racism hardened and communities polarized even further. Tougaloo College students responded by deepening their relationship with students at nearby Millsaps College, a white Methodist school. A group of Millsaps boys had tried unsuccessfully to lynch an African American. When they returned to campus, they asked their Bible professor to give them an excused absence. The professor refused, taking the opportunity to talk about biblical teachings and race relations.

After that, sociology classes from the two schools cooperated on a survey of Jackson's African American community. They launched an exchange of speakers and formed a local chapter of the Intercollegiate Council, which was committed to developing understanding between the races. Tougaloo Professor Ernst Borinski, director of the Social Sciences Forum, brought controversial speakers to the campus for monthly forums that were open to the public, both black and white, providing an opportunity that was virtually nonexistent elsewhere in Mississippi. The Mississippi legislature made Borinski the target of an investigation that also included the NAACP. During the tenure of Tougaloo President Samuel C. Kinchloe in the late 1950s, the school became a base for exposing Northerners to the realities of southern racism, plantation life, and poverty.

Ruth Barefield-Pendleton, who later served as secretary of the Central Committee for Birmingham, Alabama's civil rights campaign, spoke fondly of her time at Tougaloo. In her family, "going to college was not just a given," she said. She was the first in her family to go beyond high school. She had a high school teacher, a Tougaloo graduate, who encouraged her to enroll there.

When she told her parents her wishes, her father told her, "Boys need the education." And she replied, "I want the education, and I want to go to Tougaloo College." He told her that if she wanted to go to college, she should go to "Mr. Washington's school"— Booker T. Washington's Tuskegee Institute. "That was because his trunks had been packed to go to Mr. Washington's school," Ms. Barefield-Pendleton explained, "but he was an only child, and his mother had heard that all the young black men who were caught trying to go to school were being lynched. So they unpacked his trunk, and he rebelled. He rebelled by taking his fifteen-year-old bride and moving to Mississippi."

According to Ms. Barefield-Pendleton, Tougaloo was "the only island of light in a sea of darkness in the state of Mississippi." She had arrived from the small gulfport town of Pascagoula and met white people for the first time in her life. She joined the Paul Robeson Dramatic Club. And though she hadn't heard of Congregationalism before, she joined the Congregational church on campus. When she told her father, his response was, "When you find a black person that ain't a Baptist or a Methodist, they've been tampered with."

One of Ms. Barefield-Pendleton's fondest memories is of a professor, Florence Brumback, who took her to the Emporium in Jackson to buy her a dress for her first prom. On seeing them walk in the door, the saleswoman stated with scorn, "We don't serve colored people here, and they do not try on our dresses." According to Ms. Barefield-Pendleton, Miss Brumback, a tall and very large white woman, "stood with her very stately self and said, 'Bring a dress to fit me.'"

The saleswoman brought out two dresses. "I was brokenhearted," said Ms. Barefield-Pendleton. "Miss Brumback asked me which one did I like. I didn't like either of them, but I picked one. It had a black top—I never shall forget this—and a pale blue bottom with a big bow at the waist. The dress had to have been a size twenty." They returned to the Tougaloo campus. "She pinned that dress on me and then told me to go back to my dormitory. On Saturday morning, she called. I went over there and put on the dress. It fit, neat as could be, and the big skirt was standing out . . . I think about her now. I think about Miss Brumback."

Anticipation of the 1954 Supreme Court decision outlawing school segregation created a climate in which white leaders in Mississippi who had never been sympathetic to education for

African Americans vowed to "get" Tougaloo. A change in standards by the Southern Association of Colleges and Secondary Schools was not communicated to Tougaloo, which resulted in the loss of the school's accreditation. With help from the American Missionary Association, then Tougaloo President Harold C. Warren worked feverishly to upgrade faculty and salaries. He built Brownlee Gymnasium, named in honor of AMA Secretary Fred L. Brownlee, and revamped the library, using piles of obsolete books to kindle fires and fill the old cistern.

In the fall of 1953, Touglaoo earned back its approval rating—the only African American college in Mississippi to hold such status. It had the largest percentage of doctorates among its faculty of any college in the state, black or white.[34] Hoping to strengthen its resources, the school decided to merge with Southern Christian Institute, a Disciples of Christ school forty miles to the west, which shared a history of struggle related to race prejudice and financial uncertainty. The Southern Christian Institute campus was sold, and for a brief time Tougaloo became Tougaloo Southern Christian College.

After the 1954 *Brown vs. the Board of Education* Supreme Court decision, Mississippi became a cauldron of racial strife. African Americans were killed for registering to vote or for encouraging others to do so. In August that year, the nation's attention was riveted on the state when Emmett Till, a fourteen-year-old from Chicago spending the summer with relatives in Mississippi, was murdered for addressing a married white woman. His body—shot through the head, with an eye gouged out and a seventy-five-pound cotton gin fan wired around the neck—was dragged from the bottom of the Tallahatchie River. Despite eyewitness testimony, the killers were acquitted of their crime.

Tougaloo played a key role in the nascent stirrings that laid the foundations for the impending civil rights movement. Tougaloo graduate and chaplain William Bender became a leader in the nucleus of the first chapter of the NAACP in Mississippi. According to Larry Johnson, the current chaplain and pastor of Union United Church of Christ, Rev. Bender "got out and walked these streets in those days to help organize across the state." While Bender was president of the state NAACP, which seldom met in the same place twice so as not to be discovered, it enrolled the fifty members needed for a state charter. Rev. Bender regularly escorted students who were determined to register to vote to the courthouse, and he more than once faced down the county sheriff.

Adam Daniel Beittel's acceptance of the invitation to become the college's president in 1960 led to marked improvements in the physical plant and academic standards. His early accomplishments included a cooperative venture between Tougaloo and Brown University in Rhode Island to provide a fifth year of study for Tougaloo students who needed a firmer grounding or broader experience before entering graduate school. He also instituted a pre-college program to give talented high school graduates summer courses in writing, math, and study skills.

But Dr. Beittel's most renowned accomplishments were related to the civil rights struggle. Arriving from his post as Talladega College's president, he served on the Mississippi Advisory Committee to the U.S. Commission on Civil Rights, was secretary of the United Negro College Fund, and was vice president of the Association of Colleges and Schools for Negroes. He worked to revive Jackson's defunct Human Relations Council, and when no one else dared to serve as its president, he added that role to his responsibilities.

One year to the day after he arrived at Tougaloo, Beittel was invited to appear on a Jackson television program. A panel of journalists grilled him about his affiliation with the NAACP and Tougaloo's role as host to mixed-race groups, which had led to the protest resignation of the only white Mississippian on its board of trustees. When questioned about the Freedom Riders who were housed on the campus during their campaign to integrate buses across the South, Beittel responded that the college "simply provided hospitality to human beings who needed a place to sleep."[35]

Dr. Beittel had bailed students out of jail after they organized to the courthouse a sit-in at Jackson's public library. A panelist asked if Tougaloo's library was inadequate to meet students' needs, and Beittel responded, "I don't think the students came to the Jackson city library primarily for books."[36] He added that the students had the full support of Tougaloo's faculty, administration, and board of trustees in their effort to challenge the library's refusal to serve African Americans.

Tougaloo, which never expelled a student for civil rights activities, received several students from other schools that had put them out. It became the one public place in Mississippi where blacks and whites could meet on equal terms. When a panelist told Beittel that trouble would come if Tougaloo continued its controversial activities, he countered that education usually involves controversy but that no trouble was necessary. None would have come to the library, he said, if the authorities had simply left the students alone to read for a few hours.

Sam Bradford, who arrived at Tougaloo as a student in 1960, was one of the Tougaloo Nine who sat in at the library. He and the other eight students who volunteered to sit in "had to keep it quiet first of all," said Mr. Bradford, "because it was very dangerous. We didn't know how we were going to come out of that thing." As he spoke of their action forty years later, he said softly, "It still gets to be a little emotional for me."

The group had "enormous support," according to Bradford, and the protection afforded by members of the news media, who had been alerted by Medgar Evers, executive secretary of the Mississippi NAACP. "They came out of the bushes with cameras, and (our protest) simultaneously spread out across the country as we were doing it." On the day of the Tougaloo Nine trial, some five hundred students from Jackson State University marched downtown to show their support. "And that was the first time dogs were used against students—right here in Jackson, Mississippi," according to Mr. Bradford. "We were tried and convicted of breach of peace; we were sentenced to six months (in jail) and five hundred dollars in fines."

Mr. Bradford remembered a local couple in their nineties who had dared to register to vote and were put off their property. They were brought to the Tougaloo campus because they had no place else to go. "We were able to give them our beds, and we made pallets in the hallway and slept there," he said. "So everybody didn't get a chance to go out and do big things, but there was a reason for everybody to be involved." Bradford expressed gratitude for the many people who paved the way for the actions of the '60s: "There were those who made contributions to the civil rights effort . . . long before the so-called civil rights movement."

In December 1962, a group of students and faculty, who often met at the home of sociology professor John Salter, joined the state NAACP and others in encouraging a boycott of selected downtown Jackson stores. Salter and several students, including Anne Moody, who would later write *Coming of Age in Mississippi*, took seats at Woolworth's segregated lunch counter. A photograph of white bystanders squirting them with ketchup and mustard and dumping salt, pepper, and sugar over their heads became one of the most renowned pictures of the civil rights movement. Rev. Edwin King, Tougaloo's chaplain at that time, called Dr. Beittel, who took a seat beside the protesters when his pleas to police to protect them were ignored and helped take students who were injured from beatings at the lunch counter to his car.

The Tougaloo Movement, led by Joyce Ladner, an African American student, and Joan Trumpauer, a white student, decided to concentrate its desegregation efforts on live-entertainment establishments and churches. The students formed the Cultural and Artistic Agitation Committee. They began with Millsaps College where, much to the embarrassment of college officials, police had used dogs to prevent Tougaloo students from attending cultural programs. Beginning with an event in which sympathetic white Millsaps and Tougaloo students surrounded black students sitting in the center of the auditorium, programs at Millsaps were made increasingly available to all.

When an African American music major from Tougaloo tried to attend a concert by London's Royal Philharmonic Orchestra in Jackson, he and a companion were arrested. The British Embassy intervened, and England's *Manchester Guardian* gave the incident wide publicity, discouraging other artists from playing in the American South.

When a black student was refused a ticket for *Original Hootenanny U.S.A.*, sponsored by three local white colleges, the Cultural and Artistic Agitation Committee met the event's folk singers at the airport. Sympathetic to the students' cause, they canceled their show at great personal financial cost, performing a free concert at Tougaloo instead while some 1,500 frustrated ticket holders stood in line at Jackson's city auditorium to get refunds. Five colleges, two black and three white, later cooperated to sponsor an integrated concert in Woodworth Chapel that featured Joan Baez.

In February 1964, after weeks of correspondence with Tougaloo students, Lorne Green, Dan Blocker, and Michael Landon—the actors playing Ben, Hoss, and Little Joe Cartwright on *Bonanza*—canceled a scheduled appearance in Jackson. This prompted some local white citizens to urge others to go to church on Sunday nights rather than watch the television show. Two members of *The Beverly Hillbillies* cast made public their refusal to serve as replacements. The next day, after five thousand people had waited for forty minutes to hear Al Hirt, a man walked onto the stage and read a telegram from Tougaloo students explaining why the New Orleans jazz trumpeter had refused to appear.

When *Holiday on Ice* refused to cancel, two Tougaloo students, one white and one black, were arrested for trying to attend. They were placed in segregated jail cells. The jailer told Eli Hochstedler, the white student, to button his collar before entering his cell—a signal to the other inmates, it turned out, that he was the "race mixer." When he was released a week later, he was so terribly bruised from beatings that he was barely recognizable.

Churches proved even more difficult to integrate than auditoriums. Chaplain Edwin King, a white, Methodist, native Mississippian, was denied membership in the (white) Mississippi Methodist

Conference because of his racial views, but he was welcomed as the only white ministerial member of the black conference. In the summer of 1963, Jackson citizens and students participating in an ecumenical work camp sponsored by the National Council of Churches at Tougaloo made the first effort to integrate white churches, with little success.Groups of mixed students approached various church buildings during services until they were stopped by ushers, whom they referred to as "bouncing committees."

When ushers refused to talk with them, many students opened their Bibles and read silently while they waited for the police to arrive and arrest them. Most were charged with trespassing and disturbing a worship service. At Galloway Methodist Church, a regular member who was also a professor at Tougaloo, disguised in feathered hat and mink stole, broke through a ring of ushers and extended a gloved hand to a mixed group of visitors, welcoming them to the service and undermining the ushers' insistence that the church was united in its stand on segregation. The next day's newspaper described her as an "unidentified white lady."[37]

Crosses were sometimes burned at the Tougaloo campus gate, and cars raced through the grounds with guns firing. Faculty homes on the far west end of the campus were a frequent target. Male students organized a night patrol, armed only with whistles, although on a few occasions they secretly carried guns.

Medgar Evers was murdered in his carport in Jackson on June 12, 1963. In the aftermath of the tragedy, leaders of the civil rights movement focused their attention more intently on Mississippi. Plans were put into place for "Freedom Summer," an effort organized by the NAACP, SNCC (Student Nonviolent Coordinating Committee), CORE (Congress on Racial Equality), and SCLC (Southern Christian Leadership Conference) for a mock election in the summer of 1964. Mississippi NAACP President Aaron Henry and Tougaloo Chaplain Edwin King were selected as candidates for governor and lieutenant governor respectively. Tougaloo students turned out in droves to support the campaign.

Voter education took place in "Freedom Schools"—nearly fifty of them across the state—which were set up in shacks, stores, and churches, their purpose announced with homemade, hand-painted signs. Cardboard ballot boxes were placed in African American churches, stores, gas stations, and barber shops. Students disguised as field hands slipped onto cotton plantations to distribute and collect votes. Whites formed mobs to try to block them, chasing them and sometimes shooting at them. Police confiscated some of the ballot boxes, and arrests were made with high bail exacted.

On June 21, 1964, civil rights workers James Chaney, Michael Schwerner, and Andrew Goodman were arrested in their car after investigating the burning of a church that served as a Freedom School. They were taken to the jail in Philadelphia, Mississippi, released, and never seen alive again. Two days later, their charred station wagon was pulled—empty—from a shallow creek nearby. The search for their bodies in the swampy, snake-infested waters around Philadelphia turned up others—decomposing, unidentifiable, dumped unceremoniously in dank, backwater corners by Klansmen and law enforcement officials—exposing the grisly truth about race relations in Mississippi. Not until two months later did a bulldozer uncover the bodies of the three young men, beaten and shot, under an earthen cattle pond dam.

Between June 15 and September 15, 1964, civil rights workers in Mississippi reported more than 450 violent incidents, including eighty beatings, thirty-five shootings, thirty-five church burnings, and thirty bombings. Law enforcement officials made more than a thousand arrests. But some ninety thousand people succeeded in casting unofficial ballots during "Freedom Summer." Aaron Henry and Edwin King won with more than 99 percent of the vote. A victory rally at the Masonic Temple in Jackson displayed a new level of pride among black Mississippians who saw possibility in unity.

Fannie Lou Hamer, a fearless Mississippi sharecropper who was a leader in citizenship education and voter registration drives, and whose renditions of "This Little Light of Mine" and other freedom songs inspired courage at many civil rights marches and demonstrations, joined Henry and King as leaders of the Mississippi Freedom Democratic Party (MFDP). Ms. Hamer later received an honorary Doctor of Humanities degree from Tougaloo for her persistent bravery in the face of vicious violence, including a beating that caused injuries that eventually led to her death. In late August, the three leaders contested the seating of the regular delegates at the 1964 Democratic National Convention in Atlantic City, citing the fact that 40 percent of Mississippi's citizens had been refused the right to vote. President Lyndon Johnson ordered the FBI to infiltrate the MFDP, and convention officials refused to recognize its delegates, but the courageous three and their supporters succeeded in forcing the convention to face Mississippi's racial realities.

Mississippi state officials searched for legal ways to curtail the civil rights activities stemming from Tougaloo College, which the white opposition called a nest of communists and rabble-rousers. A close examination of the school's charter revealed a clause limiting the value of its physical plant to half a million dollars, which had been far exceeded. But an effort in the legislature to revoke Tougaloo's charter died in committee.

In June 1963, an injunction had been issued against the trustees, President Beittel, the NAACP, CORE, and others, calling for an end to "engaging in, sponsoring, inciting or encouraging demonstrations," including kneel-ins at churches. It was appealed and had no effect. Tougaloo continued to function and, at the urging of Brown University officials, unprecedented amounts of foundation money arrived to support the college.

The board of trustees' announcement in the spring of 1964 that President Beittel would be leaving in September came as a shock to many. A letter from three Mississippi religious leaders praised Adam Beittel's "forthright guidance" in making Tougaloo a "beacon light," his "unhesitating expressions of courageous insight," and his "display of moral integrity without regard to personal cost." They saw his leaving as a victory for Tougaloo's enemies and a sign of the power of Mississippi's racists. The letter concluded, "Tougaloo is finally surrendering to intimidation."[38]

Though the board asked Beittel to announce his retirement as voluntary, he refused to participate in the deception. A few years later, the white supremacist Mississippi State Sovereignty Commission, which had closely monitored activities at Tougaloo, claimed a major role in Beittel's dismissal. Members asserted that they had met privately with three of the college trustees in New York and convinced them that Tougaloo would be better off with a president who was "more concerned with education than agitation."[39]

George Owens, the school's business manager, became acting president, the first African American to fill the role. In 1966 the college received a grant from the federal Office of Economic Opportunity to conduct an Upward Bound program, designed to stimulate interest in advanced education among low-income high school students. Tougaloo opened a campus center for underachieving students and sponsored a Head Start program for preschoolers in four counties. It was awarded a grant for "Opera South," enabling Tougaloo students to appear in operas.

But dismissing Dr. Beittel didn't stop the college's activism. In the late 1960s and early '70s, Tougaloo continued its role as both a safe haven and a stage for agitation in a roiling racial climate. It was the safest place for meetings of the Mississippi Council on Human Relations. The Mississippi chapter of the American Civil Liberties Union was organized there in 1969.

A "who's who" of progressive activists, artists, and politicians— including Julian Bond, Stokely Carmichael, James Baldwin, Marian Anderson, Harry Belafonte, Ralph Bunche, Roy Wilkins, and Robert Kennedy—took their place by turn behind the podium in Woodworth Chapel. "During that period," said Tougaloo native and Union United Church of Christ member Hiawatha Douglas, "if they made it to Tougaloo, they were somewhere safe. And basically everything went on right in this church, because it was about the only facility on this campus that could hold a crowd." Tougaloo was considered the "Oasis of the South," according to Sam Bradford. "This was the one place where they could come and feel free . . . and people of all races came and participated in the process."

James Meredith—whose admission as the first black student to the University of Mississippi in 1961 drew a mob of 2,500 white rioters with clubs and guns, resulting in two deaths—launched a personal "March against Fear" across Mississippi in June 1966. Wearing a pith helmet and carrying an ivory-headed African cane, Meredith was wounded by three blasts from a sniper's shotgun on the second day of his intended 220-mile march to Jackson.

People from across the state rallied to pick up from the point where Meredith fell, facing harassment and tear gas as they made their way to Tougaloo College. Martin Luther King Jr. led twenty thousand marchers through the campus gate and moved the crowd at a spirited rally. After a night camping out on the college grounds, the marchers streamed to the state capitol in Jackson, where Stokely Carmichael electrified the nation with his famous Black Power speech.

The FBI put Tougaloo in its crosshairs, calling the college "a staging area for civil rights and militant Negro activities in Mississippi."[40] Tougaloo's Political Action Committee—a SNCC affiliate that sponsored speakers, organized voter registration drives and African culture seminars, and publicly condemned racial injustices—was listed as a target to "disrupt, discredit, or neutralize" under FBI Director J. Edgar Hoover's Counter-Intelligence Program (Cointelpro) in March 1968. After a year-long harassment campaign, the FBI announced in May 1969 that it had successfully crippled the group.[41]

Tougaloo's choir was performing in New York City's Carnegie Hall with Duke Ellington's orchestra on April 4, 1968, when an announcement was made that Martin Luther King had been assassinated in Memphis. Waves of grief and disbelief swept over the massive hall. On the Tougaloo campus, students organized three days of commemorative events, including a memorial service, rallies, and seminars based on Dr. King's book *Where Do We Go from Here?* Thirty students, chosen by drawing names from a hat, attended Dr. King's funeral.

When the county's public school students were prohibited from holding observances of the tragedy, a throng walked toward Jackson, without a plan. When highway patrolmen confronted them, they turned toward Tougaloo, where President Owens met them and invited them onto the campus. A special memorial service for Dr. King was organized on the spot.

Throughout these years of agitation and change, Tougaloo never sacrificed its standing as an outstanding academic institution. In 1966, 35 percent of Tougaloo's graduating class entered graduate schools, 36 percent took teaching positions, and 14 percent were employed in business, industry, and government. Some were among the first African American students at the University of Mississippi Medical Center. More than half of the class of 1977 was accepted for graduate professional work, causing fellow students to celebrate by tacking congratulatory handmade posters bearing the names of friends to campus trees and buildings as each was accepted into graduate school.[42]

In 1989, *U.S. News and World Report* included Tougaloo in its survey of "best colleges" in the nation, noting its highly selective requirements for admission and its development of African American leaders.[43] Today, more than 60 percent of Tougaloo's graduates enroll in graduate and professional schools.[44] Alumni of distinction include Walter Turnbull, founder of the Boys Choir of Harlem; Constance Slaughter Harvey, the first African American to earn a law degree at the University of Mississippi School of Law; and Joyce Ladner, the first female president of Howard University.

Tougaloo's impact on the surrounding community endures. Beginning in 1993, the college required community service from all its students. Its commitment to public education is evident in the fact that four schools in Jackson are named after Tougaloo graduates.[45] The George and Ruth Owens Health and Wellness Center serves twenty-six counties in central Mississippi and the Delta, offering comprehensive health care and violence prevention programs. Tougaloo serves as an undergraduate training center for the Jackson Heart Study, an unprecedented exploration of heart disease in African Americans.

Designated a National Historic District in 1998, Tougaloo College has been called "the cradle of the Civil Rights Movement."[46] It has kept alive its civil rights legacy. It hosted conferences between 1990 and 1994 to celebrate the organization of the Mississippi Freedom Democratic Party and the Freedom Rides. At a 1991 anniversary celebration of the library sit-in, members of the Tougaloo Nine returned to campus to share their story. Myrlie Evers-Williams, widow of Medgar Evers, declared their action in 1961 "the beginning of a new day for race relations in Mississippi."[47] She donated the Evers homestead, where her husband was assassinated, to Tougaloo, which, with aid from the state legislature, has developed it into a civil rights museum. At a 1994 Mississippi Freedom Summer Homecoming, art collector and former Freedom Rider Albert Gordon donated a sizeable collection of African art to Tougaloo, in gratitude for the safety, solace, and kindness he found on the campus after being released from jail thirty years before.

Perhaps no one has given more of their life to Tougaloo than Lucille Moman Fraser. She began as a student at the Daniel Hand School in 1909, moved on to the Tougaloo secondary school, and then to the teachers' training program. She was offered a position at the Daniel Hand School upon graduation and spent most of her life teaching first graders there. She is the widow of Lionel B. Fraser, the first African American academic dean at the college. Speaking in Woodworth Chapel, she said, "I graduated twice in this chapel—from high school and then from my college teachers' course. I was baptized in this church . . . and I was married in this church. And my only son was baptized and christened in this church. So many important events of my life took place right here in this chapel."

Before arriving to take the position of college chaplain and pastor of Union United Church of Christ, Larry Johnson and his wife, Norma Johnson, agreed to give Tougaloo one year. They've stayed for thirty-three. "I fell in love with the place," Ms. Johnson explained. According to Pastor Johnson, "This congregation has been an unbroken span of continuous presence here on campus . . . living out the message of the Gospel."

He enjoyed rummaging through the archives when he first arrived. He found a photograph from the school's very early days, including a particularly striking one of a little girl holding a May basket full of flowers during the annual May Day celebration. He wrote a poem about her. He mentioned it to Lucille Moman Fraser, and she began to chuckle. "You wrote a poem about me," she explained. She was the little girl standing on the steps holding her May basket ninety-five years earlier. Ms. Fraser turned one hundred last year.

Tougaloo graduates Vince and Louise Larsen, who donated a substantial sum of money to restore Woodworth Chapel, returned to "the loving arms of the Tougaloo campus," as they put it, in February 2000 to receive an award from then-president Joe Lee. Mr. Larsen gave a tribute to Tougaloo's teachers and students in his acceptance speech: "Strong faith sustained those teachers years ago during most difficult times. Teachers dedicated their lives to educate the poor, but eager, young Mississippians who came to Tougaloo from the hills, the piney woods, and the Delta country. Theirs was an unselfish devotion to others. Faith and hard work fulfilled the dreams of those students as they struggled to get an education . . . It was the Christian faith that was the foundation upon which the Tougaloo tradition was established. A tradition of serving others. And, a tradition of giving back to Tougaloo, as one generation passes the torch to the next . . . "

Dr. Van S. Allen, a 1950 graduate, similarly praised the American Missionary Association and its shining effort at Tougaloo: "The endeavors of the A.M.A . . . display the very best expression of human concern and kindness, especially since the movement was initiated soon after a time when one could lose his hands to the chopping block for teaching enslaved blacks to read and write . . . The Tougaloo story is a story of compassionate individuals, and groups of individuals, imbued with Christian principles and steeped in the concepts of the dignity of the human being and the right to equal treatment and justice under the law. All those who believe in these concepts can find in the amazing Tougaloo story at least some hope and courage to face the many challenges yet to come."[48]

9

Hearts Aflame for Education

Lincoln School's Century of Success

Union troops were anxious to leave Marion, Alabama, at the close of the Civil War, but one among them was too severely wounded to go along. Left behind in a cabin outside the town, the soldier from a Minnesota regiment soon became a curiosity to young African American children in the area, who intently watched him reading books. They begged to learn, and the maimed Union man began to teach them. "This kindled the fire," wrote long-time Marion resident Idella Childs, that had been smoldering "in the hearts of the ex-slaves."[1]

A century later, a historian researching African Americans holding doctoral degrees discovered that a disproportionate number had family roots in Perry County, Alabama, where Marion is the county seat. The city where the Confederate flag and uniform were designed, Marion was an antebellum cotton capital dependent on long hours of slave labor under Alabama's unmerciful sun, followed by the exploitation of generations of sharecroppers. That residents of this rural, isolated spot in the heart of the agricultural Black Belt and Ku Klux Klan territory achieved such success over time can be traced to the presence of Lincoln School, the roots of which were in that unknown soldier's rudimentary classes.

The spark of desire to learn, first kindled in the children, ignited the imaginations of their parents, who believed so strongly that education was the only hope for their sons and daughters that they refused to be denied in their pursuit of it. On July 17, 1867, nine men recently released from slavery formed and incorporated a school that they named for the president who had proclaimed their emancipation. "Without question," wrote Ms. Childs, "the hunger for learning" on the part of freed citizens "and the dedication of their northern teachers built Lincoln Normal School and kept it alive and active for over a hundred years."[2]

In September 1868, the school trustees sought the aid of the American Missionary Association. The AMA bought an old plantation, whose mansion at one time had been the Ku Klux Klan's local headquarters. The mansion was transformed into a teachers' residence and named Forest Home. Classes were conducted in a three-room school.

A year later, the First Congregational Church of Marion was organized in the school. Rev. George Andrews and Rev. J. Silsby of the American Missionary Association were instrumental in the founding of the church. In May 1871 the Ku Klux Klan warned Rev. Andrews and other AMA agents in the area to leave within thirty days or be hanged. Soon after, an irate white citizen grabbed Andrews by the lapel of his coat as he tried to enter Marion's post office and spat a mouthful of tobacco spittle in his face. Armed African American friends began keeping guard at his home at night. Rev. Andrews was known for holding his Bible in one hand and a rifle in the other during family worship, and he often preached with a loaded revolver on the pulpit.

An AMA teacher who visited the church wrote the following account: "The most interesting prayer meeting that I have ever attended among the Freedmen was in Alabama, in the Ku-Klux region, where they at the 'Mission Home' looked well to their guns and their rifles before retiring. I reached there on Wednesday night, the evening of the weekly prayer-meeting in the school house. 'Twas a stormy night, but with water-proofs and umbrellas we ventured. Wholly unused to bullets, I must confess, there was a little trembling under one waterproof, as we wended our way along the little path through the woods, and across a plank bridge."

Rev. Andrews opened the service, and local residents of Marion carried the worship "with a liveliness that was truly refreshing," according to the teacher. She continued her account: "(T)hey faced the danger of their being obliged to disband, for outside violence was not entirely over. But as they told of their love for their church, I could hardly help thinking of those stories we all read in our childhood, of Christians in early days, when persecutions but increased their zeal . . . And then one after another they kneeled down, and, in the most simple words of faith, asked their Father to help His children in their day of Special trouble."[3]

Rev. Thomas Steward of the American Missionary Association served as both the church's pastor and the school's first principal, a common occurrence where schools and churches grew side by side. When some local whites threatened to kill him, the AMA sent stacks of rifles and Bibles from New York. The accompanying note read: "Mr. Steward, it is our profound hope you'll have greater use for the Bibles."[4]

In addition to providing a school, the AMA bought eighty acres of land that it sold in small lots to African American families. They built homes and established gardens and orchards, giving them a rare economic foothold in a part of the South that was determined to keep property away from blacks. Much of that land is owned today by descendants of the original purchasers.[5]

By 1874 the school had grown so large that the AMA asked the state of Alabama to assume responsibility for the normal department. William Burns Paterson from Tullibody, Scotland, was invited to assume the position of principal. Paterson had come to America as a deck hand on a freighter after he discovered that he didn't have enough money to follow his hero, Scottish missionary and explorer David Livingstone, to Africa.

While he was part of a river-dredging crew in Alabama, the black laborers with whom he worked asked Mr. Paterson to teach them to read. At lunch breaks he taught the men, sitting on wagons under trees. On weekends he held classes in abandoned slave cabins, using hymnals and newspapers sent from Scotland. Soon women and children began appearing for lessons as well.

In Greensboro, Alabama, in the fall of 1872, Paterson opened the Tullibody Academy for Negroes, based on the "each one teach one" schools of rural Scotland, which encouraged every student to teach someone else to read and write, with the ultimate goal of educating the entire society. His success as an educator, organizer, and liaison between black and white communities made Mr. Paterson a perfect choice to head Lincoln School and Normal University. Together with his young wife, Maggie Flack Paterson—

who taught music, kept the books, ran the library, and supervised a large garden—twenty-eight-year-old Paterson transformed Lincoln from a small schoolhouse into a flourishing institution on a five-acre campus.

But in late December 1886, disaster struck. A fire, believed to be the work of arsonists following a disturbance between white cadets at nearby Howard University and black students at Lincoln, destroyed a large portion of the campus. Local hostility toward this thriving center of racial integration, communal living, and black education intensified. Against the vigorous protests and resistance of Marion's African American community, Alabama's state legislature voted to move the school to Montgomery, which lawmakers mistakenly deemed a less hostile environment for a black university.

The Patersons built a plain wooden house on the Montgomery campus. That is where they were, according to their great-granddaughter Judith Hillman Paterson, "the night they awoke to find a cross-shaped scarecrow burning in the yard and a note left at the door giving the 'nigger teacher' twenty-four hours to get out of town." Under threat of having their home torched with them in it, "(t)here they lay all night on the bare wooden floor and smelled the straw burning and saw the cross silhouetted on the wall and waited to hear the sound of boots hitting the porch."[6]

The next night, determined to make good on their threat to destroy the house after twenty-four hours, a group of Klansmen crept through the brush around the house. They found Will Paterson sitting on the porch in his rocking chair, with a book in his lap. Behind him were five Confederate veterans, known to be some of the best shots in the county, with guns on their knees. The vigilantes retreated quickly. Every year, for as long as the Confederates lived, even after Maggie and Will died, the Paterson family sent roses to those veterans on their birthdays.[7]

Over Mr. Paterson's protestations, the State of Alabama withdrew its support for liberal arts education at the school and shifted its focus to industrial training, a change that would last until 1969, when the school became Alabama State University. Mr. Paterson died in 1915, eleven years after Maggie was buried in the black section of the segregated Oakwood Cemetery, and just five years short of his goal "to teach the Negro fifty years." Alabama State University still celebrates Will's birthday as its Founder's Day, and the music department that Maggie started in 1878 still sings "The Blue Bells of Scotland" in their honor.[8]

Until a decade ago, according to Dr. Carl H. Marbury, a retired Alabama State professor, the university's official seal and the sign in front of its campus proclaimed its founding year as 1873. It now reads 1867, acknowledging the contribution of Lincoln School and the American Missionary Association to the university's development. In February 2002, the university's National Center for the Study of Civil Rights and African-American Culture sponsored its third symposium celebrating the legacy of the *Amistad* event and the AMA, with Dr. Patrick Pieh, a descendant of mutiny leader Sengbe Pieh, among the speakers.

Also speaking that day was Johnnie Carr, a founder of the civil rights-era Montgomery Improvement Association, who met Rosa Parks, credited with sparking the Montgomery bus boycott, in the fifth grade in 1925. They were students at the AMA-sponsored Montgomery Industrial School, popularly referred to as Miss White's School. In tribute to Miss White and all the other Northern teachers who came South, Ms. Carr asked, "Can you imagine a white person leaving the North, which was supposed to be safe, to go to the South, which was supposed to be bad, to go against the principles of most people there to set up a school to educate blacks?" Pondering what would cause a person to do such a thing, she concluded, "It can only be God."[9]

Rev. George Andrews, church planter extraordinaire, also established a First Congregational Church in Montgomery in 1872, across from Miss White's School. The new church was served for a time by Rev. Barnabas Root, the son of an African chief who had impressed the teachers at the Mendi Mission in West Africa and was sent to the United States to study theology. More than a century later, at 4:30 in the morning on April 21, 1995, a tree next to the church was struck by lightning, sparking a fire that completely destroyed the 123-year-old sanctuary. Miraculously, according to church member Beatrice Forniss, the large cross behind the pulpit was spared and the church bell was rescued from the flames. Through the dedication of its congregants and Pastor Michael Garrett, the church was rebuilt: "destruction by fire, reconstruction by faith," according to John H. Jones, a longtime member. To Faustina Jones, losing the church was like losing a family home.

As a young woman in the 1950s, Ms. Jones worked as a librarian at Alabama State University. She remembered the young, new pastor at Dexter Avenue Baptist Church showing up at the back door occasionally with batches of papers, which Ms. Jones' library colleague received and carried in the trunk of her car. "We didn't talk about it too much," said Ms. Jones. "I knew something was happening."

"Something" was indeed happening. Those papers contained information on strategies and leadership for the civil rights movement, which was about to spread from Montgomery's buses, streets, and lunch counters to every corner of the South. When young Martin Luther King Jr. showed up largely unnoticed at the library, seeming to appear out of nowhere, Ms. Jones had no idea of the role he would come to play in the movement. But, as the stories of AMA church members, the letters and journals of the teachers, and the success of the students testify, Dr. King and the other leaders didn't simply "appear out of nowhere"; the civil rights movement was built on foundations of freedom and equality laid a century before they arrived on the scene.

When the Lincoln normal department moved to Montgomery, the American Missionary Association bought the Paterson home and the five-acre campus in Marion. The home's large rooms were refurbished, and the old barn was fitted with blackboards to create classrooms for the primary and secondary grades. Lincoln School continued to grow larger—and poorer.

In 1896 Mary Elizabeth Phillips of Pittsburgh, Pennsylvania, who had been a teacher since the age of sixteen, became the school's sixth principal. AMA Field Secretary Augustus Field Beard had first sent this remarkably energetic, talented, and principled young woman to Talladega. He subsequently asked her if she would be willing to give up that promising position and "come to the rescue of a dying secondary school." Lincoln School was deteriorating, and "only a person who was willing to make every sacrifice could save it."[10] Ms. Phillips accepted the challenge.

She arrived in Marion in October 1896 to find a school of 150 children, with classes being conducted in a sagging plantation house and barn in the middle of a cornfield, and teachers living a quarter of a mile away in Forest Home. The American Missionary Association was planning to withdraw its support from what it deemed a hopeless cause. Ms. Phillips' first act as principal was to call a mass meeting of the Marion community in the Congregational Church.

The response was heartwarming. She let the attendees know that the school's future was in jeopardy. Despite their dire poverty, parents pledged seven hundred dollars and students two hundred dollars. Teachers added another five hundred dollars and, when promised that they would not starve, agreed to work without pay to keep the school open. One parent pledged a supply of eggs for the teachers, another milk, still others vegetables, meat, and flour.

Ms. Phillips telegraphed news of the $1,400 pledge to the AMA office in New York. While she and her teachers waited at Forest Home for a response, they wrote letters to Northern friends, piled them on a chair, knelt around the chair, and prayed that their appeal would bring results. Students gathered in the courtyard. At last the telegram arrived, saying that the school would remain open. The boys rushed to the school, raised the flag, and rang out the news on the school's bell that Lincoln School had been saved.

The students and their parents begged for dormitories. With sheer determination and a great deal of whitewash, they turned the Paterson home into a girls' dormitory, sleeping as many as eighteen to a room, sometimes three or four to a bed. The girls had to bring their own beds as well as their own cornmeal and bacon, which the cook tagged with names so that those who brought coveted lean meat would get their due. The construction of several other buildings followed, funded by pledges, donations Ms. Phillips solicited, and money she received from her father's estate after his death.

Livingston Hall was the first brick building on the campus. During its construction in 1901, the laborers struck for higher wages, but no additional funds were available. Ms. Phillips disappeared for a few days. When she returned, she called the students together and said, "Our new building is less than half finished, but we have no workers. In the last few days I have learned to lay brick. If you will help, we can learn our lessons while mixing cement and handling the trowel. I will be your teacher, if you will construct your own building."[11] A "line of demarcation" was clearly visible along the building's walls where experience gave way to inexperience, but the hall stood. Some of the students who learned masonry from Ms. Phillips were later among Alabama's most highly skilled and sought-after workers, assisting in the construction of some of the state's most renowned buildings.

At the age of seventy, Ms. Phillips became Mrs. Mary Phillips Thompson. She died two years later, having spent fifty-three years in the field of education, thirty-nine of them with the American Missionary Association in Alabama. She was greatly mourned by the many people, both black and white, who had come to view her as a saint. By the time of her death in 1927, Lincoln School had 596 students, twenty-six teachers, a forty-acre farm, six new buildings, and a junior college curriculum. Her one unrealized hope for the campus was an auditorium.

On the Sunday after her death, several alumni gathered and planned a memorial in her honor. AMA Secretary Fred Brownlee suggested a building. A fund was started, and money poured in—then trickled during the years of the Great Depression. On May 30, 1939, Phillips Memorial Auditorium was dedicated before a proud throng of students, alumni, teachers, and friends. Idella Childs' young daughter, Jean Childs, unveiled a bronze plaque and portrait of the beloved Ms. Phillips Thompson.

Richard Moore, a 1934 graduate of Lincoln, said of Ms. Phillips, "I remember, she was a tough customer . . . That's the way we used to say it when we were students . . . We feared her—not as somebody who was going to kill us, or hurt us—but we thought in terms of her as a top leader, a top principal, who was a strict disciplinarian, and who really knew how to operate a school."[12]

Dr. Moore remembered that, before the Depression, students had to be turned away for lack of space. But as economic hardship worsened, fewer and fewer boarding students appeared each year. Many sharecropping families were unable to afford tuition, and parents pleaded for work to be given to their children in exchange for schooling. One teacher reflected, "They are eager to work or do anything for the school and will make any sacrifice for an education."[13] Tuition was dropped from twenty-five dollars per year to nine dollars, and then again to just fifty cents per year. But still many parents had to pull their children out of school, needing their help in the cotton fields. In 1932 the school's boarding department closed.

Lincoln School was unique in Alabama with its nine-month term. In the late 1930s in the state's Black Belt, the average African American student attended school only five months out of the year. Idella Childs, who graduated from Lincoln in 1921, taught in a small, rural school down the road. She said of that experience: "Many a day I had just two or three students, for the simple reason that they were too small to work in the fields. Their parents were living on those plantations down there, and if the Boss Man said, 'We're going to pick cotton,' they'd pick cotton. And they didn't come to school until that cotton was picked. Unless it rained—that would make a difference. If the weather was too cold to plow in the spring, then school would stay open until it was warm enough for them to go into the fields."[14]

Congregational churches in the North responded to the poverty of the students and their families with generous donations of clothing and furniture. Every Saturday morning, families came to Lincoln School from all over Perry County, walking or in wagons, those without money carrying produce to exchange for clothes. Tracts distributed by the AMA and Congregational women's organizations such as the Massachusetts Women's Home Missionary Union—describing Southern schoolchildren eating dry cornbread without molasses, giving up their own Christmas tree to local orphans, and rejoicing at gifts of apples and oranges—aimed to elicit generosity from Northern schoolchildren.

Nancy Kynard, a member of Marion's First Congregational Church and a 1935 Lincoln graduate, said of the Depression days:

"We couldn't have made it if it hadn't been for some of the teachers, because I was one of the poor people, you know . . . People from the North would send down barrels of clothes and shoes and household goods. And if you didn't have a coat that was presentable, some of the teachers would take you over to the storeroom, as they called it, and get you something. You would get a coat for twenty-five cents, a good coat, and work it out after school—stay and clean, dust, put out the trash, things like that."

The church held graduations from Sunday school at the junior, intermediate, and senior levels. When she was a young girl, Ms. Kynard's family sacrificed so that she could have a new outfit for her graduation at church: "In the afternoon you would have a little ceremony, put on your little white dresses, little new shoes if you could get some at that particular time. When I graduated, my mama made me a pretty little white voile dress, and my stepfather bought me some shoes, (but) they were too little. So that Sunday morning my brother brought them back to Wilbur's over here on Lombard Street. He brought them to the store to exchange them so I could have some nice shoes to be up on the stage that Sunday afternoon."

"Lincoln and the church were our livelihood," said Jesse Billingsley, a 1941 graduate. In addition to being a place of worship, the church was a social center for the community. Young women and men were forbidden from mingling at Lincoln. "But," said Mr. Billingsley, "you could bring your girlfriend and sit in church and talk." He added with a laugh, "And after the service you could walk her home, with her parents right behind you."

Mr. Billingsley remembered visiting at Alabama State University once, and talking about the prom at Lincoln to a student there. "You're just telling a lie. You haven't danced with any white women in Alabama," the State student said in response. "But that was Lincoln," said Mr. Billingsley. "It was integrated, and integration wasn't anything new to us. It was just a different world altogether." Alberta Goree, who came from a far corner of the county to attend Lincoln, added, "We just thought we were in heaven coming up here."

The church and the school have had a close relationship since the founding of both. According to First Congregational's pastor, Eulas Kirtdoll, the church "has always stood for something in this community." Like Lincoln School, Marion's First Congregational Church has been "an institution connecting spirituality with education," according to Pastor Kirtdoll.

Under a succession of principals between 1935 and 1943, Lincoln became even more involved in the needs of the Marion community. A clinic was started, a farmers' cooperative was organized, and community groups meeting in Phillips Auditorium tackled issues ranging from transportation to a hot lunch program. Alumni established and benefited from a cooperatively owned grist mill and store, as well as a public library.

After World War II, Lincoln began a painful odyssey from being a unique and outstanding private school to becoming a public institution, as the AMA turned over responsibility for the school to the state of Alabama. The state's segregation laws made it illegal for blacks and whites to teach together in public schools, and in 1943 all the white faculty members were forced to leave. Though by then 80 percent of Perry County's population was African American, Lincoln was the county's only public high school.

Andrew Young arrived at the First Congregational Church in Marion in the summer of 1952, after his first year at Hartford Seminary. He had hoped to be in New York preparing for the Summer Olympic Trials in the 200- and 400-meter dashes, but his mother wanted him back in the South. She contacted Rev. J. Taylor Stanley, the superintendent for the Convention of the South of the Congregational Church, who had grown up in the Marion Congregational Church and attended Lincoln School, asking him to find her twenty-year-old son a summer job.

For five dollars a month, Young was hired to set up a summer Bible school and recreation program in Marion, a job and location he greeted initially with less than enthusiasm. He discovered after he arrived that he was also expected to preach every Sunday, a task that he came to enjoy and that he believed confirmed his call to ministry. After a few weeks of being hosted by church families, Young moved into an unused dormitory on the Lincoln School campus. He fell in love with Jean Childs, daughter of Idella Childs and great-great-granddaughter of James Childs, one of the original founders of Lincoln School and Marion's First Congregational Church. They were married in the church in 1954.

Jean Childs Young, a 1950 graduate of Lincoln, spoke fondly of her alma mater, which exposed its students to an expansive world beyond Marion: "We were steeped in black culture. We knew about great African kingdoms that existed prior to slavery. So we cultivated an appreciation for ourselves in the midst of segregation. I remember thinking, isn't it interesting that people would think of us as being inferior. Because we heard it from the church, we heard it from our school, and we heard it from our family that we were not inferior to anyone. We learned so much about the broader world that we knew that there was a life beyond Marion, Alabama."[15]

For Andrew Young, Marion itself was a new world. His summer there exposed him to political, social, and economic conditions that were quite different from what he encountered growing up in New Orleans and attending school in Washington, D.C., and Hartford, Connecticut. Segregation was harsher. Being in Marion, according to Young, "was the kind of experience in the rural South that let you know that there had to be something to bring about change. At that time I didn't know for sure what." The "what," of course, turned out to be the civil rights movement, which, said Young, "eventually brought me back to Selma, which is where Jean and I had our first date." [16]

On February 18, 1965, during a civil rights march in Marion, police and state troopers began beating marchers. Twenty-six-year-old Jimmie Lee Jackson, a Vietnam veteran and 1959 graduate of Lincoln School, fled with his mother and grandfather, who had been struck in the head, to a nearby café. Troopers followed them, and one hit Jackson's mother. Jackson, trying to protect her, made his way into the center of the crowd and was shot in the stomach. He died later of the wound in a Selma hospital.

Four hundred people squeezed into a Marion church for Jackson's funeral, with another six hundred standing outside in the rain. Dr. Martin Luther King offered the eulogy. After the service, the crowd walked behind the hearse down a muddy road to the cemetery. During that procession, civil rights leader James Bevel suggested that they should walk Jackson's body all the way to Montgomery and lay his casket on the Capitol steps, giving the citizens and government leaders of Alabama something they couldn't turn their heads away from.

They buried Jimmie Lee Jackson's body as planned, but the idea of a march to Montgomery caught fire. March organizers decided that starting in Marion was too risky, so a Selma to Montgomery March was announced. The day of that march—March 7, 1965— came to be known as "Bloody Sunday," as police and troopers savagely beat marchers crossing Selma's Edmund Pettus Bridge and attacked them with tear gas. SNCC leader and future Congressman John Lewis suffered a concussion that day from a blow to the head.

Andrew Young wasn't the only renowned civil rights leader to be married in Perry County, Alabama. Martin Luther King and Coretta Scott were married there in 1953. Coretta Scott King's father bragged that as a child his daughter could pick up to three hundred pounds of cotton a day on the family's farm. The Scott family suffered repeatedly at the hands of angry Perry County whites, who refused them loans, burned down their sawmill and store, and sabotaged their trucks.

Teachers at Lincoln School helped young Coretta, valedictorian of the class of 1945, to develop her talent as a vocalist and encouraged her in the direction of the New England Conservatory of Music. Years later, Coretta Scott King spoke of the impact her years at Lincoln had on her life: "I learned at Lincoln School not only the basics in terms of subject matter, but the teachers taught me values. My parents had instilled in me certain values that I have been able to use throughout my life. Lincoln School reinforced those values of love and concern for others, of sharing and giving and of honesty, and treating people the way you'd like to be treated."[17]

The values of equality, courage, and faith that Lincoln instilled in its students clearly had something to do with the activism in Perry County during the civil rights era. Idella Childs ran "a sort of bed-and-breakfast for the movement in Marion," according to her son-in-law, Andrew Young.[18] Mass meetings took place on the Lincoln School campus.

"The civil rights movement started in Marion, Alabama," said Jesse Billingsley. Mr. Billingsley is proud of being one of the first African Americans in Alabama to have registered to vote post-Reconstruction, in the late 1950s. He started sending his friends to the courthouse, "and that's when some of the trouble started," he said. A janitor at the courthouse reported to Mr. Billingsley that he discovered all the voter registration applications from African Americans in a garbage can. When word spread through the black community, massive protests were launched. Church member Nancy Kynard added that Jimmie Lee Jackson was one of the first civil rights marchers in the South to be killed, and his murder sparked one of the movement's most notorious campaigns.

Rev. Oliver Wendell Holmes, whom local historians credit with starting the Alabama civil rights campaign, was run out of Marion. Sharecroppers in the South generally stayed in perpetual debt to landowners, who exploited their ignorance of both their rights and of math. Rev. Holmes and Lincoln School were systematically teaching local people about fair prices and rental agreements, which fueled the anger of some local whites.

Alberta Goree reflected on the days of the Marion civil rights campaign: "(We were) afraid of bombs and guns and things, all of us running for cover . . . It was really much worse than what we're telling. It was awful. A lot of people lost their jobs. A lot of folks were just sharecroppers on the plantations . . . Their owners would tell them that if they were going to vote, they had to leave the farm. At that time we lost a lot of folks going north to live."

In 1970, under a Perry County desegregation plan, Lincoln School was closed, its students sent off to an integrated high school. Lincoln School was "cast away in the name of progress and racial integration," according to civil rights activist, educator, politician, and NAACP Chairman Julian Bond.[19] The city of Marion put the buildings up for auction. Fearing that Lincoln's legacy would be lost forever, Idella Childs found nine people to contribute one hundred dollars each to save Phillips Memorial Auditorium. Lincoln alumni around the country formed local chapters and raised money to renovate the building through cabaret parties, fish fries, and raffles.

Demolition crews arrived on the campus, reducing Lincoln's other buildings to heaps of rubble. According to Robert Turner, a 1964 graduate, "The community lost a leader and a focal point. Lincoln was something that black people felt like they owned. It was the shelter we felt we could go to and discuss our problems. It was a thing that we governed and ran, and we developed. With that gone, we lost a sense of togetherness; we lost a sense of community of purpose."[20]

Georgia Walker, who graduated in 1943, said sadly, "When they brought the saws there and cut those trees, it just took something out of me. It was just like piercing an area of my heart . . . Then the buildings were dismantled and torn down. It was just a sad thing, because Lincoln always to me was like holy ground."[21]

According to Julian Bond, "A dream that had taken over a century to build was destroyed in a few days. An era had indeed ended."[22] It was Dr. Bond's father, Horace Mann Bond, who had first discovered and publicized Lincoln School's rich legacy. In 1960 the U.S. Office of Education had commissioned him to examine the factors that contribute to academic success in low-income communities. He interviewed five hundred African Americans with doctorates across the nation about their backgrounds. "And something amazing evolved," observed Julian Bond. "A large number of those persons interviewed traced their ancestry to Marion, Alabama . . . From his research, my father easily concluded that Lincoln School was the foremost black secondary school that this country has ever known."[23]

In July 1988 many of these graduates, and others from around the country, gathered for a Lincoln School reunion in Chicago. They talked about the qualities they loved about the school: the care and respect of the teachers, the sense of racial pride instilled in them, the emphasis on education rather than training. They called Lincoln "a godsend" and "a school ahead of its time." According to Julian Bond, "Its teachers constantly encouraged their students to dare to achieve. They forced them to look beyond the limited horizons and opportunities provided by Perry County, and to dream the impossible dream through a strict curriculum that contained courses ranging from the arts to agriculture."[24]

Juanita Hatch, who graduated in 1938, said, "It has been said more times than you can even remember how you knew a Lincoln student at that time . . . We were motivated to not be fearful or afraid of anybody . . . You stood up for whatever you thought was good—and (the teachers) stood beside you. They were right there all the time."[25]

Evelyn Sanders, class of 1925, said that attending Lincoln "helped me to know—pardon me for saying it—that all white people weren't like these that I had lived with all my life down here. (Our teachers) were kind; they were considerate; you heard no racial slurs."[26]

Frank Perry, a 1949 graduate and president of the Lincoln Alumni Association at the time of the reunion, said, "We who grew up in the hills of Alabama knew well that education was about the only thing that we could get there that would make a difference in our lives." Robert C. Hatch of Atlanta, a 1942 graduate, said that without Lincoln School, there would have been no motivation or stimulation to achieve. Speaking of his days at the school, Dr. Hatch said, "I shudder to think what I would have been had I not had that experience. It's basic to any progress I have made subsequently."[27]

Mollie Reed, who attended Lincoln in the 1950s, said of her time there, "Everybody did something on the campus to help it to thrive and survive . . . You succeeded through prayer . . . but everybody worked. The teachers inspired you so that you never forgot it." With a rare and compelling loyalty, Lincoln alumni get together every two years, with every third meeting convened in Marion at Phillips Auditorium. According to Ms. Reed, the reunions are about trying "to pass on that legacy about what you can do for yourself, how you can do many things. It may be a struggle, but you can do it." That message is also at the heart of the museum that alumni and church members have established on the former campus, to preserve the school's courageous history and rich memories.

"It seemed to be a small effort, the founding of Lincoln," observed Julian Bond. "But actually it was the beginning of something quite remarkable—an educational institution built on the solid rock of optimism, that would guide black families to the throne of knowledge for one hundred and four years." The school, said Dr. Bond, was "an oasis where ambitions were rewarded and hopes fulfilled . . . Lincoln School's impact is one that will continue to provide incentive for many black Americans for many generations to come."[28]

10

Open Doors in Athens, Alabama

Trinity School and Church Keep a Heritage Alive

Acentury and a half after its founding, the sounds of children laughing and learning are still vibrant at the former American Missionary Association-sponsored Trinity School—now Trinity Cultural Center—in Athens, Alabama. A "Summer Time Out" program, focused on arts and crafts, games, and lessons in fairness and cooperation, reaches children ages five to twelve. Preschoolers benefit from sessions designed to prepare them for kindergarten, and high-school-age youth plan and participate in talent shows and events celebrating African American history. Thursday mornings are devoted to residents on the other end of the age spectrum. Participants in the "Ladies Coffee Break" share devotions and fellowship, and collect gifts for a local nursing home. These programs are just the initial seeds of the big dreams that Trinity graduates have for their former school.

Supported by the American Missionary Association for more than seventy years, Trinity School was organized in 1865 by Mary Frances Wells, a Mount Holyoke College graduate, Michigan teacher, and Civil War army nurse who served as the school's principal for twenty-seven years. Ms. Wells and two other teachers, who started their school in an old brick church that had been taken over as a barracks during the war, soon had one hundred pupils per teacher. The school was moved to an old hotel, a frame building near the railroad depot.

Mary Frances Wells, whose wealthy family disowned her for her work among those newly emancipated, was known to be extraordinarily brave. One night as she sat in her room above the school correcting students' papers, members of the Ku Klux Klan surrounded the building. Taking aim at the glow of her lamp through a tattered quilt that she hung every night in her doorway, the Klansmen shot a volley of bullets that whizzed past her head, while Ms. Wells calmly continued her work. They returned later and burned the building to the ground, the beloved principal barely escaping the inferno.

In the fall of 1871, Ms. Wells served in the role of matron for the first tour of Fisk University's Jubilee Singers. Accompanying her was her eight-year-old ward, Georgie Wells, who had been born to a mother who never received word of the Emancipation Proclamation and believed herself still a slave at her death two years later. Georgie was adopted by two fugitives, who took him to Union lines, where he earned food by performing improvised entertainments, consisting of somersaults, songs, and an African step from which the dance known as the Charleston later derived.

When Union troops left Nashville, a planter took Georgie in, beating him regularly and forcing him to keep watch over the garden by tying him to a gate. Georgie managed to gnaw through the rope and escape to Athens, where a Freedmen's Bureau agent found him lying on a pile of rags near the railroad tracks. The desperate boy pleaded to be taken to the legendary Ms. Wells, who opened her home and heart to him. "Miss Wells," Georgie would ask as they ate their meals together, "be this heaven?"[1]

The building that replaced the burned Trinity School was also destroyed by a suspicious fire. But flames, threats, and poverty could not deter the African American residents of Athens and their teachers from their quest for a school. According to an AMA report, education was "freedom, life, heaven to them."[2]

After the second fire, a collection was taken in the community, and labor was volunteered for the task of constructing a new school. According to a teacher at the time, who left behind many notes but not her name, when funds for the new building were secured, "joy reigned supreme, and every one was anxious to help along the work." She compared the new school's construction to the biblical story of the ancient Israelites' building of the tabernacle in the wilderness: "Willing-hearted men and women, yea, and little children, made brick, hewed timber, drove nails, carried mortar and water for the workers."

Students poured in from across Limestone County. "Some of them will sleep as did two boys from the country for months, rolled up in quilts on the floor with their feet in a box of sawdust to keep them warm," reported the teacher. "Some will wash and iron from early morning until school time, and from the time school closes until late at night, for the sake of a few hours of instruction each day. Some will walk three and four miles a day."[3]

A teacher from Boston, whose name also is lost to history, offered her first impressions of Trinity School and its environs in an American Missionary Association report: "After dinner I took my first walk in a Southern town and saw sights strange to me—cows and chickens in the front dooryards, and donkeys walking on the sidewalks. I saw cotton growing for the first time." On her second day, she was "awakened about six o'clock by the ringing of the Trinity School bell, rung long and loud at that hour to arouse people for miles around, in order that the children might be ready for school." At 8:30 that morning, she went to meet her pupils and their families, gathered in Trinity chapel for the opening of a new school year.

"All ages were there," observed the teacher, "from the minister's baby seven weeks old to the old auntie of eighty years, with bright, smiling faces and outstretched hands to welcome the new teachers." The group sang hymns and offered prayers, and graduates who had returned for the occasion spoke of their devotion to Trinity and their gratitude to be witnessing another opening. "I found it difficult to keep back my tears," wrote the teacher, "and could not until I saw a small boy in the front row giggling at me and nudging his companion."

Vandals had broken out Trinity's windows over the summer recess. When contributions were solicited to replace them, audience members began singing the spiritual "Going to Hold Out till the End" to accompany the offerings. "One after another came to the platform," reported the teacher, "making his or her little offering, some giving a quarter—and a quarter is a very great deal of money for one of these people—and the tiny ones brought their pennies which they had saved for gum and candy." The service ended with the joyful singing of the "Doxology." "I feel that there is great promise in these people," observed the teacher, "and that here especially is a splendid field to work."[4]

Louise Allyn, who became principal of Trinity in 1909 and remained for thirty-one years, oversaw the construction of the present building, erected within the ramparts of old Fort Henderson, site of the Civil War's Battle of Athens. Former military trenches soon bloomed with honeysuckle vines and trees, and threats from the local community turned into praises of Trinity. An AMA report published soon after the new school's completion stated that "the embankments . . . no longer serve to keep enemies out, for no school in the South has more of the good will of the people of the city than Trinity." The mayor of Athens praised the school as one of the city's proud possessions.[5]

Mary Frances Wells, the first principal, was also one of nine founding members of Trinity Congregational Church, which she served as its first elected clerk and treasurer. The founding documents portray a church whose members "believe(d) that the scriptures of the Old Testament are given by inspiration of God and are the only infallible rule of faith and practice"; whose government and discipline were rooted in "the principles and practices of apostles as made known in the New Testament"; and who affirmed "the endless punishment of the wicked and the endless happiness of the righteous."[6] Turning around in church on Sunday mornings after being seated was forbidden, intoxicating liquors were prohibited "as articles of drink or traffic," and "delinquent and absent members" without legitimate excuses were excommunicated.[7] Church records reveal that one member was excommunicated for "speaking harsh words to the minister," and another for refusing to stop playing his fiddle at church socials when he was requested to do so.[8]

Current members of the church—now Trinity Congregational United Church of Christ—recall that most of their teachers at Trinity were active in the church, one serving as the organist, several singing in the choir and teaching Sunday school. According to Josephine Higgins Woodson, devotions consisting of songs, scriptures, and prayers were held every morning in the classrooms, and weekly devotions were convened in the auditorium. In addition, students attended chapel services three times a week, contributed their pennies regularly to a missionary bank, and participated each year in a week of "spiritual awakening," or revival.

Celestina Higgins Bridgeforth, Ms. Woodson's sister and a 1938 graduate, said that Trinity's teachers "instilled into us every aspect of life that they could." In addition to the usual school subjects and activities, students participated in bird watching and bonfires, hikes and afternoon teas, private music lessons, poetry readings, Maypole dances, and their own version of Japanese theater. Field trips to interesting local sites were common. Kathryn Higgins Robinson said of the female members of her family, "We never went anywhere without a big bow in our hair. If there was a big bow, it was a Higgins sister."

One teacher heard about a rare, white whale that had beached itself on Alabama's Gulf shore. Knowing that the children were unlikely ever to see a whale otherwise, she arranged to have it come through Athens in a tank on a flatbed railroad car. One former student spoke of the wonder of seeing the great whale, but also of a poignant interaction beforehand. Each child had to pay a dime to see it, and her teacher knew she didn't have a dime, so the teacher discretely slipped one into her hand as the students were lining up to file past the whale.

School buses weren't available for African American students until the middle of the twentieth century. Very few cars existed among Limestone County's black community. Trinity students who did not live within walking distance of the school, or have relatives near the school who could board them, were carried to school in the beds of pickup trucks by residents who charged them a few pennies a ride.

The Higgins sisters were fortunate enough to grow up just a block from Trinity. Like the early AMA teacher, Celestina Higgins Bridgeforth remembered the school's bell, which was in a tower on the porch. "The first bell we heard rang at 7:15, and that was letting you know what time it was. The second—we called it the 'big bell'—rang at 8:15; you should be on the way to school (when it rang). The next bell we called the 'little bell.' That was the hand bell that the third-grade teacher rang. She stood on the porch and rang that bell, and you needed to be entering the building at that time."

Nelson Howell, who rang the "big bell" when he was a student, got paid fifteen cents an hour toward his $2.50-per-month tuition for that daily chore and for sweeping the halls and mopping the floors. The school taught him carpentry, plumbing, electrical work, and masonry, and he and the other students worked to close in the Civil War-era ditch around Trinity. Ms. Woodson, who also worked on the ditch, remembered several parents being upset that their daughters in dresses were right next to the boys in their neckties doing manual labor.

Ms. Bridgeforth recalled that all female students learned sewing and made their own graduation outfits. Almost seven decades later, she still remembered the details: "We had a Sunday baccalaureate service, and then the graduation service on Wednesday night. We made both dresses in the home ec(onomics) department. My Sunday dress was green eyelet—very simple, with a pink ribbon sash. My graduation dress was white organdy, in the famous style with the ruffle around the bottom." She wore a corsage of sweet peas—the class flower—pinned to her dress.

Trinity was one of the first schools for African Americans to be accredited by the Southern Association of Colleges and Secondary Schools, and it was well-known for the quality of education it provided. "We knew the freshman course by the time we got to college," said Ms. Bridgeforth. "(Colleges) were always glad to welcome students from Trinity." Patti Malone, one of the earliest graduates and a member of Trinity Congregational Church, went on to Fisk and gained fame as one of the Jubilee Singers who entertained England's Queen Victoria.

In 1956 the American Missionary Association deeded the Trinity School property to the Limestone County Board of Education for the sum of one dollar. It functioned as a public school for fourteen years. During the era of racial integration, many of Athens's African American students were bussed to the far corners of the county. Mr. Howell, who drove a school bus for thirty years, said of those days, "You weren't allowed to pass a school if the kids were eligible to go to that school." He had to take back roads, often driving six or seven miles out of the way. His typical daily route covered sixty-one miles one way.

"They made it as difficult as possible, all of this bus riding," said church member and Trinity alumnus Harvey Craig. He remembered the first countywide teachers' institute after integration. Addressing the first gathering ever of black and white teachers in Limestone County, the chairman of the board of education, referring to integration, said in his opening statement, "It is difficult to swallow this bitter pill of injustice."

Closed in 1970, Trinity School stood empty and unused for more than a decade. But from the day of its closure, hope burned in the heart of Josephine Higgins Woodson that the buildings and grounds would be used again one day for a good purpose. In 1980, county authorities proposed using the former school as a youth prison. "I couldn't stand the thought of my alma mater being used that way," said Ms. Woodson. She talked with several officials, asking the question, "Why not develop Trinity into a center to steer young people in the right directions, to prevent them from becoming offenders?"[9]

The prison plan was dropped, but the Trinity property was slated for auction and future use as an industrial facility. Trinity graduates convened a massive reunion in Athens in August 1981 and there resolved to save their school. The Athens-Limestone Community Association (ALCA) evolved from that gathering. The association, comprised of Trinity alumni and friends, raised five thousand dollars for a down payment on the property—which included a library and auditorium, classrooms, and a gymnasium on seven acres of land—and purchased it in June 1982.

The ALCA organizers stated in their founding document: "We feel that the acquisition of this property is the greatest thing that has happened to this community. It will bring pride, self-esteem, and the responsibility that comes with ownership of such a building." They desired a name that reflected the rich legacy of Trinity School and the educational, moral, and cultural gifts it imparted on generations of the community's children. They chose Trinity Cultural Center.

In 1995 Trinity Congregational United Church of Christ took possession of, and responsibility for, the property. Regarding the small church's plan to run the center and expand its programs, many observers said it couldn't be done, according to Ms. Woodson. But the church members took inspiration from the biblical story of Jesus feeding a crowd of thousands with five loaves of bread and two fish, and they trusted God for a similar miracle. A variety of fund-raising events—including fashion pageants, yard sales, gospel concerts, and bake sales—have raised enough money to keep the monthly mortgage payments flowing. Volunteer labor has taken care of ongoing cleaning and renovation.

In addition to running a variety of programs and hosting an annual Family Awareness celebration, the Trinity Cultural Center houses a museum that contains photographs and archives from the early years of Trinity School. Future dreams for the center include a senior citizen awareness program, library services, occupational workshops, and fine arts programs.

Along with the story of the miracle of loaves and fish, members of Trinity Congregational Church draw inspiration from the biblical exhortation recorded in 2 Timothy 1:6-7: "I remind you to rekindle the gift of God that is within you . . . for God did not give us a spirit of fear, but rather a spirit of power and of love." According to Rev. Gary Myers, the church's pastor, "The gift that has been rekindled here is flickering at times, and sometimes you wonder if it's going to stay lit . . . But I made a promise to myself and God that we would not be afraid of failure . . . We can take risks in order to go places, because you can't go anywhere just sitting back looking at what you did fifteen—or forty—years ago. You've got to move forward, and that's what we have done here at Trinity."

The church members have claimed the best of the tradition that nurtured them as children and used it for transformative ministry as older adults. Ms. Bridgeforth, who supervised the preschool session at Trinity Cultural Center for thirteen years, said, "What I do, I do because I love the church." Health concerns have prevented her from continuing the work, but, she said, "I nudge everybody else." Devotion is strong among other members as well. "This is my church," said Kathryn Higgins Robinson, "where I learned the truth by which I have been guided to live a brave, happy, and useful life."

This undying devotion to the church is matched by willing-to-die-for loyalty to Trinity School, as reflected in the official school song:

Ten thousand strong, we sing a song, Trinity to thee,
O worthy art thou of fame.
In lands afar, shineth thy star, setting bondsmen free.
Beloved is thy glorious name, Beloved is thy glorious
    name . . .
Ye colors old, purple and gold, kissed by gentle wind,
In victory float on high.
Or should thy form, wrestle with storm, then thy foe will
    find:
We'll conquer for thee or die, We'll conquer for thee or die.[10]

That Trinity Congregational Church still contains the original communion set and pews that were crafted over a century ago at the congregation's birth is just one sign of the importance of history here. Founder's Day was instituted in early fall many years ago to celebrate the church's heritage—and to help the congregation raise money to purchase coal, then electricity, to keep the building warm during the upcoming winter months. In 1980, for the annual commemoration, Rev. Jerry Fields, then pastor of the church, wrote in a letter: "As we reflect upon how God has used others to bless the stranger, feed the hungry, bind up the bruised, clothe the naked, care for the sick, and preach the acceptable year of the Lord, let us follow, that we may, in the years to come, be a blessing to others who shall enter these doors."[11]

In the years since, the doors of the church have remained open, and the doors of the school have reopened, inviting strangers in and allowing Trinity's light to flow out and anoint the community. Speaking at a recent Founder's Day celebration, on the church's 131st anniversary, Rev. Myers told the gathered crowd: "We must never forget our past, and we must teach the next generation that God has been with us through it all . . . Our doors are not just open on this glorious occasion, but always." By the grace of God, and the faithfulness of God's children in Athens, Alabama, Trinity's doors will remain open for a long time to come.

11
"Bright Flower of Hope and Accomplishment"
The Shining Inspiration of Dorchester Academy

From as far away as fifty miles they came, arriving on foot and horseback, in battered cars and wagons drawn by horses, oxen, and cows. For five decades, families had been making this annual trek to Dorchester Academy in Midway, Georgia, using any means of transportation available to them. Moving with pride and anticipation, guests threaded their way through dozens of colorful booths conjured for Commencement Day. Children laughed and ice cream freezers churned while the pungent aromas of frying chicken and fish mingled with the thick coastal air.

Writing in the July 1896 issue of *The American Missionary*, Rev. A. L. DeMond reflected on the school's first graduation exercises: "As amid flowers, by floral ladder, under arches festooned with the brightest buds and blossoms, and before the smiles of friendly faces the class of '96 received their diplomas from the hand of Principal Foster, a new event was chronicled in the history of this school and of Liberty county, in which it is located. Its importance is not that the county is so young, for her history extends back one hundred and twenty years; but that now after more than a century of existence she decks herself with the bright flower of hope and accomplishment.

"This is the first class either white or colored that has ever graduated in this county. These were the first graduating exercises ever held within its limits. Do you wonder that people came from far and near to behold what many of their eyes had never seen before? Do you wonder that an old gray-headed father said: 'This is what I prayed for way back yonder in the dark, that the children might have the light. Now I am so glad the light has come.'"[1]

Liberty County, known as the "cradle of the revolutionary spirit in Georgia," was named in honor of its inhabitants' patriotic zeal during the American war for independence. When the colony of Georgia failed to send delegates to the 1775 Continental Congress in Philadelphia, the county sent its own representative, along with 160 barrels of rice to aid the revolutionary cause. Two of Georgia's three signers of the Declaration of Independence hailed from Liberty County.

Nestled among giant live oaks draped with Spanish moss is Midway Church, the oldest Congregational church in the South. Its congregation was organized in 1754 by descendants of Puritan merchants from Dorchester, England, who moved to Massachusetts and founded new-world Dorchester on a windswept hill near Boston. An early observer reflected, "How the blasts roll in across the Bay with nothing to stop them this side of Ireland! Some of (the settlers) shivered themselves into the resolve to seek a milder climate and they went south as far as Georgia where they settled and again called it Dorchester."[2]

The church is seemingly misplaced, its white clapboard architecture more at home on a New England street corner than on the marshland of coastal Georgia. An early American Missionary Association pamphlet describes its environs as the "steaming, thick stickiness of southern swamps where cattle and pigs lost in the marshes return to a semi-wild state and the malarial mosquito and the alligator wait in patient silence for their prey."[3] In the early days, a reserved pew in the church cost five dollars a year—less if you could sing. Foot warmers were provided so congregants could endure long sermons in the winter.

The old church still opens with a huge, heavy brass key, available for the asking at the gas station across the street or the museum next door—which holds a fascinating array of historical artifacts: strands of mourning jewelry made of human hair; a walking cane that shoots forty-five-caliber bullets; and one of only three sets of musical glasses in the world, which, a guide will explain, were brought from England and played with vinegar on the fingertips. All the people who played them, she will further explain, "wound up in an insane asylum" because "the most sensitive part of the body is the fingertips, and the vibrations affected their minds."

The church, erected in 1792, has two front doors. The smaller one off center opens only partway, onto a set of narrow stairs that lead to what was the slave balcony. An early history records that when the settlement was established, it was comprised of 250 whites and 1,500 enslaved blacks, who were primarily engaged in growing rice. The road that passes between the church and its graveyard, with surrounding walls built of bricks carried from England, is one of the oldest in the state. Native American guides aided settlers in blazing the initial trail through the swamps. During the Civil War, after capturing Savannah on his infamous March to the Sea, Union General William Sherman and his troops came to Liberty County to forage for supplies. The cemetery's high brick wall provided an ideal corral for confiscated horses and cattle, and the troops converted the church into a slaughterhouse, using the reed organ as a meat block. They set fire to a nearby Baptist church as a signal to the federal navy that their march to the Georgia coast had reached its goal.

An elderly African American woman who had been enslaved offered this testimony: "When Massa Sherman's army came near, our own Massas ordered us down on our knees to pray for the destruction of the Yankees, and in fear we prayed. Then we went off into the swamp and prayed for the Yankees and God heard our prayers."[4] An American Missionary Association pamphlet recounts the encounter between an emancipated woman and her former mistress after the war. "Well, I am free now," she said. "Yes," replied the ex-mistress, "I know you are, but you are not my equal, for God did not make you so." "Well, maybe not," came the reply, "but General Sherman did and that's good enough for me."[5]

At the end of the war, "the white population seemed to vanish as in a night."[6]. Most white settlers had spent several months a year away from their plantations, avoiding mosquitoes and malaria, returning in the colder winter months. After the war, many of them didn't return, and freed citizens assumed responsibility for most of Liberty County's land, rebuilding in the ruins of the old plantations.

Down the highway two and a half miles from the old Midway Church is Midway Congregational United Church of Christ, formed when African Americans moved up from slavery and down from the balcony. Rev. Hardy Mobley of the American Missionary Association arrived in Liberty County in June 1867 to help organize the church and open a school on its grounds.

Rev. Floyd Snelson, a former slave from Andersonville, Georgia, and the first seminary graduate from the American Missionary Association's Atlanta University, became pastor of the church in 1874. He and his family lived in an open corn crib until he could afford to rent a three-room house. The work was demanding, resources were always tight, and new needs were continually presenting themselves. Rev. Snelson wrote to the secretary of the AMA in New York on July 18, 1874: "I am laboring very hard to get thoroughly established & to recover all of the rights & privileges that are due my people. This is being done under many disadvantages. I have a great deal of traveling to do around the county & nothing to travel with. I hired a horse for his food & have been using him since I came until two weeks ago when a ferocious horse met me in the road, turned upon me & my horse kicking & crippling both. I was compel(led) this week to hire a horse to visit the Church Trustees, who live in different parts of the county from 22 to 30 miles apart . . . "[7]

William A. Golding, a former slave who was one of the first representatives to the legislature of Georgia, gave an acre of land to the AMA for a new church building. An additional six acres were bought for Dorchester Academy for a total of twenty-eight dollars. Rev. Snelson continued his correspondence with the AMA's New York office: "Yesterday was our day for communion, & notwithstanding it being a very rainy day, we could not find shelter in the school house for the people. I was much troubled seeing them trying (to find) shelter from the rain & could not do it. We have been very busy today on the timbers; this being the best day that we have had for some time. I can see no peace of my life until I get some place for my people to worship in. I have been running ever since light this morning to urge this work on. It is now 11:30 o'clock. P.M. & I have just reached home . . . I shall watch everything and not spend a cent where I can avoid it & carry out the purpose. I have paid out very near all of the $100 which you sent for shingles, hewing brick, etc. If you can, I wish that you would send me a few dollars more soon that nothing may stop which is necessary to go on . . . "[8]

Five years after its founding, the congregation was strong in its mission and continuing to grow, as Rev. Snelson reflected in this June 1879 letter: "Nowithstanding the unpleasant situation of a church worshiping in a house unfinished and unprovided with heaters in the month of January, we determined to observe the week of prayer. Some religious interest was manifested among the young people, which was encouraged in every way possible, and one after another gave himself to the Lord, until March 23rd on our communion season, when nineteen, hopefully converted, united with the church.

"Rev. R. F. Markham, who is now in charge of the work of the A.M.A. in and around Savannah, came out by invitation, . . . preached Sunday morning, assisted in the other duties pertaining to the communion, and in the afternoon delivered a very interesting lecture on the work of the A.M.A. This was listened to with great interest by about 700 people in the house and about 300 outside who could not possibly get in."[9]

The school also grew steadily. One of the early Congregational pastors said, "I would stand by the parsonage gate of a morning and could see nothing for miles. Then I noticed what looked like clouds forming down the road. I thought a storm was coming. But they weren't clouds at all, just . . . children coming to Dorchester Academy."[10]

Consistent with other AMA schools, at Dorchester Academy religious and moral training, as well as manual work, always accompanied "book learning." A report on Dorchester in an early edition of *The American Missionary* stated, "The text-book is supplemented by the Bible, by temperance instruction, by Sunday-school work, and by the scissors and needle." Students came, according to the report's author, teacher Fred Foster, from "the turpentine swamp, the rice field, the cabin, the sawmill, and we try to make of them the all-around Christian teacher, educated in intellect, soul, heart and hand."[11]

The school day for boarders began early with breakfast, room inspection, and manual work. At 9:00 a.m. students assembled for devotions, followed by classes. By 3:20 manual work resumed, followed by a mere three-quarters of an hour of recreation, then supper, social hour, and study. The day ended with lights out at 9:30.

Eggs, a common form of tuition payment at the school, also frequently appeared in the church collection plate on a Sunday morning—as the treasurer sometimes had occasion to remember with chagrin while carrying the offering home in his pocket. One student paid her way by supplying the two gallons of syrup that the school used every day. Another arrived during the Great Depression with a box of pencils under her arm. She announced that she wanted an education, but the crops were off and her father's shop had gone out of business. She had pencils bearing her father's name, which he had printed for advertising purposes. They were good for a month's worth of schooling.

Several decades after its founding, Dorchester's students were still making great sacrifices to attend. The May 1921 edition of *The American Missionary* reported on their dedication: "The majority live five miles and more away. Two, and these among the very best, have a daily walk of nineteen miles between school and home; their paths through the cypress swamps is often ankle deep in water. They must start before light in the morning and cannot reach home until long after dark. The regular tuition fee, though very low, is more than a trifle to them, for there is precious little money there-about. Yet they deem the effort not too great nor the price too high for the privileges offered."[12]

Two long-time members of Midway Congregational United Church of Christ report that their experience during Dorchester Academy's latter years was much the same, though without the long walk to endure. According to Lillie Gillard, "We had dormitories, a girls' dormitory and a boys'. Students came from all around surrounding counties and some from other states. Some of them paid with produce—things like sugar canes, sweet potatoes, eggs, chickens, whatever they could. The parents were so concerned about having their children get an education that they found whatever means they could to take care of those expenses."

"There were nine of us," said Christine Baker. "I'm the third child. All except my two twin brothers finished from [Dorchester Academy]. This was a private school, and we had to pay fifty cents each for first and second grade, and fifty cents was hard to come by. I worked at the school, cleaning. When you worked at the school, you got ten cents an hour. When my oldest sister came, all of the teachers were white. When I came, all of them were black."

Ms. Gillard added, "People find it difficult to believe that way back in the early '20s we had an integrated faculty here at Dorchester Academy in the center of Liberty County . . . Conditions were really rough for white teachers coming down in this area teaching people of color. Nobody who was white wanted to let them have a place to live; they treated them mean." One new teacher at Dorchester described her destination as "truly at the end of the world." Arriving by train amid stifling summer heat in 1923, she wrote, "I alighted with all the pleasant anticipation of a Christian martyr about to dip into a cauldron of burning oil."[13]

Dorchester Academy had a far-reaching impact throughout the region. The 1902 AMA report made the claim, "For several years the schools of this entire county, with one or two possible exceptions, have been taught by those who at some time have received training and instruction here."[14] A century later, church member Ezekiel Walthour reflected, "This is the educational capital of this county because almost every child that would come up today is touched by someone who attended Dorchester Academy; a teacher taught the child of someone, or they taught the teacher

. . . We tend to feel that (Dorchester is) like a piece of chalk: Once you touch it, there's always a trace left."

Dorchester's most outstanding principal, and its last, was Elizabeth Moore. One local woman said to a group of visitors shortly after her arrival, "The American Missionary Association always sent us men principals. They were good men. We liked them all right. But now they sent us a woman principal and she even makes the men work. We like her fine."[15] Ms. Moore ushered Dorchester into an era of self-sufficiency that paved the way for its future beyond its life as a school, which ended in 1940. That's the year Lillie Gillard graduated from eighth grade: "I had been looking forward to going to high school at Dorchester Academy. But that was not to be. The state of Georgia decided (that year) that it would provide secondary education for students of color . . .

"The (new) school was not ready when it was time for us to begin school in September, so then the county had to negotiate with the AMA to use the buildings that were on the (Dorchester Academy) grounds . . . The AMA gave the science equipment, the library materials . . . and money to help purchase the school bus. We got one school bus, and the principal had to drive it . . . It meant we left home early in the morning and got back late in the afternoon . . . In addition to having to ride all this distance to get to school, we got the old raggedy hand-me-down books that the (white) kids had written all over.

"They sent us down to Crossroads. They didn't think we could be educated, so they decided to train us. They named our school Liberty County Training School . . . I know of two people in this community—maybe three—who graduated that year after Dorchester closed. Their diplomas do not say Dorchester Academy; they say Liberty County Training School. Those people are hurt to this day."

When Dorchester closed its doors as a school, it reopened them as a center of hope and resistance in the rural South. Dorchester Cooperative Center organized a credit union during the Depression, enabling area farmers to collectively buy a tractor and other supplies to keep their farms productive. According to a 1950 AMA pamphlet, the credit union was "the most inclusive organization in the community, cutting across denominational and social interests. It literally represented *all* the people."[16]

The center established a health clinic and led the fight to improve phone lines, drainage systems, and roads. It organized voter registration drives as early as the 1940s. Polling places were notorious throughout Georgia for making African American citizens read and interpret obscure parts of the federal or state constitution in order to qualify to vote. One man with a PhD from Tuskegee Institute read the constitution too well and was handed writings in Chinese to read.[17] Sometimes prospective voters were asked impossibly absurd questions or required to guess the correct number of jelly beans in a jar. No matter what answer was rendered, it was always deemed incorrect, and voting rights were denied. A poll tax was also a serious obstacle for many potential voters.

The state of Georgia finally repealed its poll tax in 1943. In a letter to the American Missionary Association dated April 19, 1946, Claudius A. Turner, a Fisk University graduate and then director of the Dorchester Cooperative Center, wrote of dramatic changes in Liberty County. Years before Dr. Martin Luther King Jr. reached prominence, Mr. Turner spoke of a "non-violent revolution" going on: "Well civic and political interest in this county is jumping so far as Negroes are concerned . . . The bars against voting have been let down and there is a non-violent revolution going on in this state . . . The race issue has been raised in a thousand sections of this state and so far these peddlers of race hatred have been beaten. Of course the people of Liberty County want to play their part. We have organized through the initiation of the credit union the Liberty County Citizens Council . . . Our immediate objective is to get the people registered."[18]

Mr. Turner, lamenting that he was too overwhelmed by the work to farm or even keep a garden, ended his letter with a plea for an assistant to help him with the growing workload of organizing, corresponding, collecting information, and financial reporting. "The necessities of the local situation, as I see them," he wrote, "compel me to ask for a secretary immediately. I need one now . . . The natural question is could my wife perform those functions. The answer is No!" Referring to her work in home economics training and children's programs, he continued, "It is my opinion that she is more popular in the community and the county than I am. Since it is not my philosophy to smother personalities—even that of my wife—it is not in the nature of community and county welfare to make her my secretary."

Mr. Turner also pointed out that the new assembly room being planned for the center was too small, that mass meetings in the county were drawing almost a thousand people. The center had launched an intensive educational program for prospective voters. Liberty County citizens followed the activities of legislators, keeping a chart on how each one voted on crucial issues, and interviewed candidates for public office. A hand-drawn flier titled "The $64 Question" portrayed a man down on one knee asking a woman, "Have you registered?"

The Liberty County Citizens Council was fulfilling the dream that brought it to birth: "(T)he people hoped to secure for themselves collectively those rights they had been unable to claim individually." Claudius Turner's December 27, 1947, letter to the AMA documented the council's great strides: "We are to schedule mass meetings in the various communities in the county. We shall hold instructions in government and politics at these mass meetings. We expect that within a year there will be more understanding among Negroes of government and politics in Liberty County than in any other county in Georgia . . . I think we are approaching a milestone in human relations here. As you know the average southern white man has very little respect for the intelligence of Negroes . . . We have an excellent chance to graduate the whites from that attitude in this county primary which ends January 28, 1948 . . . "

Congregational philosophy, according to a January 1950 AMA pamphlet, encompasses "a love of freedom and respect for personality" and helped lay the foundation for the democratic process evolving in Liberty County. This included respect for the voices of women: "The Congregational background created reverence for long family residence, stable family life, love for children and respect for women who . . . feel free to participate in open debate on community affairs, even when their views differ with the husbands'!" Opinions were voiced freely without fear of violence or persecution, and the debates were intense.

"Because of the New England town meeting background every Liberty County citizen believes he is a leader. In the Council everyone expects to speak his mind. Meetings, therefore, begin early in the evening and may continue until two in the morning . . . Offices in various organizations are 'passed around' to give leadership opportunities to all. When occasionally an undesirable person gains too much power, someone having the required community respect will move that all offices be declared vacant. If the motion is passed, vacancies are then refilled one by one. Those holding office previously are re-elected until the questionable officer's place comes up. Some one will then be nominated, or two or three candidates may be suggested. The office is filled with no spoken criticism of anyone; remaining vacancies are filled with those who had them. The matter is then a closed incident."[19]

This political engagement was the groundwork for Liberty County's widespread participation in the looming civil rights movement. When civil rights leader Andrew Young was looking for a site to locate the citizenship education program in 1961, he considered the Penn Center on St. Helena Island, but he ultimately chose Dorchester Academy. Considering the citizenship program "a natural extension of the historic role played by the American Missionary Association," Rev. Young called the academy a "repository of memories of the kind of hopes and aspirations we planned to revive through citizenship schools."[20] Not yet on the staff of the recently formed SCLC (Southern Christian Leadership Conference), Rev. Young preferred at that time to work through the United Church of Christ and the National Council of Churches, mentioning his desire to continue working with young people, his hope to do more writing, and his observation that the SCLC was "dominated by emotional Baptist preachers and I was a self-contained Congregationalist."[21]

The citizenship schools, according to Dorothy Cotton, one of their chief organizers, were on "a mission to make democracy mean what it's supposed to mean in this country."[22] They focused on literacy training and civic learning, apprising African American citizens of their legal rights and preparing them to vote. Many renowned leaders touched, and were touched by, Dorchester.

Fannie Lou Hamer, the outstanding Mississippi civil rights leader, was "a star pupil," according to Dr. Cotton. Bernice Johnson Reagon came to Dorchester, having been expelled from Georgia's Albany State College for her civil rights activities, and went on to found the renowned a cappella women's singing group Sweet Honey in the Rock. Septima Clark was the intrepid supervisor of teacher training at Dorchester.

Ms. Clark first got involved in voter education in Charleston, South Carolina. The law to keep African Americans from voting in primaries was passed in 1896—"just before I was born," wrote Ms. Clark in her autobiography, *Ready from Within*.[23] The U.S. Supreme Court changed the law in 1944, but Southern states were still following their own rules, according to Ms. Clark. In 1947, "(s)everal days before the election some of the whites made a statement that if blacks attempted to vote in the primary, then blood would be running down the streets like water."[24]

In the face of such threats, Septima Clark worked tirelessly for civil rights. In 1955, the South Carolina legislature made it illegal for a city or state employee to belong to the NAACP. For the dues of a dollar a year, Ms. Clark had joined the organization in 1918, when she was twenty years old and teaching on St. Johns Island, a sea island fifteen miles and at that time nine hours by rowboat from Charleston. Thirty-seven years later, refusing to rescind or deny her membership, Ms. Clark was fired from her public teaching job.

She signed her name to 726 letters, which she sent to other African American teachers, asking them to tell the state of South

Carolina that the law was unjust. "If whites could belong to the Ku Klux Klan, then surely blacks could belong to the NAACP," she wrote. According to Ms. Clark, most of the teachers "were afraid and became hostile." Only twenty-six answered her letter. Eleven agreed to go with her to talk with the school superintendent, but only five followed through. After that meeting, Ms. Clark was unable to get a job anywhere in the state.[25]

She moved to the Highlander Folk School in Tennessee, where she directed workshops and taught literacy and voter education. That's where she met and befriended Rosa Parks, who refused to give up her seat on a bus three months after attending a Highlander workshop, sparking the Montgomery bus boycott. Ms. Clark brought friends from St. Johns Island to the school and helped them buy a building, which they turned into a grocery store in front and a school in back. "We planned the grocery store to fool white people," she said. "We didn't want them to know we had a school back there."[26]

In 1957 Highlander celebrated its twenty-fifth anniversary, with Dr. Martin Luther King Jr. as the keynote speaker. Charges that the folk school was a "Communist training center," which had been leveled as early as the 1930s, escalated. In July 1959, while she was leading a workshop, eighteen police officers raided the school and carried Septima Clark away. The young people left behind added a new verse to the freedom anthem "We Shall Overcome" that night, singing "We are not afraid" as the police carried out their raid. The officers planted some moonshine, according to Ms. Clark, and then threatened to close down the school for liquor-law violations—though the real offense to the authorities was the racial integration practiced at the school.

While the police drove her over several mountains that night, Ms. Clark thought, "'Now I don't know whether I'll get to see the daylight or not . . . I do know that these young mountain boys had beaten others to death, and I had a feeling that might happen to me."[27] She spent the night in jail and was released the next day. "I wasn't going to let them scare me to death. I just wouldn't let them," said Ms. Clark after her release. She also refused to give in to anger. "I never felt that getting angry would do you any good other than hurt your own digestion—keep you from eating, which I liked to do."[28]

In 1961, citizenship training was moved from Highlander to the Dorchester Center. Septima Clark was hired to supervise teacher training. Andrew Young described her as "a no-nonsense black schoolteacher in her sixties."[29] He served as the school's adminis-trator, and Dorothy Cotton was the director. The three of them worked together as a team, according to Ms. Clark, driving all over the South to bring busloads of people to live together for five days at Dorchester. They looked for "people who are respected by members of the community, who can read well aloud, and who can write their names in cursive writing" to bring to the center and train as teachers. They had no blackboards, so they used dry cleaners' bags to record responses to questions about the needs in the various communities from which people had come.[30]

"The people who left Dorchester," according to Ms. Clark, "went home to teach and to work in voter registration drives. They went home, and they didn't take it anymore. They started their own citizenship classes, discussing the problems in their own towns. 'How come the pavement stops where the black section begins?' Asking questions like that, and then knowing who to go to talk to about that, or where to protest it."[31] Citizenship schools sprang up around kitchen tables, in barber shops, under trees in the summertime.

With grant money, the center was able to pay each student thirty dollars to come for training. "Even then we didn't have too many to come," observed Ms. Clark. "There was so much pressure from the whites in the community that too many of them were afraid. Those who came had to feel that we could get away with it or that we didn't mind if we had to die."[32]

Despite the fear that kept some people away, Dorchester Center had a remarkable impact throughout the South. In 1955, only about 25 percent of voting-age African Americans were registered in the Southern states. More than three and a half million weren't, and many of them couldn't read. Ms. Clark and her colleagues taught individuals to read in two to three months' time, and they trained hundreds to teach others. By 1970, almost two million more African Americans were voting than had been a decade and a half before.[33]

Beverly Lewis Gross, who grew up in Midway Congregational United Church of Christ, was a teenager when civil rights leaders began appearing at Dorchester. She has fond memories of those days and the people who came: "Dr. King was out there playing volleyball, sleeves rolled up but in his white shirt. Andy Young played out there, (SCLC leader Rev. Ralph) Abernathy. All of them were out there, and it was just nice. I'm glad to be part of that history."

Ms. Gross got swept up in the excitement of the civil rights movement, paying the price as a young woman for growing up in the shadow of Dorchester and being inspired by its leaders. "Alice Walker was here, an aspiring writer at that time, and we were going to Savannah one afternoon. There were several of us in the car. We stopped to get some gas. As soon as we pulled up in the service station, the guy there picked up the phone. A state trooper came and just sat there. Our car was integrated, and I guess he figured we'd start some trouble. (Our driver) got out, pumped the gas, and went inside to pay. Another car came up and couldn't get to the pump. So I got out, started up the car, and moved it up just enough for the guy to get gasoline.

"The trooper came and asked me for my driver's license. Well, I didn't have a driver's license, and I wasn't really driving, just moving the car. He took us to the police station. They didn't want a cash bond, because between us we had enough money for bond. They had already looked at the car tag and saw we were from Liberty County. They said they wanted Chatham County real estate for a bond; none of us had that. We tried to give them cash but they said, 'No, we don't want that.' They told us that if we started any trouble, 'You'll go to jail and you won't get out.' Those were their words . . . So we went to jail that night. I praise anybody who went to jail in that era, because it's really not a good feeling; to hear those doors lock behind you is not a good feeling . . .

"The next morning we had to go to court. They dropped the charges . . . When I got back home, Mom and Daddy were sitting on the porch. So many people had told me, 'You need to stay at home; you ain't got no business doing this; your mama and daddy teach school, and you're gonna make them lose their jobs.' Mom and Daddy said, 'Go ahead and do what you want to do.' They just sat there, but they were glad to see me, and I was glad to be home."

The presence of a segregated coffee shop in Liberty County moved Ms. Gross to take a personal and courageous stand. "Clyde & Betty's (coffee shop) was on Highway 17, which was a major thoroughfare at that time. When I was fifteen or sixteen, I sat in at Clyde & Betty's, and it was an experience I'll never forget . . . Mr. Strickland (a local leader in the Civil Rights movement) took us around. I was there (at Clyde & Betty's) by myself. Some of the others were in different places, because we were few in number. I went down there and I sat on the steps. They asked me to move, but I wouldn't move. So Clyde's son—he has Clyde's Wrecker Service to this day—he went and got what was at that time the emergency ambulance. It was sort of like a hearse. He had the ambulance, a German shepherd, and a shotgun, and he came to the door and asked me to move. I told him I wasn't going. He backed the hearse up toward me, pointed the shotgun at me, had the dog by his side. (A man in the coffee shop) told him, 'I don't think you want to do that. The best thing for you to do is go on back home.' About fifteen minutes later Mr. Strickland came back to check on me, and I was glad at that time to be able to get in his station wagon and leave. I was scared to death, but they said you had to stay and not be confrontational."

One of the older members of the church, who was listening to Ms. Gross recount the story, asked, "And you were only fifteen or sixteen?" Ms. Gross replied, laughing, "I have been belligerent a long time."

A few years later, she had been involved in a voter registration campaign. "I do believe we took as many as seventy or eighty people up there at one time to register them to vote. It was something that I was really proud of because we had gone door to door, and in this area the older people were just dead set on not doing anything of that nature because they were in fear of losing their homes.

"As long as I can remember, if there was a problem in the county, black people seemed to come here (Dorchester Center). They met here, they planned here. Whatever the issues were, somebody in our church was in it . . . There's a rich history here, and a lot of these people were involved in it, whether they were out front or pushing you from behind."

The NAACP met monthly on the Dorchester campus. The 1963 Birmingham campaign was planned there. Renowned for the courage of the city's children—who marched in the face of water cannons, brutal police, and vicious dogs—the Birmingham campaign was one of the first major victories of the civil rights movement. Lillie Gillard remembered the planning: "When Andy (Young) and Dr. King and the others were coming here to plan the Birmingham movement, the whole time (Dr. King) was under surveillance. Wherever he went, the FBI had him under surveillance. So whenever he came to Liberty County, they didn't announce it in advance. We had a young man in the community who'd go around from house to house: 'Dr. King will be here tonight, Dr. King will be here tonight, come on out to the Center.' This time they were planning the Birmingham movement, and even Daddy King didn't know where he was going. There were about thirteen of them, including (Birmingham leader Rev.) Fred Shuttlesworth. I think Dorothy Cotton was the only woman in that bunch. And when they got to the airport in Savannah, all of the stations were manned by FBI agents. But they planned and went on back—took their flights back and everything went according to plan."

Members of the Midway Congregational United Church of Christ, many of whom attended Dorchester Academy as children, are working together to preserve the school's long and rich history.

Bright murals that adorn the walls of the Heritage Room at the center honor the many civil rights leaders who entered its doors and document the movement's achievements. Artifacts commemorate the *Amistad* event and the rice culture that drove the county's economy for many years. The church and academy are part of the county's "Historic Liberty Trail."

In June 2004, due largely to the church members' efforts, the Dorchester Academy Museum of African-American History was dedicated. State Representative Tyrone Brooks, head of the Georgia legislature's Black Caucus, said in his address: "We should rededicate ourselves to what Dorchester stands for, to what Dorchester means. This is not just a routine ceremony, another dedication. Dorchester is a beacon, a light in the lives of African Americans . . . This is a statement from people of good will, black and white, brown and yellow, that Dorchester's mission still continues." Pointing out the many challenges facing African American children and teenagers, Rep. Brooks continued, "We're going to preach it because this new Dorchester message is our salvation."[34]

"Dorchester Days," an annual summer weekend of celebration, includes a fund-raising walkathon. The walk covers 9.3 miles, the longest distance the earliest students walked to get to the school. Lillie Gillard has a treasured photograph of the two young girls who covered that distance to school and then back again every day. The celebration both commemorates the past and ensures resources for community involvement in the future. The church members hope to build a youth educational center or retreat center nearby, to expand Dorchester's legacy.

Dorchester Academy has transformed lives through many generations, tapping people into power they thought was unattainable, igniting change in many corners. Dr. Dorothy Cotton, who serves now as director of African-American Studies at Cornell University, shared a story that highlights the center's continuing inspirational power and offers a challenge to all who know its history: "People came (for the citizenship education program) from all over the South and the border states . . . They arrived on the first day singing sorrow songs. By the third day, they were singing "I'm gonna do what the Spirit says do . . . I'm gonna vote 'cause the Spirit says vote . . . I'll go to jail if the Spirit says jail" . . .

"I was recently introduced as a colleague of Martin Luther King at a Michigan school for delinquent children. An eleven-year-old piped up, 'And y'all are still living?' That's the question for us now: Are we still living? . . . When you find yourself saying, 'Somebody ought to do something,' you need to say, 'I'm somebody.'"

12

"The People Have a Mind to Build"

Planting Living Monuments across the South

Early on the morning of September 9, 1739, a band of enslaved men and women, led by an Angolan named Jemmy, gathered at the Stono River near Charleston, South Carolina. They raided a general store for firearms and gunpowder, decapitating the proprietors and leaving their heads on the doorstep. The group marched south toward Spanish-controlled Florida, where fugitives had been granted freedom and land, carrying banners that proclaimed "Liberty!" and shouting the same. They killed white citizens as they went, adding more enslaved people to their ranks.

The Stono slave rebellion, the largest in the colonies prior to the Revolutionary War, was likely triggered by South Carolina's Security Act, announced in mid-August of that year in a Charleston newspaper. In response to the white population's fears of insurrection, the act required all white men to carry guns to church on Sundays, the only day of the week that slaves were not forced to work under their control. Fears of insurrection were well-founded. South Carolina's enslaved population was the densest among the colonies, outnumbering whites two to one, and laws governing the enslaved were particularly brutal there. Slaves caught running away the first time were whipped. The second time they were branded with the letter *R*, for "runaway," on the right cheek. The third time they were branded on the other cheek and had an ear cut off. The fourth time male runaways were castrated.[1]

Jemmy's band, numbering close to a hundred, marched ten miles before stopping in a field near the Edisto River to beat drums and sing, in hopes of drawing more enslaved people to their rebellion. Retribution was swift, as white planters and militia men descended on the group, killing thirty of the slaves by dusk. All except one of those who escaped were caught and executed. As the infuriated militia members returned to Charleston, they impaled the heads of the dead rebels on mileposts along the road. The message was clear to other slaves: fighting for freedom in South Carolina meant death.

Within months, the state assembly passed the 1740 black code, which made it illegal for enslaved people to assemble in groups, grow their own food, earn their own money, or learn to read and write. Though some of these restrictions had been in effect before the Stono Rebellion, they had not been strictly enforced.

Legislators tried to soften the blow and buy slave loyalty by reducing the length of the slave workday to fourteen hours during fall and winter, and fifteen hours during the growing season—their idea of compassion.[2]

Unrest among the enslaved in South Carolina, the only state with a black majority, continued to grow. In the spring of 1822, an insurrection was launched by Denmark Vesey, a leader in Charleston's strong African church. Vesey, the former property of a slave-ship captain, who had been forced to bring slaves ashore and transport them to the city's auction pens, had purchased his freedom with lottery money. For their part in the failed rebellion, Vesey and thirty-four other men were executed—hanged and then shot in the head by the captain of the guards when they failed to die quickly enough. The official response of South Carolina's white citizens was immediate: new public policies further restricted communication among blacks and increased punishments for slaves found reading or others found teaching them. Education, whites felt, would fuel insurrection.

In the early morning hours of May 13, 1862, Robert Smalls, a twenty-three-year-old enslaved man who worked on the Confederate steamer *Planter*, carried out a successful small-scale rebellion of his own. After the *Planter*'s white captain and crew went ashore for the night, Smalls commandeered the boat, which was loaded with weapons for rebel forts. He gathered up his family and a dozen other slaves, donned the captain's wide-brimmed straw hat and mimicked his stance, and navigated the boat through Charleston Harbor, sounding the correct whistle at each Confederate fort he passed and raising a white flag when the closest Union blockading vessel came into view. The resourceful Mr. Smalls later served in both the South Carolina Senate and House of Representatives.

Charleston, with a reputation for being both charming and aristocratic, was a flashpoint for rebellion among white citizens as well. In this city the Articles of Secession were written, ushering South Carolina out of the Union—the first state to leave. Off its shore the first battle of the Civil War, for Fort Sumter, was engaged. And in its largest park a monument was erected after the war to John C. Calhoun, the proslavery U.S. senator and vice president who had helped to craft the colonies' Articles of War against England.

The Calhoun monument was replaced in 1896 with a towering eighty-foot-high statue on a massive granite pedestal, apparently because African Americans regularly defaced the original. Calhoun is said to have revealed the repugnance of his racism with the offensive remark, "Show me a nigger who can conjugate a Greek verb and I will admit that he is a man."[3] Fortunately, Calhoun's monumental prejudice didn't cast a shadow as far as Bull Street. There, on October 1, 1865, the American Missionary Association opened the Avery Institute, named for the AMA's first large-scale outside donor, Rev. Charles Avery of Pittsburgh. Within its walls sat a thousand children who were on their way to learning how to read, write, and conjugate verbs. An "insurrection" of a different sort.

Plymouth Congregational Church, the first church established by the American Missionary Association in the South, came to birth soon after the founding of Avery Institute. Before the Civil War, Charleston's black and white Congregationalists worshiped together in downtown Circular Church, founded in 1681. In 1861 a great fire swept through the city, leaving the church in ruins, and the Civil War soon followed with more devastation. After the war, black members of the congregation withdrew to form Plymouth Church, organized on April 14, 1867. The members moved around for five years, meeting in various places, including the chapel at Avery Institute.

Under the leadership of Rev. James T. Ford, who served as both the church's pastor and Avery Institute's principal, the congregation built a church. At its dedication on March 10, 1872, Rev. Ford placed in the cornerstone a Bible and documents of the church's founding, as well as copies of the Social Compact that the Pilgrims made before landing at Plymouth Rock, the Emancipation Proclamation, and the Thirteenth, Fourteenth, and Fifteenth amendments of the U.S. Constitution, which outlawed slavery and protected suffrage and citizenship rights. Two hundred church members and some 1,800 onlookers sang a hymn as the cornerstone was lowered into place.

Avery's first principal was Thomas W. Cardozo, an antebellum free black, who put the school on solid footing and led it well until a sex scandal surfaced from his past. The AMA replaced him with his brother, Francis L. Cardozo, who was lauded for his tireless work, his commitment to training service-oriented Christian teachers and community leaders, and the school's academic excellence. Within a year, half of Avery's faculty members were African American.[4] For several decades Avery was the only institution in Charleston preparing black students for college. It survived relentless financial woes, entrenched white opposition, and an earthquake that damaged its buildings in 1886.

Septima P. Clark, a 1916 graduate who would become renowned as a fearless civil rights leader, called Avery "black Charleston's version of the Massachusetts Institute of Technology."[5]

A decade later, when the American Missionary Association was considering closing down the school, Avery principal Benjamin Cox noted that two-thirds of the teachers in Charleston County's black public schools, and 85 percent in the city's black schools, were Avery graduates.[6] South Carolina had the highest illiteracy rate in the nation, and Avery, whose staff and faculty by that time were entirely African American, was the only fully accredited high school, black or white, in Charleston. It was the largest AMA-operated secondary school in the nation, with double the number of high school students as the next in size.[7] AMA officials were persuaded of Avery's importance, and the school stayed open until 1954.

Plymouth Church members Inez Fields, who graduated from Avery in 1930, and Gracie Lee Dobbins, who was born in 1906 and outlived all her classmates, remembered that tardiness was not tolerated at the school. The gates were locked at 9:00 sharp, and if you were late you had to stay outside. "Then you'd be let in," said Ms. Dobbins, "to clean windows, or sweep the floor, or empty the trash" for penance. "Sometimes boys would climb over or go under the gate to get to the grounds," said Ms. Fields, "but no girls, to my knowledge." When she was in eighth grade, a classmate of Ms. Dobbins released a horde of fiddler crabs in the classroom, a prank that disrupted the school's strict discipline for a while, until all the creatures were caught.

Avery graduates predominated in the leadership of Charleston's NAACP, founded in 1917, and the organization's meetings took place in both the school and Plymouth Church. In 1944 Avery alumnus John H. Wrighten Jr., a disabled World War II veteran, coordinated a letter-writing campaign that challenged discriminatory admission policies in South Carolina colleges. During the 1950s and '60s, Averyites were in the forefront of the civil rights movement.

Septima Clark was a major force in citizenship schools, which were estimated to have trained one hundred thousand African Americans in literacy and voter rights. During Arthur J. Clement Jr.'s tenure as Charleston's NAACP president, the fight to desegregate the city's parks and public schools was engaged. The legal battle was coordinated and led by J. Arthur Brown, who like Clement was an Avery graduate and businessman who headed Charleston's NAACP for a time. Two Averyites, Eugene C. Hunt and J. Michael Graves, inspired Charleston's 1960 sit-in movement targeting downtown lunch counters. Former Avery teacher Ruby B. Cornwell was arrested in an attempt to integrate Fort Sumter Hotel in 1963.

Plymouth Church member Anna Smalls said, "When I first went to Avery, I was a little timid person, who would not speak out for any reason. But I don't do that anymore." Ms. Smalls remembered when thousands of people came through Charleston in 1963, heading from Alabama to the March on Washington. The city's streets were lined with people cheering them on, and church members prepared meals for the marchers. Ms. Smalls often visited the islands off Charleston's shore at night, holding clandestine meetings and training people to vote, returning after midnight. "It was risky," she said, "but it's what needed to be done."

Kathy Robinson-Nelson, who was invited to Plymouth Church by James R. Fields, who served as its pastor for almost thirty years, arrived with four small children. The church "took me under its wing," she said, and provided clothes and Christmas presents when her family needed them. One day she came home and found several beds on her porch—donated by Rev. Fields and other church members. "There's a feeling at Plymouth that whatever you're going through, there's someone there to uplift you," said Ms. Robinson-Nelson, who succeeded Rev. Fields as pastor of Plymouth Church. Ms. Robinson-Nelson, who received nonviolence training at the Highlander Center and was arrested at civil rights protests, said that, at the church, "The message was always, 'You are somebody. Don't let anyone take that away from you. Because God created all of us, and we're all entitled to the same rights.' We were told, 'Hold up your head and be proud.'"

Florence Miller, who was born in 1930, said that when she was young, "segregation was just something you lived with. You knew that when you went to the movies, you were going to sit upstairs. And you knew that when you rode the bus, you were going to sit in the back. And you were going to drink from the colored fountain." When she drove to Alabama with her family, they always had to pack enough food for the trip because there was nowhere safe to stop. There was no place to eat out on Sundays, so she always had to get her children dressed for church and have dinner ready before they left so they could eat as soon as they got home. These days, Ms. Miller never cooks on Sundays. Plymouth Church was crucial to the change, she said. "Plymouth always had an 'open door policy' for anyone that needed to use our church or needed our support."

In 1969 the NAACP provided leadership for the Charleston Hospital strike, in response to the low wages paid to its African American nursing assistants, dietary staff, orderlies, and janitors, and to discriminatory practices at the Medical College of South Carolina. The strike was sparked when negotiations between the employees' labor union and the hospital administration broke down, leading to the firing of a dozen worker activists. Septima Clark was instrumental in uniting leaders from the union and the Southern Christian Leadership Conference, including Coretta Scott King and Ralph Abernathy, whose arrest galvanized Charleston's black community behind the strike. The 113-day strike was settled when the hospital administration agreed to rehire the fired workers, raise its minimum wage, and establish an employee grievance procedure.

Plymouth Church member Deborah Harris was a senior in high school during the year of the strike. "There was a curfew on at that time; I don't think any African Americans went to their senior prom that year," she said. "We were threatened with not being eligible to graduate if we were ever arrested. Teachers and guidance counselors told us that it would affect the possibility of getting financial aid [for college], so that was scary." But despite the threats, Ms. Harris and many other students attended rallies in support of the hospital workers, encouraged to do so by the church's leaders.

"Plymouth Church has always been steadfast," said Ms. Harris. "Plymouth has a huge extended family in the community, and everyone knows Plymouth as a strong driving force in the community. We've never had over a hundred members, but the entire community is aware of who we are and what we're all about. At some time or another, a large segment of the community has crossed our threshold." Delores Wainwright said that had largely to do with the charismatic leadership provided by Rev. Fields over almost three decades. "If you need him, he'll come," she said. "No matter who you are, no matter where you are, he'll do his best to get to you—and you don't have to be a member of this church."

In 1978 Avery graduates organized the Avery Institute of Afro-American History and Culture, a community-based historical society. In 1985 members of the institute cooperated with the College of Charleston to found the Avery Research Center for African American History and Culture, located in the former school building. The center, which houses extensive archives, is dedicated to collecting and preserving the unique African American heritage of South Carolina's coastal Low Country.

Just a short jaunt down the coast from Charleston is First Congregational United Church of Christ in Savannah, Georgia, located on a historic and picturesque city square. Founded by the American Missionary Association in April 1869, the church held services at Beach Institute, Savannah's AMA-sponsored school, for the first five years of its life. Always committed to education, First Congregational hosted a kindergarten program when it built a church and organized a popular Bible school and training center for prospective ministers. When Beach Institute closed in 1919 and African American children were without a high school, church members opened a school in cooperation with other Savannah citizens. Less than a year later, the county board of education assumed operation of the school, signaling the beginning of public high school education for the city's black children. Many of the first teachers in the public school system were members of First Congregational Church.

Dorothy L. DeVillars taught school for thirty years. She said, "The AMA has touched me all my life." She grew up down the street from the church and attended kindergarten there. "In my generation, almost everyone I knew came here for kindergarten," she said. "It was one of the best in town." When she was in high school during the 1940s, the NAACP and other groups "met at this church when they couldn't meet at other churches, because this was a liberal church, and people felt comfortable here."

Church member Eugene H. Gadsden, who was born in 1912, worked as an assistant city attorney and was the first African American judge on Georgia's Supreme Court, which he served for three terms. Judge Gadsden was involved in five lawsuits to integrate Savannah's schools and police force. Though he became the target of pipe and package bombs and needed the protection of a body guard, he refused to back down from his civil rights activities. "I just kept on 'til some of the white people got to be Christians," he reflected wryly.

Helen H. Washington joined Savannah's First Congregational Church in 1958. Born in Tougaloo, Mississippi, to a father who collected rosin from coastal pines and a mother who taught kindergarten, Ms. Washington attended the Daniel Hand School on the campus, then Tougaloo high school and college. Looking back on her graduation, she said, "I remember walking across the stage, and the announcement was made by the president that 'Here's a graduate who has attended our institutions from kindergarten on up to college graduation.' At the time I did not think that it was such a glorious experience because I was ready to leave after all those years in the same place. But I must say, the longer I live and the more I move around the country, I have certainly learned to appreciate all that Tougaloo College, the Daniel Hand School, and the Tougaloo community had to offer."

Like many other loyal AMA graduates, Ms. Washington felt so tied to the tradition that she immediately sought out a Congregational church when she relocated. "It's my first and only religious affiliation," she said. She has served on the trustee and deacon boards of the Savannah church, and as moderator of the congregation. She worked for many years as a social worker, with a particular concern for child welfare and housing for low-income families. She has made an annual contribution to Tougaloo College since 1969. "The AMA instilled in me a desire and belief to give back to one's community," she said.

Almost on the Florida border, in the rural plantation belt of South Georgia, sits the city of Thomasville, a popular resort at the turn of the twentieth century. The AMA-sponsored Allen Normal and Industrial School was moved there in 1886, after the old hotel in which it was established in nearby Quitman was burned to the ground just six weeks after it opened. Supported generously by Congregational women's auxiliaries in Connecticut, the institution was initially called the Connecticut Industrial School for Colored Girls, then renamed in honor of Mrs. F. L. Allen of Waterbury, Connecticut, who donated the hotel property to be refurbished into a school.

The Quitman arsonists struck in the middle of the night, piling up furniture and using barrels of kerosene. A fire engine that responded to the alarm came only to save the adjacent property. The school's superintendent, Rev. J. H. Parr, and the teachers, who lived above the classrooms and barely escaped alive just before the roof fell in, were left standing on the sidewalk, thinly clad, in the cold night air for more than an hour. When at last they were taken into a local hotel, their welcome was mixed with insults and charges that Rev. Parr had set the fire. The only item that survived the blaze was a carriage, upon which local residents later piled rails to burn it as well. "The carriage is no longer an element of danger," wrote one of the teachers ruefully. "It will not harness itself up to ruthlessly run over any of those who are afraid of a chariot of civilization. It has furnished what light it could amidst great darkness."[8]

Indignation and sympathy arrived from some corners, including from the mayor of Thomasville, who offered a large plot of land just outside the city for a permanent school for girls. The school, which emphasized strict discipline, offered nursing and teacher training, as well as sewing, basketry, and rug weaving. "We do our tasks well," wrote a student in a composition, "because, if we don't, we do them over again. This is to make us nice girls for life."[9]

One particularly generous student gave a classmate a pair of her shoes. When her mother discovered them missing over Christmas break, her daughter explained, "Well, Mother, one of the girls had shoes so worn they wouldn't stay on, and I couldn't keep two pairs." The mother was unable to chide her generous daughter, since she herself had been given a pair of shoes twenty years before, by a classmate who went on to become one of her daughter's teachers at Allen School.[10]

Early one Easter morning, the students opened all the doors to the teachers' rooms, then gathered on the stairs to sing spirituals and tell the Easter story. "Singing voices wakened us," wrote one teacher, "and we found the room filled with music and dawn light together. Softly, clearly, tenderly as the light, came the resurrection story . . . When they had finished they slipped quietly away, leaving us with our loveliest memory of Easter music."[11]

Allen School emphasized pietistic religion, and early in its history plans were in place to organize a church. One of the students who was most keenly interested in Christian faith became quite ill, and the rites of baptism and communion were offered to her as she sat propped up with pillows in her bed. Teachers and schoolmates, standing and kneeling around the bed, "sang with subdued voices the sweet songs she loved, it seemed not far from the pearly gates."[12] Later that evening the school's chapel was filled, and many young students entered into a solemn covenant with God and one another, bringing to birth Bethany Congregational Church. Officials from the American Missionary Association were on hand to offer recognition and welcome and to celebrate communion with the new congregation.

"Education and Christianity have worked hand in hand in our denomination," said Forenza Chatmon, who has been a member of Bethany Church since 1972. Church members have recently taken a renewed interest in the children in a public housing project adjacent to the church. They've begun a mentoring program, exposing the children to elements of African American history and culture, including the spirituals. They also host a very active quilting ministry, giving the quilts as gifts or auctioning them and donating the proceeds to charities. "For the future, we intend to be a vibrant force in this community as we once were," said Mr. Chatmon. "We intend to have an identity that we're proud of, and we intend to be a community that God will be pleased with."

Norma H. Scott joined the church in 1956, fresh out of nursing school at Grady Memorial Hospital in Atlanta. She was hired by Archibald Hospital in Thomasville, but when she arrived and the hospital supervisors took note of her race, they told her that the nursing dormitory was filled. Risking her job, Ms. Scott and three other members of Bethany Church spearheaded sit-ins at the hospital to desegregate its snack bar. She also participated in boycotts of local stores until they changed their discriminatory hiring practices.

Andrew Young, newly married and just graduated from Connecticut's Hartford Seminary, was the pastor of the church when Ms. Scott arrived. She laughed when she remembered her sister-in-law meeting her pastor and saying, "Oh, no, that's nothing but a little old boy." But Ms. Scott expressed gratitude half a century later that Rev. Young helped her young husband find work, driving him to job interviews around the area.

Andrew Young also served Evergreen Congregational United Church of Christ in nearby Beachton, spending two Sundays a month with each congregation. The Evergreen congregation had its beginnings in Alabama. In 1911, the church's minister, who had been trained in an American Missionary Association school, was found teaching his congregation to read, write, and count. Local whites instigated a terror campaign and gave him twenty-four hours to leave the county. He left—but took the whole congregation with him. In one night they all packed up and moved to Beachton, just above the Florida line. The only work available there was on plantations, but the adults wanted their children to be educated, and the AMA's Allen School was nearby.

Cherry B. Grohom of Evergreen Church remembered when Rev. Young would bring the children from Bethany Church for Bible School. "He had a little red car, and he would have it packed to the brim," she said. The children helped during the day with chores around the farm where Ms. Grohom was raised and studied the Bible at night. Rev. Young also reached out to older youth in the communities, providing popular social and religious activities. "The church always taught you that you could do anything or be anything you wanted to be," said Ms. Grohom, who attended Talladega College with the church's encouragement.

Rev. Young's early sermons were modeled on his seminary training, until a deacon of the church told him, "Some of our folks don't trust a preacher with a whole lot of paper. The Lord doesn't need that paper to make Himself heard."[13] The young pastor offended some of the other local ministers by playing on the YMCA basketball team, one denouncing him from the pulpit for "running up and down some floor half naked."[14] And he temporarily alienated a few of his church's trustees when he proposed building an indoor toilet, after the church's outdoor toilet caved in a year after he arrived. Through thorough research, he learned that an indoor toilet could be built less expensively, but his proposal was unanimously defeated. His eyes were opened to the realities that indoor toilets were considered a luxury and that several of the trustees did not have them in their homes. Lessons learned in his first churches—about faith, the effects of racism, and the precarious lives of his congregation of mostly tenant farmers—served Rev. Young well as he moved on to work with the National Council of Churches and become a leader in the Southern Christian Leadership Conference.

Evergreen Church member Martha Carter was a high school student in 1968, when she was "drafted" out of an all-black school to attend the local white school. It was a very difficult time for her. Both classmates and teachers were often cruel. On the school bus, many of the students "would rather stand up than sit in the seat with you," she said. Insults were hurled at her regularly, fist fights broke out occasionally, and she was made to feel unwelcome at football games, the prom, and other events that high school students usually look forward to. "You learned how to deal with it, and how to live it . . . and you tried to learn as much as you could," said Ms. Carter. It was all worth it, she said, to move from the African American school, where there were "raggedy books, and not enough for the students," to the white school, where they had "books galore, new books—so new you could smell them." Her family and the church helped her through the difficulty. "I had to rise above that, and I did that with the guidance of the people at the church . . . They continued to encourage me and pray that I would make it through high school. I definitely give credit to the members of the church for believing in me."

Adella Clark, a longtime member of Evergreen Church, also remembered difficult times when she was growing up, as well as the Harvest Home Festival that took place every November when she was young. People didn't have money to support the church, so they would bring "sacks of all kinds of things that they grew," she said. Her father always planted an extra field of corn, and whatever he earned from selling it went to the church. "My dad would always quote 'Silver and gold have I none, but such as I have . . . '—and that's what he would bring: corn and meal, and chickens. And (other church members) would kill hogs and bring a portion of that." When asked if Artis Johnson, who has served as pastor of the church since 1974, gets paid that way, Ms. Clark laughed and said, "We like to just cut him a check."

Rev. Johnson has continued the church's rich heritage of dedication to children and youth, who participate actively in all aspects of the church's life. In addition to the programs the church offers, Rev. Johnson and his wife, Myrtle Johnson, have been foster or adoptive parents to thirteen children. According to Rev. Johnson, Evergreen Church is on "a journey, as Isaiah says, 'untrod, unknown'; but in the end the results will count . . . I tell my white brothers and white sisters, and black brothers and black sisters, that we are all God's children . . . And on this journey you've got to continue to study, you've got to continue to improve, your walk has got to line up with your talk. And most of all, you've got to learn how to empower others to act when we are gone."

Many miles north of Thomasville, in a decidedly different geographical space of Georgia, is Rush Memorial United Church of Christ. Organized in 1913, the church sits on the edge of the Atlanta University Center, ringed by Spelman College, Morehouse College, and the Interdenominational Theological Center—all prestigious, predominantly African American institutions in urban Atlanta.

During the civil rights era, Rush Memorial Church was uniquely situated to offer meeting space and other forms of support to Atlanta's growing student movement, known as the Committee on Appeal for Human Rights. The committee provided leadership in a campaign that registered five thousand voters in one month and successfully desegregated more than seventy Atlanta lunch counters, restaurants, theaters, and stores. NAACP Chairman Julian Bond, and Children's Defense Fund Founder and President Marian Wright Edelman, along with other civic leaders, got their start in political work in the Atlanta student movement.

Alethea Boone, who was the wife of Rev. Joe Boone, the pastor of Rush Memorial at the time, explained how the students came to meet at the church: "Lonnie King had been elected the president of the student group of the Atlanta University Center. Things were getting a little hot, so (the university president) called Lonnie and told him to get those students quieted down . . . So Lonnie was coming down the street, and Joe was putting the numbers out there on the bulletin board, and they spoke. Joe asked him how things were going, and Lonnie told him that the president said they had to disband, that they couldn't meet on the school grounds. Joe said, 'No problem, you just come on right here' . . . A lot of the ministers and congregations wouldn't let them have all the rabble rousing going on at their churches. So Joe said they could have the rabble-rousing here."

Ms. Boone was a member of the Interdenominational Ministerial Wives Alliance, which offered support to civil rights protesters in jail. Spelman College students made strides toward desegregating a downtown Atlanta shoe store with the group's aid. African Americans weren't allowed to sit down to try on shoes, but several students sat in the white section of the store and insisted. Befuddled clerks brought them shoes, and the women students kept sending them back, asking for a different size, style, color.

They tied up the business until police came and took them to jail. Ms. Boone made sure they all had soap and toothpaste for their stay. She explained: "I had two children, and I didn't walk the picket lines, but all the things I could do behind the scenes, I did. My husband would bring the (movement) workers home. 'Alethea, fix these folks some food'—like I had Jesus's power. So I would go to the store for 'five loaves and a couple of fish.' I'd go to the store and I'd buy a great big cabbage for a quarter, and a fryer for a dollar, and I'd buy about five white potatoes, a big thing of lemonade. And I would stew that chicken, fix those potatoes—you know how you do—spread them out on the plate with a big thing of cornbread, and make that lemonade real sweet. And they were very happy. A lot of us did that."

Operation Breadbasket, the relief arm of the Southern Christian Leadership Conference, met at the church until the SCLC acquired its offices on Auburn Avenue. Rush Memorial Church organized the first African American Boy Scout troop in Atlanta. During the Vietnam War, Morehouse students who were conscientious objectors to the military draft found refuge there. The college's president expelled them from school. In protest, they pitched a tent on Morehouse land. When the college threatened to put them in jail, they moved their tent to a vacant lot by the church. For the weeks of their protest encampment, they cooked over an open fire, used the church's restroom facilities, and received other forms of support from the congregation. A generation later, when several of Atlanta's children turned up murdered, the Missing and Murdered Children's Campaign was launched from Rush Memorial.

Members are proud of their courageous legacy and the impact the church has had in almost a century of existence. They have hopes of renewing their connection with the vibrant community that surrounds them. "We don't want to live in the past," reflected Pastor Lawrence E. Calbert Sr., "but we do want to learn from it."

Not far from Rush Memorial, at the corner of Courtland Street and John Wesley Dobbs Avenue in downtown Atlanta, is First Congregational United Church of Christ, the second church established in the South by the American Missionary Association. Founded on May 27, 1867, the initially integrated congregation worshiped in the chapel of the AMA's Storrs School. In reaction to growing racial tensions during Reconstruction, a separate white church was established in 1882 (now Central Congregational United Church of Christ).

Storrs School, the precursor of Atlanta University, was begun when Rev. Frederick Ayer, who had been an AMA missionary among the Ojibway nation in Minnesota, joined with James Tate and Grandison B. Daniels, former slaves who had started a small school. The three established a second classroom in an abandoned railroad boxcar, which the American Missionary Association purchased for $310. A former Confederate commissary building that was moved from Chattanooga to Atlanta provided the first permanent school building. When a Cincinnati Congregational church, pastored by Rev. H. M. Storrs, gave a generous contribution, the school was bestowed with his name.

Amy Williams, known for her competence and compassion, served as the principal of Storrs School for seventeen years. Years after she left, a former student was asked if she remembered Ms. Williams. Her face lit up as she said, "Oh yes; she gave me my first Bible."[15] Ms. Williams walked miles to check on her students. When a colleague accompanying her one evening urged her to return home, she replied, "I must go on a mile further to the home of a poor boy who ran away and has been sleeping in my schoolroom two nights, because his father beats him so he does not dare go home."[16] That boy, John W. Whittaker, graduated in 1884 and became a pastor, serving First Congregational Church in New Orleans. When her health became a concern and she returned north, Ms. Williams wrote, "My heart just aches to go back South. Every other work seems insignificant."[17]

The school was determined to sound for its students "a constant call to become learners of Christ," according to Edmund Asa Ware, an education superintendent with the Freedmen's Bureau who became the first president of Atlanta University.[18] "The children in school have been deeply moved, and for many days, of their own impulse, a band of thirty or more of them devoted the half-hour of recess to a prayer-meeting under their own direction, giving up the opportunity to play and eat their lunch," wrote C. W. Francis, a colleague of Ware.[19]

One brave mother, Harriet Lynch Wright, walked almost two hundred miles from Cuthbert, Georgia, to Atlanta, with three children in tow so that her son Richard could attend Storrs. A year after its founding, General O. O. Howard addressed the school's pupils on the importance of education. When he asked what he should tell his friends about the students when he returned to New England, young Richard Wright stood proudly and declared, "Tell them we are rising!"[20]

Richard Wright graduated from Atlanta University in 1876. He went on to become one of the most influential educators in the post-Reconstruction era, giving testimony before the U.S. Senate Committee on Education and Labor regarding the historical contributions of African Americans to religion, math, and culture. John Greenleaf Whittier immortalized young Wright's declaration of confidence with a poem called "Howard at Atlanta":

O black boy of Atlanta!
But half was spoken;
The slave's chains and the master's
Alike are broken;
The one curse of the races
Held both in tether;
They are rising—all are rising—
The black and white together.[21]

Another student of note was James Weldon Johnson, who studied race relations at Atlanta University under W. E. B. DuBois and graduated from the school in 1894. Johnson became a poet, a diplomat, an educator, an activist, and a leader in the Harlem Renaissance. With his brother John Rosamond, he composed "Lift Every Voice and Sing," which came to be known as the Black National Anthem.

Storrs School hosted First Congregational Church in its early years. In 1894, Henry Hugh Proctor, a graduate of Fisk University and Yale Divinity School, became the church's first African American pastor. While still a student at Fisk, Proctor was called upon to introduce the great temperance lecturer J. C. Price. When Dr. Price rose to speak, he declared, "If I could make the impression on this audience which my friend has made in my introduction to you I would count myself an orator."[22]

Under Dr. Proctor's quarter century of visionary leadership and eloquent preaching, the church flourished, its membership growing from one hundred to one thousand. After a race riot devastated Atlanta in 1906, Dr. Proctor led efforts to restore order to the divided city and was instrumental in establishing the Atlanta Racial Commission. A tribute written in 1914, titled "The Church that Saved a City," recounted the despair that African Americans felt after the riot that Atlanta would never accept them: "There will be no opportunity for us in Atlanta from now on; the disease is checked, but there remains the wound, ugly, glaring, a bitter reminder forever that we are different, that we are set behind the veil, that we may go thus far and no farther. Whatever we have gathered together here that cannot go must be sacrificed, for we must seek out a new city where there is no scar."[23]

Dr. Proctor refused to accept this posture of defeatism. "Let's show them the men we are," he declared to Atlanta's African American community. "Let's begin by erecting a church as has never been erected by colored men before, an institutional church embodying all that is modern and approved in church work. Let that be the answer to the riot; let's begin now."[24]

The ground breaking for the church building, a magnificent stone structure, took place in May 1908. Booker T. Washington, who had helped to secure financial resources, was the guest of honor. The building, listed as a landmark on the National Register of Historic Places, was hailed by two U.S. presidents who made visits, William Howard Taft and Theodore Roosevelt.

First Congregational Church, called "one of the most progressive centers of Christian social action in the nation,"[25] was believed to be the first African American "institutional church" in the world.[26] It ran a kindergarten and offered classes in business education and domestic science. It contained a gymnasium, a model kitchen, and the only lending library for African Americans in Atlanta. The church organized an employment bureau, classes for the blind, two prison missions, and six neighborhood missions throughout the city. It sponsored a home for young African American women working in Atlanta and a "Trouble Department," whose mission was to "render any service possible to those in trouble."[27]

The church made available to the community its auditorium, the largest in the South at the time—"with a seating capacity of 1,000; provided with grand pipe organ; heated by steam; lighted by electricity; open for any good thing designed for the betterment of the race."[28] It hosted annual music festivals for African Americans in Atlanta and across Georgia. In a time of entrenched segregation, when access was denied in other quarters, First Congregational Church provided virtually every service that the African American community needed.

Many of the church's members are part of the third or fourth generation in their families to attend First Congregational. Katie J. Daniels, who was christened more than ninety years ago with water that Dr. Proctor brought back from the Holy Land, remembered that when the church was built, the pews were soaked in water so they could be curved to face the altar and the minister. First Congregational provided a trough under a shade tree on the corner for horses, and a water fountain close to the building for passersby who wanted a drink—the only integrated water fountain in Atlanta at the time. The bulletin board in front of the church was known as "The Wayside Pulpit" then, according to Ms. Daniels. The streetcar would stop at the corner, and people would read the popular Bible verses and proverbs posted there, many of them later sending letters to thank the church for its brave witness on that corner.

Ms. Daniels also recalled lying flat on her back on the center pew as a child and looking up into the church's magnificent dome at the stained glass window there. "It's full of angels and color," she said. The Dome of Charity window honors AMA Secretary Michael E. Strieby. A unique Emancipation window in the sanctuary depicts Abraham Lincoln, and the Gethsemane window—donated by St. John's Congregational Church in Springfield, Massachusetts, where John Brown worshiped for three years while a fiber merchant in that city—is dedicated to the fiery abolitionist. But most of the windows honor AMA history and personnel. Talladega College students donated a window, and Fisk University students dedicated one in the balcony that depicts Jubilee Hall to Erastus M. Cravath. Others honor Amy Williams and Edmund Asa Ware for their contributions to Storrs School and Atlanta University.

Appreciation for the AMA is reflected in the lives of the church's members as well as its windows. "I thank God for the American Missionary Association," said Dosh R. Jackson, who graduated from Ballard Normal School, an AMA institution in Macon, Georgia, in 1928. "I had dedicated teachers . . . They gave their lives to become teachers in the American Missionary Association." Tuition at the school was three dollars a month, which was hard to come by then. "I used to fire the furnace," Mr. Jackson said. "I kept the coal furnace going all winter long. And every morning at time for school, I'd go up in the tower and ring the bell. That's the way I earned my three-dollar tuition."

Richard Grigsby, an Atlanta attorney and member of First Congregational, recalled hearing about the AMA from his father, J. Howard Grigsby, who passed away at the age of ninety-two in late 2002. One of twelve children, the elder Mr. Grigsby attended the AMA's Brewer Academy in Greenwood, South Carolina. "His father claimed to have invented the trailer," said his son. "He put a crossbeam on wheels and loaded a piano crate on top. Every fall he loaded it up with cows, pigs, and chickens. Dad milked cows and collected eggs every morning." School officials recorded his contributions and credited them to his tuition. And every spring he carried the livestock home again.

Homer C. McEwen Sr. served the church for thirty-two years, beginning in 1947. Rev. McEwen faced his first major challenge when an influential group of white businessmen approached the congregation with a lucrative offer to purchase the church building and property. In exchange, the church would have to relocate and surrender the name "First" to a local white congregation. Rev. McEwen persuaded the congregation to reject the offer.

Rev. McEwen had a strong ally in Rev. Edward M. Brown, who tirelessly gave decades of his life to desegregation work among students and congregations across the South. The two men worked to bring together members of Rush Memorial Church, Central Congregational Church, and First Congregational Church, matching people by their professions and encouraging meetings in one another's homes as a way of breaking down prejudices.

Racial barriers were being dismantled on the national level as well, as Congregational and Christian churches were merging with Evangelical and Reformed congregations to form the United Church of Christ in 1957. Rev. J. Taylor Stanley, who was superintendent of 215 African American congregations scattered over twelve states, and Rev. Erston M. Butterfield, who served 127 white churches in six states in the same capacity, were in the eye of the storm as the new denomination restructured its associations based on geography rather than race. For his role in the process, Rev. Butterfield received threats, faced a group of angry men with shotguns, and had a burning cross thrown on his windshield while he was driving one night near Anniston, Alabama.

First Congregational Church in Atlanta continued its legacy of activism by publicly protesting lynching. During the 1960s, the church sponsored mass meetings that led to the inclusion of African Americans on the Atlanta police force. In 1961 a boycott of downtown businesses was launched from the church. Andrew Young was a member of First Congregational Church while he was involved with the Southern Christian Leadership Conference, and after his service as Atlanta's mayor, in the U.S. Congress, and as ambassador to the United Nations, he served as minister for church renewal on the church's pastoral team from 1996 to 1999.

Given the congregation's commitment to mission and its embrace of African American music, it is not surprising that it called the multitalented Dwight Andrews as senior minister in 1999. Like Dr. Proctor, Dr. Andrews graduated from Yale Divinity School. In addition to pastoring the church, he is a professor of music at Emory University and an award-winning composer and jazz instrumentalist, who has served as the musical director for several Broadway productions of Pulitzer Prize-winning August Wilson's plays. The church is packed when quarterly Jazz Vespers are held there.

Under Dr. Andrews's leadership, the congregation has grown in number and diversity, youth programs have increased, a capital campaign for restoring and expanding the church has been launched, and outreach to the greater Atlanta community has taken new directions. "Through struggle and strain, and commitment and love, this church was born," said Marguerite Simon, who has taught Sunday school at First Congregational since 1943. "This church is strong as the Rock of Gibraltar," she stated proudly. Its founders "built a building that would stand and withstand."

Elizabeth Mitchell Clement, a church member who served as minister of church life and education on First Congregational Church's pastoral team during the late 1990s, spoke of the church's history and future. Like the ancient Israelites seeking a home after release from bondage, soon after General Sherman and his troops destroyed Atlanta in 1864, people "came amidst the smell of a burning city, so deep was their hunger for that strange promised place of God." Some, reflected Rev. Clement, "were drawn from the North, to see the world differently. And some came from the region to *be* that difference. They were all drawn by the promise of milk and honey, the sweet abundance of God's land."

On the corner of Courtland Street and John Wesley Dobbs Avenue, they "put the work of God into hearts and hands and heads and homes," said Rev. Clement. "They were told, 'The land you are about to enter is not like the one you left.'" With courage, they persisted in this new land, so that now, according to Rev. Clement, "in the doorway of the twenty-first century, their story is still our story. And we remain on that corner the suggestion of God's promised goodness."

The biblical book of Nehemiah tells of the destruction of the ancient city of Jerusalem, its wall broken down, its gates destroyed by fire. When Nehemiah, a Jewish official, heard news of the devastation, he sat down and wept, then fasted and prayed for days, and finally went to the city to ask the people to rebuild the wall. When their enemies heard about their plan, they mocked and ridiculed the people. "Will they revive the stones out of the heaps of rubbish—and burned ones at that?" they asked disparagingly. (Neh. 4:2) They hurled insults at the builders, called the people "feeble," and declared that a fox could break down their wall. But the workers persisted, because, as the scripture declares, "The people had a mind to build." (Neh. 4:6)

Those words are inscribed on the cornerstone of First Congregational Church. Amid the charred ruins that were Atlanta—its walls destroyed, its buildings burned—a school and church emerged from cinders and ashes. In other settings of equal devastation, all across the South, the story repeated itself, as longing and dedication met compassion and faith. South and North, black and white, rural and urban joined together, overcoming ridicule and hostility, tearing down walls of prejudice and building up living monuments of hope. The American Missionary Association story stands as a testimony to the greatness that can be achieved when people have a mind to build.

Epilogue

According to ancient mythology, Zeus, ruler of the Greek gods, announced that he would offer the prize of immortality to the person he judged the most useful to humankind. Competitors for the coveted reward thronged the court on Mt. Olympus. In came the soldier who risked his life for his country and the philanthropist whose deeds made him universally beloved, the artist who bestowed the gift of beauty and the musician who lifted the people's spirits. An old man looked on with interest to see who would walk away with the prize. Zeus inquired who he was. "I am only a looker-on," replied the sage. "These competitors were my pupils." "Then," declared Zeus, "this is my judgment: crown the faithful teacher with the prize awarded to the most useful to humankind!"[1]

Though few people throughout history have been acquainted with the extraordinary story of the late-nineteenth-century missionary teachers, these indeed have won immortality. With raw courage and sheer determination, they transformed the social landscape of the nation at a time of crisis and launched a legacy of hope and possibility that continues to this day. "A worthier band has never furnished theme or song for sage or bard. Their courage, their self-sacrificing devotion, sincerity of purpose, and purity of motive, and their unshaken faith in God were their pass keys to the hearts of those for whom they came to labor," wrote one of their devoted students more than a century ago. "It is said that gratitude is the fairest flower which sheds its perfume in the human heart. As long as the human heart beats in grateful repose to benefits received," he continued, these teachers shall not lack "a monument of living ebony and bronze." The student reflected appreciatively, "They gave the highest proof that the nineteenth century, at least, has afforded, that Christianity has not yet degenerated into a dead formula and barren intellectualism, but it is a living, vital power."[2]

That vitality persisted into the twentieth century, with the American Missionary Association upholding its noble witness for more than a century and a half. In its latter years, it continued to shine the light of justice on a variety of concerns: supporting farm workers and women coal miners, joining the effort to combat AIDS, establishing a theological seminary in Puerto Rico and an office that celebrated the arts and religion. Among its enduring gifts is the Amistad Research Center, initially housed at Fisk University and now at Tulane University in New Orleans, with more than ten million original documents, including correspondence from the Tappan brothers about the *Amistad* event, hundreds of letters from the early missionary teachers, and several collections celebrating African American history. The story is being preserved for future generations.

In 1996, in celebration of the AMA's 150th anniversary, several leaders in the American Missionary Association and the United Church of Christ gathered for a conversation about the importance of the AMA's witness. They commended its sense of mission, its compassion toward people perishing on the margins of society, and its commitment to empowerment. At its heart, reflected Thomas E. Dipko, the American Missionary Association called the nation back to its founding vision, affirming that all people are endowed with human rights. "It was always a vision about every-day, ordinary people and the kind of justice that they were entitled to every ordinary day of their lives. It was about the kind of human community we are entitled to be embraced by."[3]

A motivating factor among the early AMA leaders, according to F. Allison Phillips, was "the need to 'speak truth in love,' to name unjust issues. They refused to maintain the status quo . . . AMA founders put the issue as a challenge to God's people: whether American churches have the moral power to meet the moral prob-lems of America."

In our era, the same question can be asked of our communities of faith. Rhetoric is rampant and rancorous about the "divided nation" in which we live. Racism and economic injustice persist, part of the enduring legacy of slavery. Once again—still—the times summon us to claim the liberating power of education and faith, the moral force of justice; to draw inspiration and strength from the stories of those who went before us, showing a way where there seemed to be no way.

In 1988, when Jesse Jackson was a candidate for president of the United States, Cleo Fields, then a twenty-five-year-old state sen-ator from Louisiana, addressed the Democratic National Convention. He offered this observation: "Booker T. Washington started to teach so Rosa Parks could take her seat. Rosa Parks took her seat so Fannie Lou Hamer could take her stand. Fannie Lou

Hamer took her stand so Martin Luther King Jr. could march. Martin Luther King marched so Jesse Jackson could run."[4] Every movement for change is carried on the shoulders of the daring individuals who blazed a path for those who would come later and pick up the journey, extending the reach of justice a little farther. And so the story continues.

We have in our history, in the last years of the nineteenth century, a witness to the power of living faith that provides both inspiration and invitation. A hundred years ago, Booker T. Washington said of those brave souls at the heart of the educational campaign, who took their stand and beckon us to match their courage: "The history of the world fails to show a higher, purer, and more unselfish class of men and women . . . Whenever it is written—and I hope it will be—the part that the Yankee teachers played in the education of the Negroes immediately after the war will make one of the most thrilling parts of the history of this country."[5]

Indeed.

Notes

Introduction

1. Charles Johnson, Patricia Smith, and the WGBH Series Research Team, *Africans in America* (New York: Harcourt Brace & Company, 1998), 29.
2. Howard Zinn, *A People's History of the United States* (New York: HarperCollins Publishers, 1980), 24.
3. Augustus Field Beard, *A Crusade of Brotherhood* (Boston: The Pilgrim Press, 1909), 121.
4. Joe M. Richardson, *Christian Reconstruction* (Athens: The University of Georgia Press, 1986), 5.
5. Beard, *A Crusade of Brotherhood*, 123-124.
6. Richardson, *Christian Reconstruction*, 11.
7. Beard, *A Crusade of Brotherhood*, 124.
8. W. E. B. DuBois, *The Souls of Black Folk* (New York: Vintage Books, 1990), 76.

Chapter 1

1. Howard Jones, *Mutiny on the Amistad* (New York: Oxford University Press, 1987), 4.
2. Helen Kromer, *Amistad* (Cleveland: The Pilgrim Press, 1973), 9-14.
3. Connecticut Historical Society, Amistad Exhibit, from deposition, September 20, 1839, Hartford, quoted in *New York Morning Herald*, September 23.
4. Jones, *Mutiny on the Amistad*, 15.
5. Ibid., 24-25.
6. Kromer, *Amistad*, 31.
7. Ibid., 33.
8. Amistad Research Center archives, #F1-4595.
9. "Amistad: The Story," www.amistadamerica.org.
10. New Haven Historical Society, description accompanying portrait of Sengbe.
11. Jones, *Mutiny on the Amistad*, 66.
12. Kromer, *Amistad*, 12.
13. Connecticut Historical Society, Amistad Exhibit.
14. Jones, *Mutiny on the Amistad*, 97.
15. Kromer, *Amistad*, 72.
16. Arthur Abraham, "The Amistad Revolt," pamphlet.
17. Kromer, *Amistad*, 78.
18. Ibid., 81.
19. Amistad Research Center archives, #F1-4990.
20. www.amistadamerica.org.
21. Fred L. Brownlee, *New Day Ascending* (Boston: The Pilgrim Press, 1946), 22.
22. Connecticut Historical Society, Amistad Exhibit.
23. "The Amistad Event," pamphlet.
24. Connecticut Historical Society, Amistad Exhibit.
25. Howard Jones, speech, "The Amistad Education Legacy: National Symposium III," February 21, 2002, Alabama State University.
26. www.amistadamerica.org.
27. www.ucc.org.
28. Kromer, *Amistad*, 97.

Chapter 2

1. Brownlee, *New Day Ascending*, 270.
2. Jacqueline Jones, *Soldiers of Light and Love* (Athens: The University of Georgia Press, 1992), 97.
3. "Brief History of Dixwell Avenue Congregational United Church of Christ, Inc.," pamphlet.
4. "Our Goodly Heritage," pamphlet, 2.
5. *The American Missionary*, October 1846, quoted in Brownlee, *New Day Ascending*, 258.
6. Brownlee, *New Day Ascending*, 259.
7. *The American Missionary*, October 1846.
8. Brownlee, *New Day Ascending*, 23.
9. Richardson, *Christian Reconstruction*, 88.
10. Brownlee, *New Day Ascending*, 98-99.
11. John G. Fee, *An Autobiography*, 14, quoted in Brownlee, *New Day Ascending*, 82.
12. Brownlee, *New Day Ascending*, 88.
13. Ibid., 85.
14. Ibid., 87.
15. Ibid.
16. "History of the American Missionary Association," September 1874 report, Amistad Research Center archives, 8.
17. Ibid., 9.
18. Brownlee, *New Day Ascending*, 88.
19. Ibid.
20. Ibid., 92.

21. Beard, *A Crusade of Brotherhood*, 110.
22. Ibid., 112.
23. Ibid.
24. Ibid., 113.
25. Ibid., 116.
26. www.tulane.edu.
27. Beard, *A Crusade of Brotherhood*, 117-118.

Chapter 3

1. Willie Lee Rose, *Rehearsal for Reconstruction* (New York: Vintage Books, 1964), xix.
2. Ibid., 7.
3. Ibid., 117.
4. Ibid., 10.
5. Edith M. Dabbs, *Sea Island Diary* (reprint, Avery Research Institute archives), 113.
6. Elizabeth Jacoway, *Yankee Missionaries in the South* (Baton Rouge: The Louisiana State University Press, 1980), 24.
7. Ibid., 118.
8. Rose, *Rehearsal for Reconstruction*, xiii.
9. Ibid., 12.
10. Ibid., 109.
11. William S. Pollitzer, *The Gullah People and Their African Heritage* (Athens: The University of Georgia Press, 1999), 182.
12. Rose, *Rehearsal for Reconstruction*, 20.
13. Ibid., 25.
14. Ibid., 26.
15. Ibid., 30.
16. Ibid., 31.
17. Ibid., 34.
18. Ibid., 35.
19. Ibid., 45.
20. Ibid., 47.
21. Ibid., 55.
22. Ibid., 66.
23. Ibid., 173.
24. Margaret Washington Creel, *A Peculiar People* (New York: New York University Press, 1988), 192.
25. Jacoway, *Yankee Missionaries in the South*, 30.
26. Rose, *Rehearsal for Reconstruction*, 233.
27. Jacoway, *Yankee Missionaries in the South*, 48.
28. Rose, *Rehearsal for Reconstruction*, 233.
29. Ibid.
30. Ibid., 220.

31. Ray Allen Billington, *The Journal of Charlotte L. Forten*, (New York: W. W. Norton & Company, 1953), 139.
32. Ibid., 142.
33. Ibid., 144.
34. Ibid., 145.
35. Ibid., 164.
36. Ibid., 146.
37. Ibid., 177.
38. Ibid., 11.
39. Art Rosenbaum, *Shout Because You're Free*, (Athens: The University of Georgia Press, 1998), 1.
40. Ibid., 3.
41. Billington, *The Journal of Charlotte L. Forten*, 169.
42. Ibid., 203.
43. Ibid., 181.
44. Ibid., 160.
45. Ibid., 187.
46. Ibid., 191.
47. Ibid., 203.
48. Ibid., 207.
49. Ibid., 210.
50. Ibid., 171.
51. Dabbs, *Sea Island Diary*, 172-174.
52. Jacoway, *Yankee Missionaries in the South*, 87.
53. Billington, *The Journal of Charlotte L. Forten*, 175.

Chapter 4

1. Rose, *Rehearsal for Reconstruction*, 244-247.
2. Ibid., 223.
3. Ibid., 249.
4. Ibid., 259.
5. Billington, *The Journal of Charlotte L. Forten*, 213.
6. Ibid., 214.
7. Ibid., 217.
8. Ibid., 215.
9. Rose, *Rehearsal for Reconstruction*, 258.
10. Ibid., 269-270.
11. Ibid., 283.
12. Ibid., 286.
13. Ibid., 290.
14. Ibid., 291.
15. Ibid., 294.
16. Ibid., 292.
17. Ibid., 316.
18. Ibid., 317.
19. Ibid., 321.
20. Ibid., 322.
21. Ibid., 325.
22. Ibid., 331.
23. Ibid., 337.
24. Ibid., 339.
25. Ibid., 343.

26. Ibid.
27. Ibid., 360.
28. Ibid., 346.
29. Ibid., 347.
30. Ibid.
31. Ibid., 348.
32. Ibid., 385.
33. Ibid., 387.
34. Ibid., 386.
35. Ibid., 405.

Chapter 5

1. Buddy Sullivan, *Early Days on the Georgia Tidewater* (Darien, Georgia: McIntosh County Board of Commissioners, 1990), 183.
2. Johnson, Smith, and WGBH Research Team, *Africans in America*, 357.
3. Ibid., 359.
4. Ibid., 433.
5. Ibid., 434.
6. William S. McFeely, *Sapelo's People* (New York: W. W. Norton & Company, 1994), 99-100.
7. Joseph T. Glatthaar, *The March to the Sea and Beyond* (Baton Rouge: Louisiana State University Press, 1985), 6.
8. Ibid., 118.
9. Ibid., 74.
10. Rose, *Rehearsal for Reconstruction*, 332.
11. William T. Richardson, letter, January 25, 1865, Amistad Research Center archives.
12. Jones, *Soldiers of Light and Love*, 74.
13. Ibid., 75.
14. Brownlee, *New Day Ascending*, 101.
15. "Our Goodly Heritage," pamphlet, 6.
16. Jones, *Soldiers of Light and Love*, 2.
17. Richardson, *Christian Reconstruction*, 167.
18. J. E. Twitchell, "The Amistad Captives and the Origin and Growth of the American Missionary Association," 6.
19. Jones, *Soldiers of Light and Love*, 32.
20. Wayne E. Reilly, ed., *Sarah Jane Foster* (Charlottesville: University Press of Virginia, 1990), 14-15.
21. Allis Wolfe, "Women Who Dared," dissertation, ARC archives, 16-17.
22. Joe M. Richardson, "American Missionary Association Teachers in the South During the Civil War and Reconstruction," *New Conversations* reprint, 9.
23. Donald Brown, letter, January 20, 1865, ARC archives.
24. J. Warner, letter, October 9, 1867, ARC archives.
25. Sophia E. Russell, letter, November 12, 1867, ARC archives.
26. E. B. Montague, letter, May 21, 1868, ARC archives.
27. Unsigned letter, 1874, ARC archives.
28. ARC archives #20939.
29. Richardson, *Christian Reconstruction*, 13.
30. Wolfe, "Women Who Dared," 167.
31. Unsigned letter, January 8, 1868, ARC archives.
32. Richardson, *Christian Reconstruction*, 174.
33. Ibid., 171.
34. Ibid.
35. AMA 1874 annual report, 59.
36. Ellen E. Adlington, letter, March 3, 1868, ARC archives.
37. AMA 1874 annual report, 70.
38. A. Knighton Stanley, *The Children Is Crying* (New York: The Pilgrim Press, 1979), 143-144.
39. Unsigned letter, March 3, 1868, ARC archives.
40. Jones, *Soldiers of Light and Love*, 176.
41. S. W. Magill, letter, April 21, 1865, ARC archives.
42. Jones, *Soldiers of Light and Love*, 180.
43. ARC archives, #48 and #49.
44. Jacqueline Jones, "The Great Opportunity," dissertation, ARC archives, 69.
45. Ibid.
46. Richardson, *Christian Reconstruction*, 179.
47. Wolfe, "Women Who Dared," 107.
48. Richardson, "American Missionary Association Teachers," 7.
49. Wolfe, "Women Who Dared," 105.
50. Jones, *Soldiers of Light and Love*, 29.
51. Richardson, "American Missionary Association Teachers," 11.
52. Wolfe, "Women Who Dared," 104-105.
53. AMA 1874 annual report.
54. Wolfe, "Women Who Dared," 111.
55. Richardson, *Christian Reconstruction*, 137.
56. "Missionary Milestones," pamphlet, 54
57. Reilly, *Sarah Jane Foster*, 13.
58. Unnamed AMA secretary, letter, 1869, ARC archives.
59. Unnamed teacher, letter, 1870, ARC archives.
60. Jones, "The Great Opportunity, 448
61. William S. Clark, letter, November 19, 1867, ARC archives.

62. AMA 1874 annual report, 54.
63. Jones, "The Great Opportunity," 239.
64. "Does Cotton Valley Pay?" AMA pamphlet.
65. M. L. Roth, letter, May 15, 1867, ARC archives # 20700-02.
66. Douglas G. Risley, letter, August 6, 1867, ARC archives #20818.
67. W. L. Eaton, letter, September 21, 1865, ARC archives.
68. Jones, "The Great Opportunity," 239.
69. Wolfe, 108.
70. James D. Anderson, *The Education of Blacks in the South, 1860-1935* (Chapel Hill: The University of North Carolina Press, 1988), 10.
71. AMA 1874 annual report, 61.
72. Wolfe, "Women Who Dared," 156.
73. Richardson, *Christian Reconstruction*, 13-14.
74. Wolfe, "Women Who Dared," 158.
75. Ibid.
76. Richardson, *Christian Reconstruction*, 37.
77. Ibid., 49.
78. Ibid., 38.
79. AMA 1874 annual report, 59.
80. Stanley, *The Children Is Crying*, 42.
81. Jones, "The Great Opportunity," 142.
82. Ibid.
83. Richardson, *Christian Reconstruction*, 22.
84. Ibid., 191.
85. Clara Merritt DeBoer, "Be Jubilant My Feet," dissertation, 1994, quoted in AMA anniversary calendar.
86. *The American Missionary*, September 1876.
87. "A Brief Timeline for the AMA Story," *New Conversations*, Summer 1996, p. 6.
88. Brownlee, *New Day Ascending*, 275.
89. George A. Wilcox, "A Sketch of the Life of Mr. Daniel Hand," 11-12.
90. Booker T. Washington, *Up From Slavery* (New York: Signet Classic, 2000), 1.
91. Ibid., 36.
92. David Levering Lewis and Henry Holt, "W. E. B. DuBois," *Biography of a Race*, Volume 1:1868-1919.
93. Washington, *Up From Slavery*, 153,155-156.
94. Ibid., xiv.
95. Brownlee, *New Day Ascending*,181.
96. Ibid., 167.
97. Richardson, *Christian Reconstruction*, 139.
98. Ibid., 57.
99. Ibid., 259.
100. DuBois, *The Souls of Black Folk*, 24, 76.
101. "Andersonville," pamphlet.
102. Judith A. Shearman, letter, May 13, 1867, ARC archives.
103. William T. Richardson, letter, January 25, 1865, ARC archives.

Chapter 6

1. Maxine D. Jones and Joe M. Richardson, *Talladega College* (Tuscaloosa: The University of Alabama Press, 1990), 15.
2. Ibid., 2.
3. Ibid., 1.
4. Beard, *A Crusade of Brotherhood*, 173.
5. Ibid., 174.
6. "Talladega College Historic District," pamphlet.
7. Jones and Richardson, *Talladega College*, 4.
8. Ibid., 51.
9. Ibid., 9.
10. Ibid., 95.
11. Ibid., 56.
12. Ibid., 34.
13. Ibid., 6.
14. Beard, *A Crusade of Brotherhood*, 175.
15. Jones and Richardson, *Talladega College*, 14.
16. Ibid., 15.
17. Ibid., 27.
18. AMA 1874 annual report, 36.
19. Jones and Richardson, *Talladega College*, 49.
20. Ibid., 53.
21. Ibid., 25.
22. Ibid., 39.
23. Ibid., 57.
24. Ibid., 63.
25. Ibid., 65.
26. Ibid., 89.
27. Ibid., x.
28. Ibid., 103.
29. Ibid., 107.
30. Ibid., 93.
31. Ibid., 111.
32. Ibid., 119.
33. Ibid., 113.
34. Ibid., 124.
35. Ibid., 121.
36. Ibid., 148.
37. Ibid., 145.
38. Ibid., 175.
39. Ibid., 194.
40. Ibid., 182.
41. Ibid.

42. "Birmingham's Racial Segregation Ordinances," pamphlet.
43. Cicely Savery, "Two Girls' Work," AMA pamphlet.

Chapter 7

1. Andrew Ward, *Dark Midnight When I Rise* (New York: Farrar, Straus and Giroux, 2000), 4.
2. Ibid., 5.
3. Ibid.
4. Peggy Robbins, "Saved by a Song," *The World & I*, February 1993, p. 411.
5. Ward, *Dark Midnight*, 5.
6. Ella Sheppard Moore, "Negro Womanhood: Its Past," 4.
7. Ward, *Dark Midnight*, 82.
8. Ibid., 53.
9. Ibid., 32.
10. Ibid., 37.
11. Ibid., 76.
12. Joe M. Richardson, *A History of Fisk University, 1865-1946* (The University of Alabama Press, 1980), 2-3.
13. Ibid., 3.
14. Richardson, *Fisk University*, 22.
15. Ibid.
16. AMA pamphlet, untitled, 6.
17. Ward, *Dark Midnight*, 110-111.
18. Ibid., 110.
19. Ibid., 113.
20. Herbert Fox Jr., "The Jubilees Forever!" *Nashville* reprint, 1.
21. Ward, *Dark Midnight*, 121.
22. Ibid., 23.
23. Ibid., 64.
24. Ibid., 81.
25. Ibid., 90.
26. Ibid., 119.
27. Ibid., 121.
28. Richardson, *Fisk University*, 26.
29. Ward, *Dark Midnight*, 126.
30. Ibid., 197.
31. Robbins, "Saved by a Song," 408.
32. Richardson, *Fisk University*, 28.
33. Ward, *Dark Midnight*, 132.
34. Ibid., 134.
35. Ibid., 135.
36. Robbins, "Saved by a Song," 409.
37. Fox, "The Jubilees Forever!" 1.
38. Richardson, *Fisk University*, 28.
39. Ward, *Dark Midnight*, 149.
40. Ibid., 153.
41. Fox, "The Jubilees Forever!" 2.
42. Ibid.
43. Ward, *Dark Midnight*, 156.
44. Ibid., 157.
45. Ibid., 165.
46. Ibid., 166.
47. Ibid., 168.
48. Ibid., 383.
49. Ibid., 168.
50. Richardson, *Fisk University*, 30.
51. Ward, 190-193.
52. Ibid., 286.
53. Ibid., 385.
54. Richardson, *Fisk University*, 33.
55. Ward, *Dark Midnight*, 407.
56. Ibid., 325.
57. Ibid., 391.
58. Fisk University, display, Nashville, TN.
59. Ward, *Dark Midnight*, 394.
60. Ibid., 187.
61. Ibid., 300.
62. Ibid., 374.
63. Richardson, *Fisk University*, 47.
64. Ward, *Dark Midnight*, 155.
65. Ibid., 157.
66. Richardson, *Fisk University*, 69.
67. Ibid., 72.
68. Ibid., 71.
69. Ibid., 66.
70. Ibid., 79.
71. Ibid., 84-87.
72. Ibid., 88.
73. Ibid., 50.
74. Ibid., 48.
75. Ibid., 92.
76. Ibid., 103.
77. Ibid., 119.
78. Ibid., 114.
79. Fisk University brochure (Nashville, TN), 7.
80. Richardson, *Fisk University*, 144.
81. John Lewis, *Walking with the Wind* (New York: Harcourt Brace & Company, 1998), 72.
82. Ibid., 102.
83. Ibid., 109.
84. Ibid., 111.
85. "Study at One of America's Truly Great Universities," Fisk University pamphlet (Nashville, TN), 6.
86. "The Lincoln Bible," pamphlet, Fisk University archives (Nashville, TN).
87. "After Forty-five Years," article, ARC archives #A1460.
88. Richardson, *Fisk University*, 27-28.
89. Fisk University, "Great Universities," 8.
90. DuBois, *Souls of Black Folk*, 138.
91. Ward, *Dark Midnight*, 202.

Chapter 8

1. Clarice T. Campbell and Oscar Allan Rogers Jr., *Mississippi: The View from Tougaloo* (Jackson: The University of Mississippi Press, 2002), 7.

2. Ibid., 18.
3. Ibid., 19.
4. Ibid., 16.
5. Ibid., 13.
6. Ibid., 30.
7. Ibid., 143.
8. Ibid., 37.
9. Ibid., 36.
10. Ibid., 38.
11. Ibid., 108.
12. Ibid., 60.
13. Ibid., 61.
14. Ibid.
15. Ibid., 68.
16. Ibid., 71.
17. Ibid., 82.
18. Ibid., 83.
19. Ibid., 87.
20. Ibid., 136.
21. Ibid, 98.
22. Ibid., 99.
23. Ibid., 101.
24. Ibid., 79.
25. Ibid., 81.
26. Ibid., 193.
27. Ibid., 93.
28. Ibid., 112.
29. Ibid., 116.
30. Ibid., 138.
31. Ibid., 126.
32. Ibid., 135.
33. Ibid., 165.
34. Ibid., 181.
35. Ibid., 198.
36. Ibid., 198.
37. Ibid., 206.
38. Ibid., 217.
39. Ibid., 217.
40. Ibid., 229.
41. Ibid., 230.
42. Ibid., 224.
43. Ibid., 277.
44. Ibid., 309.
45. Ibid., 239.
46. "The American Missionary Association Colleges," brochure.
47. Campbell and Rogers, *Mississippi*, 288.
48. Ibid, xii-xiv.

Chapter 9

1. Idella Childs, "Lincoln Normal School," reprint, 1.
2. Ibid., 2.
3. J. Taylor Stanley, *A History of Black Congregational Christian Churches of the South* (New York: United Church Press, 1978), 34.
4. *Where Once We Stood: The Lincoln School Story*, video (produced by the University of Alabama, 1989).
5. Brownlee, *New Day Ascending*, 124.
6. Judith Hillman Paterson, "To Teach the Negro," *Alabama Heritage*, Spring 1996, 6.
7. Ibid., 7.
8. Ibid., 17.
9. Johnnie Carr, speech, "The Amistad Education Legacy: National Symposium III," February 21, 2002, Alabama State University.
10. "Lincoln Normal High School History," pamphlet, p. 1.
11. Brownlee, *New Day Ascending*, 125.
12. *Where Once We Stood*.
13. Ibid.
14. Ibid.
15. Ibid.
16. Ibid.
17. Ibid.
18. Andrew Young, *An Easy Burden* (New York: HarperCollins Publishers, 1996), 352.
19. *Where Once We Stood*
20. Ibid.
21. Ibid.
22. Ibid.
23. Ibid.
24. Ibid.
25. Ibid.
26. Ibid.
27. Ibid.
28. Ibid.

Chapter 10

1. Ward, *Dark Midnight*, 126.
2. AMA 1904 annual report.
3. Ibid.
4. Ibid.
5. "Holding the Fort at Athens, Alabama," pamphlet.
6. "Articles of Faith," Trinity Congregational United Church of Christ archives, 3.
7. "By-laws," Trinity Church archives, 2.
8. "Homage to a Fruitful Heritage," reprint, 2.
9. Elma Bell, "Old School is Reborn as Budding Cultural Center," *The Birmingham News*, June 3, 1984.
10. "Homage," 2.
11. Jerry Fields, letter, 1980.

Chapter 11

1. *The American Missionary*, July 1896.
2. "Dawn in Dorchester," AMA pamphlet.
3. Ibid.

4. Ibid.
5. Ibid.
6. Ibid.
7. Ibid.
8. Floyd Snelson, letter, January 25, 1875, DC archives.
9. Floyd Snelson, letter, June 1879, DC archives.
10. Brownlee, *New Day Ascending*, 161.
11. AMA annual report, May 1902.
12. Ibid.
13. *The American Missionary*, January 1924.
14. AMA annual report, May 1902.
15. Brownlee, *New Day Ascending*, 161.
16. AMA pamphlet, untitled, 1950.
17. Septima Clark, *Ready from Within* (Trenton, NJ: Africa World Press, Inc., 1990), 67.
18. Claudius A. Turner, letter, April 19, 1946, DC archives.
19. AMA pamphlet, untitled, January 1950.
20. Young, *An Easy Burden*, 134.
21. Ibid., 131.
22. Dorothy Cotton, speech, United Church of Christ Georgia-South Carolina Association Annual Meeting, Savannah, Georgia, September 2000.
23. Clark, *Ready from Within*, 24
24. Ibid., 25
25. Ibid., 37
26. Ibid., 47
27. Ibid., 57.
28. Ibid., 34.
29. Young, *An Easy Burden*, 133.
30. Clark, *Ready from Within*, 63.
31. Ibid., 64
32. Ibid., 65
33. Ibid., 70
34. Jennifer Swain, "Organizers Open African-American Museum," *The Coastal Courier*, June 16, 2004.

Chapter 12

1. *Slavery and the Making of America*, PBS documentary.
2. Johnson, Smith, and the WGBH Research Team, *Africans in America*, 106.
3. "Avery Institute," AMA pamphlet.
4. Edmund L. Drago, *Initiative, Paternalism, and Race Relations* (Athens: The University of Georgia Press, 1990), 61.
5. Ibid., 155.
6. Ibid., 165.
7. "Avery Normal Institute History," AMA pamphlet, 1.

8. *The American Missionary*, May 1886, 131.
9. Mrs. F.M. Jencks, "An Inside View," reprint.
10. Ibid.
11. Ibid.
12. Young, *An Easy Burden*, 91.
13. Ibid., 83.
14. Ibid., 84.
15. "A Look at First Congregational Church Through Its Stained Glass Windows," pamphlet, 5.
16. Ibid.
17. Ibid.
18. AMA 1872 annual report, 29.
19. Ibid.
20. Jones, *Soldiers of Light and Love*, 127.
21. DuBois, *Souls of Black Folk*, 59.
22. AMA pamphlet, untitled, 8.
23. Homer C. McEwen Sr., "For the Good of Man and the Glory of God," *Atlanta Historical Society Bulletin*, Spring 1977, quoting Bruce Barton.
24. Ibid.
25. Ibid., 134.
26. A.K. Stanley, *The Children Is Crying*, 84.
27. "First Congregational United Church of Christ," 134th Anniversary booklet, 18
28. Ibid., 6.

Epilogue

1. Beard, *A Crusade of Brotherhood*, 161.
2. Ibid., 234.
3. "Round Table: The Legacy of the American Missionary Association," *New Conversations*, Summer 1996, 39.
4. Jim Wallis and Joyce Hollyday, *Cloud of Witnesses* (Maryknoll, NY: Sojourners and Orbis Books, 1991), xvi.
5. Washington, *Up from Slavery*, 39, 42-43.

Acknowledgments

Many hands, hearts, and minds contributed to the creation of this book. I offer my deepest gratitude to my colleagues on the staff of the Southeast Conference of the United Church of Christ—especially to Conference Minister Timothy Downs, who birthed and nurtured the vision for this project; to Gerri Ryons-Hudson, administrative assistant extraordinaire, who faithfully and graciously transcribed many hours of interview tapes; and to fellow Associate Conference Minister Kathy Clark, who gave many helpful and insightful editing suggestions on the manuscript—all of whom offered generous doses of guidance, encouragement, and chocolate when needed.

I also extend my warmest thanks to Susan Mitchell and Milton Hurst, delightful traveling companions and partners in the collection of oral histories. I am grateful to Elizabeth Mitchell Clement, whose eloquence danced through this project from the earliest glimmer of a vision to the final pages of the book, and to the members of the advisory board—Annie Neal, Helen Washington, Odessa Woolfolk, and Jerome Gray, along with Milton Hurst. I thank Andrew Young for inspiring me as a teenager, pastoring me as an adult, and enhancing this book with his fine foreword.

On the Heels of Freedom would not exist without the generous support of many donors, especially the Southeast Conference, the Women in Mission Partnership Fund, and the former Board for Homeland Ministries—now Office of Local Church Ministries—of the United Church of Christ. The Connecticut Conference, the Rhode Island Conference, the Southern Conference, and the Massachusetts Woman's Home Missionary Union reaffirmed the partnership that made possible the late-nineteenth-century educational crusade through their contributions. I extend special thanks to John Thomas, Robert Noble, Lorin Cope, Thomas Dipko, Jose Malayang, Davida Foy Crabtree, Bennie Whiten, Daehler Hayes, Rollin Russell, Ervin Milton, F. Allison Phillips, William Land, Theodore Trost, and Fay Coker Walker. I am extremely grateful to the Louisville Institute and its executive director, James Lewis, for providing a generous and crucial grant for travel and writing expenses.

I thank Clifton Johnson and Brenda Square of the Amistad Research Center for making available their archives, including hundreds of original letters from the Amistad Committee and the early missionary teachers. I am grateful to the Avery Research Center for African American History and Culture, and to the Dorchester

Center, for sharing additional pieces of history; to Helen Caver and Talladega College for granting permission to use the stunning Amistad murals on the book cover; and to Carol Ganz, John Henry Scott III, and Martha Smalley for their help with the New England aspects of the research.

It was a delight to work with my good friend Roy M. Carlisle, senior editor at Crossroad Publishing, on this book, and I rejoice that he and his creative colleagues so deeply honored the story. I thank my agent, John Talbot, whose persistent efforts helped to get it published. I feel blessed by my co-pastors, Nancy Hastings Sehested and Ken Sehested, who shouldered extra burdens while I wrote, and by all the dear friends who are part of Circle of Mercy congregation in Asheville, North Carolina. The prayers, pasta, and potato casseroles of Mary Etta Perry and Mary Cowal kept me going—as did encouraging words from my mother, Ann Hollyday, and my sisters, Kay Filar and Debra Link, and their families.

My profoundest admiration and appreciation are reserved for the scores of people all across the Southeast Conference who shared their personal stories of trial and triumph. I regret that space limitations make it impossible to include every testimony in this book; all are worthy, and each is an integral part of the inspiring, larger American Missionary Association story. To those who welcomed my colleagues and me—and our tape recorder—I can only say that I have been blessed by your generosity and openness, and changed by your courage and faithfulness. Thank you.

The following people were interviewed for *On the Heels of Freedom:*

King's Chapel United Church of Christ, Alpine, Alabama: Harvey Calhoun, Josie Calhoun, Ovell B. Calhoun, Mildred Wheeler

Trinity Congregational United Church of Christ, Athens, Alabama: Celestine Bridgeforth, Mildred Brown, Harvey Craig, Nelson Howell, Betty S. McDaniel, Clarence H. McDaniel, Gary L. Myers, Josephine H. Woodson

First Congregational Christian United Church of Christ, Birmingham, Alabama: Ruth Barefield-Pendleton, June Fox Davis, J. Mason Davis, Juanita O. Hixon, Marilyn T. Jones, Beverly Richardson, Kathryn Robinson, Odessa Woolfolk

First Congregational United Church of Christ, Marion, Alabama: Jesse Billingsley, Lorenzo Curry, Alberta W. Goree, Eulas Kirtdoll, Nancy Kynard, Earline Lapsley, Cheryle Williams

First Congregational United Church of Christ, Montgomery, Alabama: Beatrice M. Forniss, John H. Jones, Faustina W. Jones, J. G. Pendarvis, Jean Pendarvis

First Congregational United Church of Christ, Talladega, Alabama: Reginald Brasher, Willie Brown, Lillian W. Duncan, Emmett L. Gray, Milton S. Hurst, Mable C. Moore

Central Congregational United Church of Christ, Atlanta, Georgia: Edward M. Brown

Rush Memorial United Church of Christ, Atlanta, Georgia: Launa B. Bacon, Alethea W. Boone, Ethelyn Barksdale, Johnatham Barksdale, Beverly Calbert, Lawrence E. Calbert Sr., Candice Giles, Betty K. Foster, Blake Foster, Samuel O. Jackson, Phillip Jenkins, Shirley Jenkins, Lois Montgomery, Otis Montgomery, Mavis W. McMullen

First Congregational United Church of Christ, Atlanta, Georgia: Harriet N. Chisholm, Ann N. Cooper, Claire Greene Crooks, Katie J. Daniels, Richard Grigsby, G. Johnson Hubert, Dosh R. Jackson, Dorothy N. Mitchell, Lucius R. Mitchell, Walter L. Mitchell, Marie Saxon, Marguerite Simon, Louisa J. Williams

Evergreen Congregational United Church of Christ, Beachton, Georgia: Martha Carter, Ned Carter, Adella Clark, Cherry B. Grohom, Artis Johnson, Kelvin Johnson, Myrtle Johnson, Stephanie Johnson, Gary Metcalf, Glendell Mills, Marcus Walden

Midway Congregational United Church of Christ, Midway, Georgia: Christine Baker, Loretta Baker, Deborah A. Dawson, Lillie W. Gillard, Annette L. Givens, Annie B. Givens, Eloise Green, Beverly Lewis Gross, Gladyse W. Harris, Dorothy Lewis, Franklin R. Lewis, James A. Lewis, Jeraldine Maxwell, Samara Mohassan El Bey, Dorothy D. Mosely, Abraham Mullins, Alberta Mullins, Inez Powell, Sallie W. Richardson, Deborah Robinson, Sandra Hicks Sheffield, Annie M. Stewart, Ezekiel Walthour, Ethel M. Wright

First Congregational United Church of Christ, Savannah, Georgia: Barbara Baker, Dorothy L. DeVillars, Ora Pinkney Ford, Connell J. Stiles, Jordan W. Stiles, William E. Stiles, Helen H. Washington

Bethany Congregational United Church of Christ, Thomasville, Georgia: Denise Brown, Emma Chatmon, Forenza Chatmon, Jack Hadley, Juanita Jackson, Rosa Rone, Norma H. Scott, Pinkie Wilkerson

Union United Church of Christ, Tougaloo, Mississippi: Sam Bradford, Shirley F. Bradford, Lillie McKinney Cooley, Hiawatha Douglas, Sarah L. Douglas, Henry Thornton Drake, Diane Brou Fraser, Lucille Moman Fraser. Larry L. Johnson, Norma Johnson, Annie S. Smith, Beverly Williams

Plymouth Congregational United Church of Christ, Charleston, South Carolina: Gracie Lee Dobbins, James R. Fields,

Inez Fields, Deborah Harris, Florence Miller, Ruth Miller, Kathy Robinson-Nelson, Anna M. Smalls, Delores T. Wainwright

Howard Congregational United Church of Christ, Nashville, Tennessee: Wanda Akins, William Alexander, Dorothy H. Baker, Howard Harris, Ernestine Holiday, Newton Holiday Jr., Beth Howse, Annie W. Neal, Mary Welch, Wilson Q. Welch Jr.

Fisk University, Nashville, Tennessee: Cheryl Hamberg, Lillian A. Lawson, Jean Welch-Wilson

Pleasant Hill Community Church, Pleasant Hill, Tennessee: Erston M. Butterfield

About the Author

Rev. Joyce Hollyday is an Associate Conference Minister for the Southeast Conference of the United Church of Christ. A nationally known writer and retreat leader, Joyce is also co-founder and co-pastor of Circle of Mercy, an ecumenical congregation in the mountains of western North Carolina. She serves on the national steering committee and faculty of "Word and World: A People's School," a social transformation movement for faith-based activists. Joyce has worked as a court advocate for survivors of domestic violence and a chaplain for children with cancer.

Reverends Mitchell, Hurst, and Hollyday celebrate the completion of their five-year "Rekindle the Gift" oral history project in Tougaloo College's historic Woodworth Chapel. Rev. Susan Mitchell and Rev. Milton Hurst collaborated with Joyce in collecting the stories that appear in On the Heels of Freedom.

During her fifteen years as Associate Editor of *Sojourners* magazine, Joyce traveled widely in the United States and around the globe to write about struggles for justice and freedom. She was a founding member of Witness for Peace and a member of the first team to establish a nonviolent, prayerful presence in Nicaragua's war zones in the 1980s. She went to the Middle East in 1997, and she visited South Africa twice—once to cover the persecution of the church under apartheid and a decade later to observe that nation's unprecedented Truth and Reconciliation Commission. She is at work on a book documenting the work of the commission and the newly launched Truth and Reconciliation process in Greensboro, North Carolina, the first of its kind in the United States.

Joyce holds a B.A. in religion from Bates College and an M.Div. from Candler School of Theology, Emory University. She was a Rockefeller Fellow at Yale Divinity School for one year and a Woodruff Scholar at Candler. In 1996 and 1997, she served as an Adjunct Professor of Homiletics at Columbia Theological Seminary in Georgia.

Joyce is the author of *Clarence Jordan: Essential Writings* (Orbis Books, 2003); *Then Shall Your Light Rise: Spiritual Formation and Social Witness* (Upper Room Books, 1997); *With Our Own Eyes: The Story of Jubilee Partners* (Herald Press, 1996); and *Clothed with the Sun: Biblical Women, Social Justice, and Us* (Westminster/John Knox Press, 1994). She has written a spiritual memoir entitled *Turning Toward Home: A Sojourn of Hope* (Harper & Row, 1989), and is the co-editor of *Cloud of Witnesses* (Orbis Books, 1991) and *Crucible of Fire: The Church Confronts Apartheid* (Orbis Books, 1989).

A Word from the Editor

Usually I am in trouble as an editor. Well, until recently that is. The reason is that I actually make a distinction between my "calling" and my employment. It is a distinction made possible, even demanded, because I am seminary trained and ministry oriented and my calling is very important to me. As is my employment. But confusion can and has resulted in the working out of this distinction. Fortunately, I work for a few of the most wonderful people in religious publishing and they not only understand my calling but support it. I am allowed to honor my calling to nurture and support writers and authors in the creative process of writing and publishing, and also enjoy the sheer unmitigated pleasure of my employment by The Crossroad Publishing House in New York.

Unfortunately there is a pervasive tendency in many corporate publishing houses today to treat authors as an afterthought, almost as if the house could get along without them. Or at least think that there is always a new author coming around the corner so who cares if we alienate the current one. No one in corporate publishing would cop to this attitude but it is rampant and in smaller publishing gatherings it even gets voiced.

For me, the writers and authors are my reason for being. The publishing house is second on the loyalty list and must always be so. Book publishing doesn't exist without writers, though I shouldn't have to even say that, and I never want to forget the current writer or author and his or her concerns just because maybe another one is coming around the next corner. Or the publishing house has forgotten its priorities for a few moments. So I am always remembering writers and authors I have worked with in the past and trying to catch up with them if possible. In fact you would find that this is true on my current list of authors with books by writers I have worked with many years ago at different houses and Joyce is one of them.

We did meet many years ago back in the 80s when she was affiliated with Sojourners magazine and I encouraged her to do her first book, Turning Toward Home. She was a naturally talented writer and a gifted journalist. Her columns in the magazine were one of its most popular features and many Christians throughout the country, and especially those who were involved in social justice issues read and grew from "listening" to Joyce's wise and thoughtful voice. It made sense for her to tell a larger story in a book back in the mid-80s. Which she did. Then even after her affiliation with Sojourners magazine ended she went on to do other wonderful books with other publishing houses, as she worked out her literary calling and her ministry. There was a hiatus in our connection but I never forgot about Joyce nor did I forget about her wonderful ministry nor about that lyrical talent for language.

In one of those moments that can never quite be fathomed as happenstance or providential, I decided to contact Joyce again with no idea what she was doing or even if she was working on a book. Thank goodness for email. I sent a missile out into the North Carolina woods (otherwise known as Asheville) and a response came back. I was surprised and elated. Subsequent phone calls with her and her agent led to a deal that finally resulted in what you have in your hands, On the Heels of Freedom. Joyce had been working on this project for many months and had gathered a team of people together to help her do the research, but the enormous job of sorting the material and writing the narrative had fallen on her most capable shoulders.

The more I read the more excited I got about this project. Joyce was not quite finished with the manuscript when we finally had agreed to move ahead with publication. And then the phone call happened that put us on an express train to Atlanta. Joyce wanted the book to be completed and ready for distribution by the time her denominational convention rolled around by mid-year in Atlanta. Normally the bookmaking process is accomplished in few months and we would have to make a decision to compress that schedule into a few weeks. It meant that every phase of the publishing and production process had to be choreographed to happen as quickly as possible. Crossroad agreed, if Joyce could finish the ms in record time.

Frankly, I don't know how she did it. I imagine she went without sleep a lot, worked long hours beyond counting and in the midst of it all, she kept her humor and her wits about her. All I can do in this short piece is salute this magnificent woman and her amazing dedication to this project. She has done an invaluable service to the men and women who populate this story and she has challenged all of us to live beyond racial prejudice. Her contribution will be a legacy that will inspire generations to come and her eloquent writing will give us all new eyes to see the courage and commitment of a people so often neglected and so often marginalized. Thank you, Joyce, for being faithful to your calling; we are all in your debt.

ROY M. CARLISLE
SENIOR EDITOR